5
6
7
8
9

Expropriation in the Americas

OTHER VOLUMES IN THE
COLUMBIA UNIVERSITY
INTER-AMERICAN LAW CENTER
PROJECT ON PRIVATE PROPERTY
IN THE AMERICAS

**INFLATION AND
PRIVATE INVESTMENT:
Brazilian Solutions
edited by Norman S. Poser
Vice-President, American
Stock Exchange, Policy
Planning and Government
Relations Division**

Volume I—Monetary Correction

Volume II—Capital Market

Expropriation in the Americas

A Comparative Law Study

edited by
Andreas F. Lowenfeld

DUNELLEN

New York

Columbia University Inter-American Law Center
Project on Private Property in the Americas—Henry P.
de Vries, Director

International Standard Book Number 0-8424-0035-4.

Library of Congress Catalogue Card Number 79-148701.

Printed in the United States of America.

Expropriation
in the
Americas

Contents

Foreword and Acknowledgments   ix
About the Editor and Authors   xi
A Note on Method   xiii

Introduction   xv
    Andreas F. Lowenfeld
Argentina   11
    Agustín A. Gordillo
Brazil   49
    Miguel Seabra Fagundes
Chile   81
    Alamiro de Avila Martel, with Manuel Salvat Monguillot
Mexico   113
    Julio C. Treviño
Peru   159
    Jorge Avendaño Valdés, with Domingo Garcia Belaunde
Venezuela   199
    Enrique Perez Olivares, with Allan-Randolph Brewer-Carias,
    Hildegarde Rondón de Sansó, and Tomás Polanco Martinez
United States of America   241
    Robert K. Greenawalt
Concluding Remarks   307
    Andreas F. Lowenfeld

Foreword
and
Acknowledgments

The Inter-American Law Center of Columbia University, established with a Ford Foundation grant, exists to encourage the development of more effective communication between the United States and Latin America through comparison of legal systems. As part of the Parker School of Foreign and Comparative Law it shares the School's facilities for training and research in comparative law. The Center's major project, examination of the role of private property in the economic development of the Americas, has led to two initial studies, both to be published in 1971.

This book is the result of the first study. A second study, to be published shortly, explores the effects of inflation on private investment in a single vast and complex country - Brazil.

Professor Andreas F. Lowenfeld as Editor of the present study, has surmounted the difficult task of compressing elaborate country reports in Spanish and Portuguese into a meaningful synthesis of problems, procedures, and solutions in the taking of private property by the State.

Professor Robert Kent Greenawalt and Dr. Fernando J. Figueredo assembled the distinguished group of collaborators and prepared the initial outline that formed the basis for their papers. Dr. Figueredo also gave unstintingly of his time and effort in correspondence with the various authors, in assembling materials for use by the editor, and in coordinating the necessary translation and research.

As is explained in more detail in the Note on Method, the manuscripts from Latin America essentially went through two stages of translation, first a literal rendition into English of the manuscripts as they arrived, second a rendition into idiomatic and professional English suitable to this book. The second version was the principal task of the editor, working both from the originals and from the first English version, at the same time as he was editing and revising. The first version was prepared by our two able translators Benjamin Varela and Margarita L. Kenny, supplemented by Mrs. Alice McCarthy with the Spanish texts and Miss Yaya A. Hamar with the Portuguese text.

A number of students at the Columbia University School of Law with interest in Latin America and abilities in Spanish or Portuguese helped with this project. Mr. Thomas Skola proved invaluable in preparing the final manuscript, and in tracking down the many authorities cited by the various contributors. Mrs. Ilda Aviles took over for Mr. Skola in the final stages.

Miss Yaya A. Hamar, Miss Carolina Martinez and Mrs. Alice McCarthy, the secretaries at the Inter-American Law Center, did more than anyone could expect in putting up with a variety of temperaments, languages, and styles in the process of turning a massive set of manuscripts into a book. Without them, too, the project would have been impossible.

Finally, we realize that the authors in Lima, Santiago, Caracas, Buenos Aires, Rio de Janeiro, and Mexico City also had research assistant, secretaries, and collaborators. Though we do not know them by name, we express our gratitude and appreciation to them.

Henry P. de Vries
Director
Columbia University Inter-American Law Center

About the Editor and Authors

Andreas.F. Lowenfeld is Professor of Law at New York University. Previously he was Deputy Legal Adviser in the United States Department of State. Professor Lowenfeld specializes in International Law, Conflicts of Law, and International Economic Transactions. He is co-author with Professors Chayes and Ehrlich, of *International Legal Process (1968-69)*.

Agustín A. Gordillo (Argentina) is Professor of Administrative Law at the National Universities of Buenos Aires and of La Plata. Formerly he was Chief Attorney for Administrative Law in the Office of the Solicitor General of the Nation. Among his publications are *Derecho Administrativo de La Economia (1967): Procedimiento y Recursos Administrativos (1964);* and *Empresas del Estado (1966).*

Miguel Seabra Fagundes (Brazil) is a practising attorney and Professor of Administrative Law at the University of Guanabara. Formerly he was a Judge in the Court of Appeals in Rio Grande do Norte. Among his works are *O Contrôle dos Atos Administrativos pelo Poder Judiciário (1968); Da Desapropriação no Direito Brasileiro (1942); Dos Recursos Ordinários em Matéria Civil (1946);* and *O Poder Judiciáro na Atual Constituição (1967).*

Alamiro Avila Martel (Chile) is Professor of Legal History at the University of Chile in Santiago and Director of the University Libraries. Among his works are *Derecho Romano: Organización*

Judicial y Procedimiento Civil (1962) and *Esquema del Derecho Penal Indiano (1941)*. He was assisted in his paper by Professor Manuel Salvat Monguillot of the University of Chile.

Julio C. Treviño (Mexico) is engaged in the practice of law in Mexico City.

Jorge Avendaño Valdés (Peru) is Dean of the Law School at the Catholic University of Peru in Lima. Previously he was a member of the Commission to Revise the Civil Code of Peru (1967).

Enrique Perez Olivares (Venezuela) is Dean of the Law School of the Central University of Venezuela in Caracas. He was assisted in the work by his colleague Allan-Randolph Brewer-Carias, Professor of Administrative Law and author of *La Expropriación por causa de Utilidad Pública o Interés Social* (1966) and by Professors Tomás Polanco Martinez and Hildegard Rondón de Sansó of the University of Venezuela.

Robert Kent Greenawalt is Professor of Law at Columbia University, New York. Professor Greenawalt specializes in Constitutional Law and is the author of a number of works in that field, with emphasis on political and civil rights.

A Note on Method

Every editor of a collective work faces the problem of whether to keep his own activity to a minimum, at the risk of ending up with a collection of disparate elements, or to try to achieve a unified book, at the risk of altering the authors' contributions to reflect his own style and preferences. The problem was particularly serious in this book, because the seven contributors (other than the editor) are from seven different countries, wrote in three different languages, and had very different concepts of what the book or, at any rate, their contributions to the book should be. Some thought the main emphasis should be on theoretical distinctions in public and private law, some stressed historical development, and some emphasized "the real world" as contrasted with the statute books. Some thought of expropriation as a subject separate and distinct from the development of law generally, while others thought that expropriation could be understood only in the context of a thorough treatment of the history, geography, and sociology of the country. And some contributions arrived three hundred typewritten pages long, others at first contained as few as forty.

As a result, the editor's job—at least as this editor carried it out—became much greater than first contemplated. To achieve a more or less balanced and symmetrical book, a substantial amount of rewriting was done. Doubtless some of the individuality of the various contributors was sacrificed in the process, hopefully none of the accuracy. But—and perhaps this is the hallmark of any multilateral comparative study—editing meant translating, not just from Portuguese and Spanish into English (which was in fact done initially by professional translators), but from the contributors' legal and educational thought pattern—I almost said from the Latin American pattern—to that of the lawyer trained principally in the United States. I say "almost" because like so many persons working with Latin America, I soon concluded that the superficially similar pattern—the grammar of the law, in Professor Mirjan Damaska's phrase—concealed differences not only in substantive solutions to particular problems like valuation, payment of compensation, and judicial review, but in the approach and presentation of the individual contributors. Whether there is nonetheless a "Latin American pattern"—whether for example Argentina in this area resembles Mexico more than it does the United States—I leave for the concluding chapter. At this point I want to note only the editor's concern that the double translation through which all of the manuscripts (except that of the contributor from the United States) passed may have distorted the possibility of judging degree of diversity or community of approach.

One final word by way of preface seems in order. Though many of the topics covered in the chapters of this book are quite technical, detailed, and dry, it turns out that in nearly every country—least in the United States—expropriation is a highly political subject. How a person—even a scholar—thinks about expropriation tells a good deal about how he thinks in general about the role of government and probably what he thinks of the governments that he has observed in his own country. Some of the contributors to this volume tried to keep their own views out of their papers in the name of objective scholarship; others did not hesitate to comment on what they regarded as fair or unfair, progressive or backward. It should be stated that none of the authors was selected for his political views, and indeed these views were usually not known to the organizers of the project. So far as we know none of the contributors was censored in any way at the source; none of the editorial revisions at this end were designed to alter any of the assessments, conclusions, or commentary of the authors of the individual chapters. So far as the editor has any views on the subjects covered, these are set forth in the introductory and concluding chapters bearing his name. No political or jurisprudential considerations went into the editorial process. Neither this book nor the Inter-American Law Center has any party line except the promotion of comparative legal scholarship.

A. F. L.
September 1970

Mirjan Damaska, "A Continental Lawyer in an American Law School: Trials and Tribulations of Adjustment," *116 U. Pa.L. Rev.* 1363, 1365-7 (1968).

Introduction

Andreas F. Lowenfeld

I. Purpose of the Study

There are a number of reasons for an examination in detail of the law of expropriation in the Western Hemisphere:

First, perhaps better than any other single topic in the law, the law and practice of expropriation of private property throw light on (perhaps reflect would be more accurate) the relationship between the citizen and the state.

Second, as redistribution of existing wealth and attraction of new capital compete for favor among those who would better the economic lot of backward lands, the law and procedures of expropriation are vital to both.

Third, as an old problem develops new aspects, particularly as the forms for transfer of small holdings are sought to be applied to efforts at large scale social change, each country may well study the experiences of others with profit. In particular, while the study of most aspects of Latin American law has limited practical usefulness for North Americans, either because the North American institutions are so much further developed or because the traditions are so different, the taking of private property by the state for purposes of social change has just begun in the United States, whereas at least in some of the Latin American countries there has been a great deal of experience. Thus, the comparative study of Latin institutions has in this area more of the aspect of "how to do it" (or "how not to do it") for North Americans than is the case with most studies of Latin American institutions.

A final reason may be stated for studying the law and practice of expropriation in the Americas--we are careful not to call it the first. It has become more and more apparent that there is today no real agreement on the international law applicable to expropriation; that is, on the obligation of states to other states or to citizens of other states whose property may be the subject of governmental taking. Indeed, the United States Supreme Court has said, "There are few, if any, issues in international law today on which opinion seems to be so divided as the limitations on a State's power to expropriate the property of aliens." In declining to make its own pronouncement on these issues, the Supreme Court added its view that there is no area "which touches more sensitively the practical and ideological goals of the various

1

members of the community of nations." * If international law is to be built in this area—some would say rebuilt—on the basis of some kind of consensus, then the best place to begin would seem to be the practice of states toward their own citizens. Only when we have such knowledge can we reach meaningful conclusions about the possibility of a consensus, about the elements of such a consensus, about the effect and limits of the exhaustion of remedies principle, and about the question—by no means obvious—of whether an international law standard should be higher, lower or equal to the standard applied by states vis-à-vis their own citizens.

II. A Realistic Law of Expropriation?

1. The Philosophical Bases

What should a modern effective law of expropriation consist of? Some would argue that this all depends on one's attitude toward private property. For example, if private property is considered in effect a revocable concession from the state, the answer would be very different from what it would be if private property is considered an "unalienable right." One can emphasize the "social function" of private property; one can take as his point of departure that private property is an inherent social good to whose preservation the state is dedicated. As the papers in this volume show, Latin Americans are much more inclined than North Americans to reflect on such questions. In the United States, for instance, lawyers are quite content to learn the intricacies of the Rule against Perpetuities without asking very much about its relation to the freedom of property ownership or the social goals it was designed to achieve. North Americans would much rather have de facto inroads into the traditional concepts of the sanctity of private property than to have anyone tamper with the traditional 18th-century formulation of these concepts. In Latin America, by contrast, there can be long scholarly debates about the relationship between state and private purpose, and rather considerable differences in the formulation of this relationship without, necessarily, great differences in the substance of the

---

* Banco Nacional de Cuba v. Sabbatino (376 U.X. 398, 428, 430 (1964).

actual arrangements. It is the present editor's thesis—perhaps reflecting his culture-bound insensitivity to doctrinal disputes—that a model framework for a law of expropriation can be constructed based not entirely on neutral principles but nevertheless adaptable to different countries, different social philosophies, and different legal absolutes.*

2. Public Purpose

Much is made in constitutions, treaties, and, indeed, in the individual papers in this volume of public purpose or social utility as a requirement for taking of property by the state. But, except in context of a Trujillo turning a state into his own private preserve, it is hard to see the concept of public purpose as more than a tautology. Everything a state does—whether the decision is made by judicial, executive, or legislative power—is presumably made for a reason of state, as the decision-maker views it. Correspondingly, the only kind of state taking that could be excluded by a public purpose test would be one designed to punish—that is, where the state has no real use for the property but merely wants to deprive the private owner of it. If the state wants or needs the property, it does not really matter whether it wants to convert that property to a new use—such as farmland being used to build a road or pasture land turned to grain production, or whether the state wants to preserve the same use by assuming control—such as a privately owned electric power or telephone company being transferred to public ownership. This is why in none of the countries with which the papers in this volume deal is there ever a truly effective legal challenge to a taking on the grounds that the taking is not for a public purpose. The issue of public purpose is a true legal question only in the procedural sense; that is, with respect to who is to make the decision of public purpose, and to what extent there is to be review of or appeal from that decision.

We will see in the individual country papers a variety of answers to this question. Separate agencies or ministries, such as the Bureau of Roads or the Ministry of Agriculture, may be given the power to take private property in connection with the execution of the duties assigned to them; the Executive Branch as a whole may

---

*To avoid any doubt, let it be reiterated that no effort has been made to impose these principles on the various contributors to this volume.

be authorized by a general expropriation law to take private property, subject to certain procedural rules; the Legislature may itself decide that certain property or certain classes of property shall be taken by the state; or the power to take property may be viewed as an inherent state power of the sovereign, without any explicit legislative grant. In any case, the taking authority makes the decision that ownership (or use) of the property in question is to be transferred to it (or to the state), and no effective judicial review of this decision is possible. The only issue on which a court could render a meaningful judgment is whether the agency has acted within its power—for instance, whether the petroleum law gives the Ministry of Petroleum jurisdiction over natural gas fields, or whether the Agriculture Ministry can build a road. But this is really a different issue, that of abuse of a subdivision's powers. So long as there is no defined limit on the functions of a government as a whole, there is probably no real way the public purpose or public utility of a taking can or should be challenged judicially. The only requirement in our model would be a kind of self-policing of government officials by means of a requirement that the purpose of the taking be clearly stated and that, where applicable, the specific authority for the taking be set forth.

If, then, judicial review of public purpose is limited, a good case can be made for another kind of review. For example, a requirement that all takings by a given Ministry must be approved by the Minister or that all takings over a given amount must be approved by the President, by the Legislature, or by a Committee of the Legislature may serve as a check on the executive or officials of the Executive Branch. Similarly, a requirement of public notice, even without a specific mode of appeal or review, may serve as a check on arbitrariness and improve confidence in the fairness and rationality of state action.

3. Notice

No action of the state to take private property should be taken without effective notice to the property owner. This means, first, that the state must make a real effort to find the property owner, and not just post a notice on a bulletin board somewhere. It means further that the notice must come sufficiently in advance of the actual taking so that the property owner can inquire into means available to him to secure such rights as he may have, not only to

4

challenge the taking itself but to secure a fair determination of compensation and to negotiate about the extent of the taking. The time period will obviously vary from place to place, but a fair approach might be a minimum of 30 days' notice before the next step, followed by an additional period of 90 to 120 days if the owner has signified his intention of taking issue with part of the procedure.

The substance of the notice ought to contain at the least an accurate description of the property taken, a recital of the authority under which it is taken and, as discussed above, a statement of the purposes for which the property is to be used. The notice should also contain a tender of compensation or, alternatively, an invitation to the owner to make a proposal which could then be discussed with the taking authority.

4. Compensation

All of the countries of the Americas (with the exception of Cuba) recognize in principle the need to pay for property taken by the state. Most of them also have requirements under their constitutions that the payment--sometimes called compensation, sometimes indemnification--shall be completed prior to the taking. But these pronouncements by no means prove that there is general agreement that there must be cash payment of full value in advance of taking. Indeed, if there were such agreement, a great range of options as to social organization and distribution might be denied to sovereign states. A firm commitment that there shall be a taking of property only when there is a willingness and ability to pay full value for the property, cash on delivery, would mean that for most countries or subdivisions there simply would not be any opportunity to make major expropriations.

But if the principle is to be wholly abandoned, the commitment of the state to ownership of property by individuals or firms, and with it the encouragement of savings and investment, would have to be abandoned as well. The aim, therefore, must be to achieve a compromise between absolute commitment to the letter of full prior cash compensation and the notion that reasons of state or exercise of sovereignty override all such principles.

Leaving aside for the moment the problem of valuation, one approach would be to recognize frankly that there is a basic difference between taking a small piece of property—say, a homestead or a gasoline station needed for highway construction--and taking large haciendas or industrial establishments. The owners of the former probably would require full cash payment, in order to resettle or start a new business; typically, this presents no insuperable problem to the taking authority. Owners of the latter may well be able to get along with part in cash and part in deferred compensation. Because of the constitutional provisions in many countries calling for prior indemnification, there has been much argument about whether bonds are equivalent to cash. The difficulty with such a proposition, of course, is that bonds do have a market value. If the interest rate on bonds offered to expropriated owners is less than the going interest rate, the discount value for these bonds is likely to be considerably below the face value stated to be equal to the property taken. Thus, as an effort to meet constitutional requirements for prior compensation, the argument in favor of bonds is generally inadequate. The real issue, however, is not whether bonds are fully convertible or how close they come to being equal to cash. The issue is how some form of compensation can be worked out that allows the state to carry out its purposes without repudiating its obligations--in the most neutral sense of the term--to the prior owner of the property.

Suppose, for instance, a scale is established whereby the first x thousand dollars or pesos worth of property taken must be compensated in cash; the next y thousand dollars worth may be compensated by payment over a five-year period; the next z thousand dollars worth may be compensated by payment over a ten-year period and so on. Suppose, further, that there is a provision to protect against inflation—for example, by linking the deferred compensation to some index, which might well be the revenue from the seized property.

Under such a system, the issue of a cash value of the deferred compensation would not arise. The interest on the deferred compensation might well not be equal to the rate of return the property was previously earning. By definition, an expropriation is designed to accomplish a change. But the point here is, first, that it may well make sense to distinguish between different kinds of property and different kinds of taking rather than to try to fit all takings into the mold established for removing small houses from roadways; and, second, that prior compensation as a necessary condition for expropriation is often unrealistic and has led to inaccurate and sometimes disingenuous analysis.

Needless to say, no one pattern or formula for compensation can be established for all countries or even for all situations in a given country. The effort here is merely to try to strike a balance between security for property owners and a range of options for governments.

5. Valuation

Valuation is, of course, the other side of the question of compensation. 100 per cent compensation of 50 per cent of value is the same as 50 per cent of compensation of 100 per cent of value of a given property. But if valuation presents many practical problems, it seems to present fewer ideological problems than does the issue of compensation itself.

It is clear that no single formula for valuation of property fits all circumstances. Market value, for example, may well be meaningless in a situation where there is no market. Replacement value may be grossly distorting where the cost of acquisition was substantially less, and vice versa. The attempt of some countries to base valuation for purposes of expropriation on values declared for tax purposes has a surface appeal, based on a kind of rough retributive justice. But on reflection, this too turns out to be unsatisfactory, for if the tax rate has been set to take account of a prevailing pattern of undervaluation for tax purposes, then there is nothing improper if a property owner conforms to that pattern, and an effort by the state to use that pattern for other purposes amounts to a kind of punishment. Similarly, book value for commercial property is only rarely a fair measure of the worth of a going concern, and exclusive reliance on book value would reward or punish according to accounting practices that ought not to be chosen with one eye on possible expropriation.

Probably the best approach is to set out a series of factors to be considered in arriving at just valuation. The list would include "book value," "market value," replacement cost, acquisition cost, purchase price of similar properties in a recent period, and average production, revenue, or profit over a stated period. In general, future profits as an ingredient of valuation should be disregarded, except as they appear as an underlying assumption in using past earnings as a guide to valuation. On the other hand, a formula based solely on capital invested less earnings should probably be rejected, since it would result in rewarding the unsuccessful as contrasted with the successful enterprise, and since such a formula disregards the expectation of profits altogether as an element in stimulating the enterprise.

The difficulty is, of course, not in listing the factors, but in determining how much regard is to be given to one rather than another factor. But a list of criteria, plus a procedure for weighing them, is probably all that can be accomplished without making arbitrary rules that will not fit particular cases. This itself may be a substantial achievement, however. If the state and the individual or firm both know the criteria, and therefore the range within which they must work, there is a fair chance of negotiating a price. The chance is likely to be greater if there is a time limit on the negotiations and an organ to make the decision within the same range and according to the same guidelines if the parties cannot agree. Probably this organ should be an administrative body, either composed of experts or entitled to call upon experts, and separate from the taking agency. Except in emergencies, no taking should be effected until there has been either a negotiated agreement or a determination of price by the administrative organ created for that purpose. Both the state and the property owner should be allowed to appeal to courts from the administrative decision on price, but normally appeal ought not to entitle the private owner to delay the taking. The state, however, should be permitted to postpone the taking if it considers the outcome of the judicial decision regarding price as sufficiently critical.

As in arbitration, there are arguments both for and against a statement by the administrative body of the basis for its decision. On balance, it probably serves to develop confidence in the integrity of the procedures and the fairness of the state in dealing with property owners if the basis of an award is spelled out. If the full basis of the administrative decision is stated on the record, review by courts may be limited—though it need not be—to the record and to the method of calculation—i.e., without the possibility of re-examining the evidence.

The proposal here, then, is not very specific. It would encompass a list of criteria used in valuation, a time period for negotiated settlement, a further period for administrative decision with opportunity for each party to present evidence, and, finally, the possibility of judicial review. Within this framework, rules would presumably develop on the basis of administrative and judicial decisions attaching greater or less weight to different factors in recurring types of situations. No one would be left in the dark with regard to the basis for valuation, and in each case the stated object would be to arrive in full valuation, without regard to ability or method of compensation.

III. The Problem of Alien Ownership

Divorced from what are popularly considered facts of life — the lack of adequate capital in all of the countries of the Western Hemisphere except the United States, increasing fear of expropriation, and recurring experience with inflation and devaluation — the problem of alien ownership would be very simple. As an abstract proposition, it is hard to quarrel with the rule of nearly all Latin American states that all persons are equal before the law, and that therefore no special obligations are due to aliens who own property in a country. No one is forced to hold property in a country other than his own, and if he does he ought to be content to be bound by that country's laws and customs. Surely North Americans would be very surprised if any of the many foreign interests that hold investments in the United States were to claim rights not possessed by United States citizens or residents.

An important condition must be attached to the proposition, however. If aliens are not to be entitled to special privilege or protection, the law in which they share as equals must be fundamentally fair, both as written and as administered. Furthermore, there must be no arbitrary restrictions on the rights of aliens—both individuals and firms—with respect to ownership and disposition of property, and no restrictions on the opportunity of aliens to avail themselves of the administrative and judicial processes open to citizens.

The general principle may be unsatisfactory if—and this is not necessarily to be accepted without question—the objective is to attract new foreign investment. In part, of course, this may be less true if the capital importing countries adopt and implement an expropriation law following the model outlined here. But beyond this, the suggestion here would be that such guarantees in addition to equal treatment as seemed necessary to particular countries be contained not in the expropriation law, but in investment laws or investment guarantees. Thus, for example, assurances that in the case of expropriation of property owned or acquired by aliens the proceeds will be free from exchange control or protected against devaluation, or that a certain investment will not be subject to expropriation for a stated period should be made separately. The only reference in the expropriation law relevant to this issue might be a provision that limitations on the powers of the state to expropriate not contained in the expropriation law may be authorized and will be binding, if they are contained in special legislation or approved by stated officials.

IV. A Disclaimer

Every book on the Hemisphere, whether the focus be law, politics, history, or wildlife, warns somewhere in the first chapter or introduction that, of course, there are twenty-one independent countries, that the differences are greater than the similarities, and that one really cannot speak of "Latin America." From Chapter 2 on, however, nearly every book does just that. Here we try to avoid falling into the trap by presenting individual studies. It might be argued that without a contribution from Central America or the Caribbean we cannot claim to have a representative sample; similarly, the fact that we do not have a contribution from Bolivia, which has undergone a complete "revolution," may be a serious omission. But our effort has been to present the problems and some of the techniques for their solution, and to do so within the confines of a single manageable volume. Whether this effort is successful will be for the readers to judge.

Let it be said here only that the suggestions for a model law are not an effort at synthesis. We have too much respect for the comparative method and for the diversity of the countries represented here for that. The suggestions made in the introduction are an effort only to find a common ground for the future, and to put in a brief form a set of criteria against which to measure the much more detailed presentations that follow.

Argentina

Agustín A. Gordillo

Contents

I. The Framework for Expropriation in Argentine Law   15
  1. Various Concepts of the Right to Own Property   15
  2. The Distinction Between Civil and Administrative
    Law Restrictions on Property Rights   15
  3. Expropriation and the Legal System of Argentina   17
II. Expropriation   18
  1. Historical Foundations   18
  2. The Constitution of 1853 and the Civil Code   19
  3. Legislative Bases for Expropriation   20
  4. Types of Property Subject to Expropriation   22
  5. Mining Rights   24
III. The Bases for Expropriation   25
  1. The Concept of Public Utility   25
  2. The Decision as to Public Utility   26
  3. The Scope of Judicial Review   27
IV. Compensation and Valuation   29
  1. The Duty to Compensate   29
  2. Limitations on the General Principle   29
  3. Criteria for Just Compensation   30
  4. The Relevant Time for Purposes of Valuation   33
  5. The Requirement of Prior Compensation   33
  6. Payment   34
V. Expropriation Procedure   35
  1. Effort at Out-of-Court Settlement   35
  2. Commencement of Judicial Proceedings   36
  3. Determination of Just Price   37
  4. The Court Hearing   39
  5. Rights and Remedies of Third Parties   39
  6. Failure To Use the Expropriated Property
    for Its Intended Purpose   40
  7. Irregular Expropriation   41
VI. Rights of Aliens   42
Conclusion   43
Notes   44

I. The Framework for Expropriation in Argentine Law

1. Various Concepts of the Right to Own Property

It is difficult to tell which of the numerous existing concepts concerning the nature, extent and limits of the right to own property are reflected in current Argentine law. Different provisions of the law can be traced to different and often conflicting sources of law, including Roman, law, classical European civil law, and varying conceptions of the social function of property as developed in Latin America in the nineteenth and twentieth centuries.

For example, until 1968 the Civil Code defined the right to own property as in principle "absolute" (Article 2506 n.), "exclusive" (Article 2513), and "perpetual" (Article 2507, 2510). In 1968 Article 2513 was modified to limit the right to possess, use, and dispose of property to "regular exercise." Though this formulation is vague, it is clearly intended to get away from the old concept that even abuse of property (ius abutendi) was included within property rights. Even before the amendment, however, the Roman law characterizations were not adhered to strictly even within the Civil Code itself. The Code contained (and still does) a number of limitations on the exclusive, absolute, and perpetual character of property, divided in two main groups: limitations imposed by law for the benefit of other private parties—for example, for the benefit of adjoining land owners; and limitations imposed by law for the benefit of the public interest. The first category of limitations is governed by civil law, the second, according to Article 2611 of the Civil Code, is governed by administrative law.

2. The Distinction Between Civil and Administrative Law Restrictions on Property Rights

Some idea of the distinction between the two kinds of restrictions on property rights may be obtained from an illustrative list of limitations on the right of property: for example, among limitations contained in civil law are restraints against excavations. that might endanger adjoining property or cause landslides (Article 2615) and restraints against drilling wells, for whatever reason, against a party wall or other wall without erecting an additional wall (Article 2624). On the other hand, a property owner may not prohibit the erection of scaffolds or other

15

provisional structure needed by an adjoining property owner, it being understood that the person erecting the scaffold is liable for any damages caused (Article 2627); again, the property owner may not put trees within three meters of his property line (Article 2628), and the construction of drainage work or dikes cannot be carried out in such a way as to cause either flooding or erosion on neighboring land (Articles 2634, 2651).

As for administrative restrictions, it is important to note that administrative law is local; that is it is subject not only to national but to state and local regulation as well. Thus it is not possible to catalogue these restrictions precisely, since they vary from place to place. Typically, however, restraints on property thought to fall within administrative law include restrictions on the height of buildings, restrictions on the use to which property may be put, or requirements that fire escapes be provided and that certain construction standards be met.

A second category of restrictions on property is the so-called administrative servitude. Among these, for example, are requirements that riparian owners must leave room on the banks of the river in connection with public navigation (Article 2639 of Civil Code) restrictions specifying that owners of property bordering on railroad tracks are forbidden to carry out certain types of work near the tracks; restraints on the height of structures near airports; and, interestingly, a requirement that any ruins and archeological discoveries belong to the state regardless of who finds them or where they are found.

Another form of curtailment of property, much debated by writers though not very important in practice, is the right of a public authority to occupy private property temporarily. In contrast to some other countries where this practice is relatively normal, in Argentina occupation of private land or buildings by public authority is exceptional, typically related to emergency flood control or similar measures.[1]

By far the most important administrative restraint on property comes under the category of expropriation. For one thing, expropriation can affect any kind of property, not just immovables. For another, expropriation is permanent; that is, it extinguishes property rights and does not merely affect them. Before going into further detail on expropriation, it is worth mentioning just briefly two other administrative categories of interferences with property: *Requisition* is similar to temporary occupation except that it applies to movables; in times of public need, it may be carried on by the military. Compensation is called for and is usually determined by decree of the Executive Branch, without participation by the Judiciary. *Decomiso* is a public sanction implying loss of ownership of a movable object without compensation. Typical instances of decomiso are seizure of merchandise imported without payment of duties, forfeiture of weapons used in connection with a criminal act, and confiscation of property in connection with enforcement of sanitary regulations such as milk unfit for drinking.[2] Decomiso, in other words, is expressly a penalty. Expropriation, conversely, is not designed to be penal and as a matter of principle is always compensable.

3. Expropriation and the Legal System of Argentina

The question of whether expropriation belongs in the realm of public or private, administrative or civil law is not only a formal one in terms of differing legal theory but, under the Argentine Federal System, has important practical consequences. If expropriation is conceived as of a civil law nature, it would be governed by the Civil Code, and interpretations made by the national Supreme Court would have to be accepted in the provinces. If, on the other hand, expropriation is conceived as exclusively of public law character, then each of the provinces would have complete freedom to issue whatever rules it wanted concerning expropriation, subject only to the requirements of the federal Constitution (Article 17) which under the supremacy clause in the Constitution (Article 31) would prevail in case of conflict. The prevailing view is that expropriation has elements of both public and private law; consequently, there are only a few national principles of constitutional origin, and it is open to the provinces to fashion their own rules with respect to procedure and with respect to compensation.

In this connection, it is worth saying a word about the role of courts in Argentina in developing the governing legal rules. As in most civil law countries, decisions of the courts ("jurisprudence") lack the binding quality typically attributed to case law under the common law system. Strictly speaking, decisions of a court (except for decisions of the full bench) do not even bind that court itself, since rigid adherence to prior decisions is thought of as interference with the independence of the court to decide according to its own judgment. But on the other hand the decisions of the Supreme Court and many decisions of lower courts are published, and courts regard the interpretive criteria formulated with approval by other or higher courts as persuasive. Thus case law in fact not only serves to illustrate the law but also serves as an important source of public law.[3] An interesting aspect of the role of courts in the Argentine federal system has been that typically provincial courts deciding cases brought about by expropriation on the part of provincial or municipal authorities have tended to be more imaginative and also more solicitous of the individual property owner than have the national courts, particularly, the national Supreme Court. The technique for recognizing safeguards that might not have been recognized by the national Supreme Court has been to interpret the provincial constitution rather than the national constitution, even though the two documents contain the same basic guaranties.[4]

II. Expropriation

1. Historical Foundations

The Colonial Period. The first expropriation on record in what is now Argentina was ordered by the Cabildo (city council) of Buenos Aires in 1605, decreeing the appropriation of certain private properties in order to supply an expeditionary army. The decisions stated that persons whose property was taken would receive in payment "what justly and appropriately appears to be due to them, as is the custom." It is interesting that this first recorded expropriation already introduced the concept of just compensation, and apparently the concept of market value. A number of comparable decisions by the Cabildo of Buenos Aires were recorded in the course of the seventeenth century. The records of the colonial period do not reveal any systematic articulation of the values pertinent to a law of expropriation. However, such records of individual expropriations as survive suggest that the two primary concepts—the supremacy of the public interest and the protection due to private property—were implicit, if not explicit, throughout the period of Spanish rule.[5]

The First Years of Independence. The first constitution of Argentina of 1819 was strongly influenced by the liberal currents running through Europe. With respect to property, the Constitution of 1819 gave strong emphasis to the right of individuals to own property, but said (in Article 24)

> when the interest of the State requires that the property of any village or private individual be dedicated for public use, the owner shall receive just compensation therefor.

Particularly in relation to later expressions, it is worth pointing out that the formulation in the Constitution of 1819 follows very closely the formulation in the Fifth Amendment to the Constitution of the United States, both in its use of the term "public use" (*uso público*) and in its emphasis on "just" compensation. [6]

2. The Constitution of 1853 and the Civil Code

The Constitution of 1819, though on the whole a liberal and democratic document, did not survive the civil wars and struggles for power in the new nation. For more than twenty years starting in 1829, the country was dominated by a military dictator, Juan Manuel de Rosas, with most constitutional guaranties, including the guaranty of ownership of property, in effect subjected to the will of the dictator. Rosas' fall in 1852 led to a new constitutional convention. The constitution of 1853, with some amendments and with interruption during the Peron years in the mid-twentieth century, remains in effect today.

The Argentine constitution of 1853 is, perhaps more than any other in Latin America, based on the model of the United States Consititution, with a bicameral legislature, a president elected through an electoral college, and with some powers assigned to the national government, others to the provinces. With respect to property rights, the Constitution states (in Article 17)

> Property is inviolable, and no resident of the nation may be deprived of property but pursuant to a judgment based on law. Expropriation by reason of public utility must be authorized by law and is subject to prior compensation.

Some commentators have pointed out that in this formulation, the Constitution of 1853 omits the word "just" which is in the Constitution of 1819. However, the sound view is that the omission of the word "just" has no significance. The Spanish word *in-*

demnización, derived from the Latin *damnum* (damage) makes it clear that the object is to leave the former property owner "without damage." If, then, the compensation he receives is unjust, he is not left without damage and therefore has not been given *indemnización* as required by the Constitution. The other change in the 1853 Constitution from the 1819 version is replacement of the term "public use" by the term "public utility," *(utilidad pública),* similar to the term used in many other Latin American constitutions.

The Civil Code. The Argentine Civil Code was adopted in 1869 to go into effect as of January 1, 1870, and with various amendments, notably the 1968 reform referred to earlier, it has remained in effect until today. The Code contains a number of provisions pertinent to expropriation. Most important, Article 2511 states

> No one may be deprived of his property but for reason of public utility and by just compensation prior to transfer. In such case just compensation shall mean not only payment of the actual value of the property, but also of direct damages resulting from the loss of the property.

Despite the expansive tenor of Article 2511 it was thought not to repeal the Expropriation Law of 1866 (See Section II (3)), and accordingly, the Civil Code has been less important than one might expect with regard to expropriation.

3. Legislative Bases for Expropriation

The First Expropriation Law. The first expropriation law following the Constitution of 1853 was Law 189 of 1866. This law authorized the Executive to pay the property owner, if he agreed, "the value which [the Executive] considers to be the just price on the basis of prior assessment or report of experts" (Article 5). In the event no agreement could be reached, the price was to be determined judicially. Article 8 of Law 189 provided that after the trial was finished and an amount equal to the compensation fixed had been deposited with the court, the property was deemed to have been transferred to the taking agency. In order to arrive at the amount for compensation, the judge could appoint experts. The criteria for valuation were quite broad, including all the damages consequent upon the expropriation, the value of plants or buildings on the property, and depreciation through division of the property. However, hypothetical future profits could not be taken into account.

In case of emergency, Law 189 provided that occupation by the state need not await agreement or judicial determination of compensation. The state could take possession upon deposit of an amount equal to its offer, subject, however, to the obligation to make whatever additional payment might be decreed by the Court (Article 4).

Finally, Law 189 expressly provided (in Article 19) that the private owner could, upon returning the compensation received, demand return of the expropriated property if it was not being used to fulfill the purposes for which it had been taken.

Though Law 189 was not changed for eighty years, gradually the liberal or private property oriented outlook of nineteenth century Argentina gave way to the more state-oriented conceptions of the twentieth century. Numerous examples could be adduced for this trend, by no means limited to the subject of expropriation. To cite only two examples, the Supreme Court of Argentina in a "leading case" in 1922 sustained a law extending the period of urban leases,[7] and in 1934 sustained a moratorium on mortgages.[8]

The Expropriation Law of 1948. The liberal tradition which, at least in theory, has been dominant in Argentina since 1853 was, of course, broken by the government of Juan Perón in the 1940's and early 1950's. Perón, while putting some important social reforms into effect, not only substantially increased the powers of the state and impaired individual rights and freedoms but developed an ideology based on the functions and duties of the state. The Peronista Constitution of 1949 survived the fall of Perón by less than one year. However, Law 13,264, the Expropriation Law passed under Perón, remains in effect. The detailed provisions of the Expropriation Law of 1948 will be discussed throughout the remainder of this paper. It is pertinent at this stage only to point out that the reduction in the absolute power of the state following the fall of Peron did not immediately extend to law or to the decisions of the courts in the area of expropriation. In particular, while writers were unanimous that the consequences of devaluation of currency should be taken into account in arriving at just compensation when payment is made after—and often long after—the state takes possession of private property, this step was not taken by the Supreme Court of Argentina until June 26, 1967;[9] that is, after its reconstitution following the entry into office of the government of General Onganìa. Thus, while the new government again broke the theoretically liberal political tradition of Argentina, it reinstated some economic private rights that had not previously been fully respected.

4. Types of Property Subject to Expropriation

Article 4 of the Expropriation Law of 1948 states

> all property appropriate or necessary for the satisfaction of "public utility," whatever its legal nature and whether or not it is used in commerce or is a thing may be the object of expropriation.

It has been argued that Article 4 of the Expropriation Law is excessively broad, in that the Constitution speaks of "property" whereas the definition in the Expropriation Law may go beyond normal concepts of property. But this is a two-edged argument. If the concept of property as used (but not defined) in the Constitution is considered narrower than the sum of rights that a person may possess, then the scope of expropriation may be narrower; but so correspondingly would the fundamental guarantee in Article 17 of the Constitution stating "property is inviolable."[10] The most persuasive resolution of this dilemma would seem to be that expropriation extends only to those rights covered by the guaranty of property, whereas other rights guaranteed by the Constitution, for example the rights (in Article 14) to work and exercise any lawful trade; to petition the authorities; to enter, live in, transit, and exit from Argentine territory; to publish one's ideas in the press without prior censorship; to worship freely; to teach and to learn . . . all are rights not falling within the guaranty of property rights and therefore not subject to abridgment by the state on the ground of public utility as permitted under the concept of expropriation.

Perhaps the most difficult question in distinguishing between personal and property rights is the question of author's rights. In this writer's opinion, the state does not have the right to the work of an author, inventor, or discoverer in the sense that it can take a writing or invention and modify it for its own use. To put the case bluntly, expropriation for public utility cannot be resorted to in justification of literary or artistic censorship.

Immovable Property. Among the appropriate objects of expropriation, the most important are, of course, immovables. With respect to immovables, the Expropriation Law contemplates total or partial expropriation of particular property, and also expropriation of subsoil without expropriation of the surface land. Article 8 of the Expropriation Law provides that if in the case of partial expropriation of immovable property the remaining part is inadequate for rational use or exploitation, the expropriated party may require the expropriation of the entire property. With respect to urban lands, inadequate remainders are defined as lots which cannot be used for buildings because under the relevant local ordinances or customs the front, rear, or surface is less than what is authorized. This criterion seems to work well in cities.[11] With respect to rural immovables, Article 8 provides that the Executive Branch shall decide whether or not the remaining property is adequate for rational exploitation. This provision has been criticized in that an arguably judicial function is given to the Executive, which, needless to say, has an interest in the decision. However, this decision is subject to judicial review.

It was formerly argued, and occasionally held by courts[12] that an expropriation for purposes of erection of a public project could only take the property immediately needed for such project, and not adjacent or surrounding property. Article 7 of the 1948 law provides that expropriation may extend to adjacent property "with the purpose of carrying out plans of social improvement authorized by law." While it may still be possible to question in the courts the extent of a proposed expropriation, the provision of Article 7 eliminates a substantial range of objections.[13] In view of the characteristic of public projects to outgrow their original plans, this provision, in the writer's view, makes sense with respect to immovables; however, the concept of expropriating more than is presently needed has no place with respect to movable or intangible property.

Movable Property. Some writers have cast doubt on expropriability of movable goods at all, since in so far as movable property may be replaced or interchanged, it is difficult to show public need for any particular property. In fact, not much use has been made of expropriation of movable property in Argentina. However, there may be and indeed have been instances of shortages of particular property—for example, food or drugs during an epidemic—when the public authority has acted through expropriation to make the property available to the public.

Abuse of this authority may occur in a dictatorial government, as happened when the newsprint of a private newspaper was expropriated on the grounds that the paper was needed for official publications.[14]

Rights Other Than Ownership. In addition to ownership interests, other interests held by private parties may be subject to expropriation. For example, if an immovable subject to an easement is transferred to the state, the state may by expropriation take the easement.[15] Interestingly, if a private immovable is taken by expropriation, the lessee or tenant is not made the subject of a separate expropriation. The leasehold is simply deemed to cease to exist,[16] the value of that interest is in theory included in the compensation paid to the owner, and the tenant will look to him for his interest.

One special but not infrequent case of expropriation of personal rights is the taking by a state authority of the right to perform certain kinds of public services. Since such a right is typically derived from a franchise or concession, it might be sounder to speak in this context of retrocession of the franchise or concession, rather than of expropriation. However, Article 9 of the Expropriation Law contemplates expropriation in this circumstance, and provides that it may include the property used to perform the service in question.[17]

Taking of Government-Owned Property. There has been no dispute about the right of the nation to expropriate public property belonging to provinces or municipalities.[18] This too is specifically authorized in Article 5 of the Expropriation Law of 1948.

The reverse situation, in which a province might attempt to expropriate property of the nation, has not yet occurred in practice. At least one author, however, considers that in case of "vital" pre-eminence of the need of the province, expropriation of the national property would be permissible.[19]

5. Mining Rights

The Mining Code of 1886 provides (in Article 7) that "mines are private property of the nation or the provinces depending on their location." Thus under Argentine law mines as well as oil and natural gas wells can never be privately owned and expropriation of mines as property cannot take place. However, the nation now has the right under the Mining Code and under the Law of Hydrocarbons to enter into certain types of contracts with private persons or concerns for the exploitation of mineral properties.[20] Such contracts, presumably, are subject to expropriation. There has been some question whether the nation can renounce its power to expropriate or, in other words, whether it can give a guarantee to a contract or concession holder that the contract or concession will not be terminated before a stated period. This writer's view is that since expropriation belongs exclusively to public law, a contract cannot abridge this right. Even if a renunciation of the power to expropriate (or guarantee of the duration of a concession or contract) were contained in a law passed by the Congress, it would not alter the right of a later government to expropriate a concession or contract, since the authority to expropriate comes from the Constitution itself and therefore cannot be diminished by a mere statute. From the point of view of the investor or the contractor seeking to protect itself, it would seem that the best way to do so without running the risk here described would be to agree in advance on a special procedure for determination and payment of compensation. Such a procedure, whether contained in the contract or concession itself or in a law, would not, if reasonable, be open to constitutional objection, since the manner of determining the compensation due and the procedures for payment are governed solely by statute and not by the Constitution.

III. The Bases for Expropriation

1. The Concept of Public Utility

As already noted, the concept of public necessity never appeared in Argentine law, and "public use" only appeared briefly in the Constitution of 1819. Since the Constitution of 1853, the basis of expropriation in Argentine law has been public utility. Article 1 of the Expropriation Law of 1948 defines public utility in terms of "all those cases in which the satisfaction of a requirement determined by social improvement is aimed at." This vague and

25

imprecise definition is not made more explicit by Article 6 which states that "expropriation may include not only property necessary to the principal purpose of the expropriation, but also property convenient for such purpose." Nor has case law made the definition of public utility more specific. While particular kinds of public utility could be defined by statute—for example, the need for agrarian reform or urban renewal—no such legislative definition exists at present. In general, the courts have sustained nearly every kind of public utility as determined by the expropriating authorities.

2. The Decision as to Public Utility

Under Argentine law the branch of government empowered to declare when public utility exists is always the Legislative Branch. The courts have taken differing views about their power to review the declaration of public utility. In one instance, the Supreme Court declared that the question of public utility was nonjusticiable in that it concerns the propriety and correctness of the exercise of a power exclusively vested in the Legislature.[21] In another case, the Supreme Court of Argentina upheld a declaration of public utility regarding a military installation alleged by the property owner to be unnecessary, without examining the challenge on its merits, but simply stating that only extreme arbitrariness justified judicial interference. If the property owner wished to pursue his challenge the remedy was with the Legislature.[22] Finally, in a case involving the confiscation of a racing car for alleged nonpayment of customs, the Supreme Court said

> It is appropriate to bear in mind that no expropriation may be carried out, according to clear statement in the Constitution, but for reasons of public utility as stated in law. And whatever might be the opinion concerning the powers of judges to examine whether said cause exists, a question on which each of the [members of the court] would rely on prior opinions, it is indisputable that powers of review exist in cases of serious arbitrariness, for example, when it is clear that the State under color of the exercise of the power to expropriate actually takes property away from one person in order to give it to another for his private use, that is, without any public benefit. In such a case the judges before whom the matter is brought for review must adjudicate the question and in appropriate cases invalidate the action of expropriation.[23]

To this writer, the existence of adequate judicial review of the criteria set down by the Congress seems indispensable for assurance of compliance with the Constitutional requirement of public utility. As one writer has said, "We achieve nothing by saying that expropriation must be just, because injustices, if they exist, could not be redressed by declaration of unconstitutionality if we were to admit that the declaration of public utility were non-justiciable."[24] The racing car case quoted above can be considered a firm statement by the Supreme Court—at least up to the present—that judicial review will always exist to prevent manifest arbitrariness. Whether or not such judicial review will be effective in any given case depends on the attitudes of the members of the court. But it is certain that they have the power to exercise due judicial control of the reasonability and constitutionality of an expropriation. In this sense the role of the courts is the same as it is in reviewing other administrative or governmental acts, and in essence, raises the same issues concerning the scope of judicial review.[25]

Under Law 189 of 1866 a special law was required for each project that required expropriation, including reference to plans, professional reports, and other data describing accurately the property to be expropriated. The 1948 law, however, is much more general: Article 2 says

> The declaration of public utility shall be made in each case by a law referring to specific property. Whenever the declaration has been approved in a generic sense, the executive branch shall identify the specific property required for the purposes of the law, referring to descriptive plans, technical reports and other material sufficient for this purpose.

Thus the 1948 law permits generic characterization of public utility and leaves it up to the Executive to identify the property coming within the general description and destined for a particular expropriation. Clearly this criterion is more dangerous than the nineteenth century version, but, on the other hand, it is obvious that it cannot be known exactly what properties will be appropriate or necessary for a given public work until all of the relevant plans have been completed in detail.

3. The Scope of Judicial Review

If Congress has described the property specifically on the basis of concrete plans and with respect to a specific public project, the scope of judicial review is simple. The judiciary must simply check whether the purpose is reasonable and whether the Executive has carried out the mandate of the law, and not whether the property in question is the one most suitable for the purpose.[26] On the other hand, if Congress has merely made a general description of public utility the question becomes much more complex:

Determination of the Project. First it is necessary to know whether Congress has described specifically the public project to be carried out, just leaving to be filled in the details of the private property to be appropriated to that project. For example, the Congress might authorize the construction of an airfield in the national capital, without specifying which particular pieces of property shall be used. On the other hand, Congress might be more general and simply authorize construction of airfields where convenient.[27] Probably, under current Supreme Court rulings, the latter authorization would not be sufficiently specific to justify a subsequent expropriation, whereas the former one would be.[28]

Determination of the Properties to be Taken. In general, under Article 2 of the 1948 Law (and corresponding provisions of provincial legislation) the Executive identifies particular property for the purposes of the public project. The Legislature may, however, assign this task to a particular agency concerned with the public project in question or, for example, to the municipality directly concerned with the project. The courts will not normally interfere with either method.

The Question of Delegation. The general delegation of power by the Congress to the Executive to determine the details of an expropriation is no longer questioned.[29] But suppose a public project is operated by a private concession holder. Can the power to determine the character and extent of an expropriation be delegated to such a concession holder? This writer's view is that the delegation authorized in Article 2 of the Expropriation Law does not extend that far, so that the concession holder cannot exercise these powers. However, assuming the decision is made by the Congress or the Executive, it is clear that the beneficiary of the expropriation may be a private concession holder engaged in activity affected with public concern. Reasoning by analogy from this practice, it has been held that expropriation of a tract of land for subdivision and allotment to individual small holders is within the power of expropriation, and does not come under the prohibition of taking of property from one private person for assignment to another.[30] This issue is one on which the courts are competent to rule although, as suggested above, the chances for upsetting the expropriation once begun are not great.

IV. Compensation and Valuation

1. The Duty to Compensate

The general principle in Argentine law is clear: Compensation for expropriation must cover precisely the damage caused to private owners, without either increasing or diminishing their wealth. In other words, expropriation cannot be a source of profit either to the expropriating agency or to the previous property owner. This means that compensation shall include not only payment for the value of the expropriated property, but also for damages caused by extinction of property.[31] The principle is put in the Expropriation Law of 1948 as follows

> Compensation shall only comprehend the objective value of the property and those damages that are a direct and immediate consequence of the expropriation. Circumstances of a personal character, sentimental value, and hypothetical gains are not to be taken into account. Future profits shall not be compensated. With respect to immovables, scenic view or value derived from historical events shall also be disregarded.
> The value of property shall be estimated as if the public project had not been executed or authorized. (Article II).

2. Limitations on the General Principle

Case law has produced a series of limitations on the general principle:

(i) *It is not the goal of compensation to enable the purchase of goods similar to those expropriated.* Various formulations have been made of this point. For example, the Supreme Court has said that expropriation and compensation therefor do not constitute a purchase and sale transaction and that the compensation is not a price. Again, just compensation has been held not to require that the condemnee be placed in a situation in which he may replace the expropriated property with property of equal value. What just compensation means is that the economic sacrifice must be made good in accordance with some objective determination of value.[32]

(ii) *Compensation must not enrich the expropriated party.* Under the criterion of objective value rather than replacement cost, it would be possible in theory for the expropriated party to gain from an expropriation. However, the prevailing rule is that this shall not happen; thus, in effect, the rule for compensation is replacement cost or original cost, whichever is lower.[33]

(iii) *Criteria for compensation are to be laid down by the Legislature.* The Argentine Supreme Court has held that the elimination of the term "just compensation" from the 1853 Constitution as contrasted with the 1819 Constitution and the Fifth Amendment to the United States Constitution means that the Legislature and not the courts determine the formula for compensation, the only constitutional requirement being that the compensation be prior.[34] This statement is evidently in contradiction to other statements of the Supreme Court, that the judiciary may always review actions of the Legislature whenever arbitrary action is charged. Accordingly, commentators have criticized the statement suggesting that the Legislature can provide for unjust compensation.[35] The context in which this question was most often raised concerned depreciation or devaluation of the national currency from the time of taking to the time of the final decision concerning compensation. As is discussed in Paragraph 4 below, this problem has now been resolved by the Argentine Supreme Court in a way favored by most of the critics; that is, to recognize and compensate the owner for the loss of value of the currency during the pendency of an expropriation proceeding.

(iv) *Compensation may not exceed the claim of the expropriated party.* This principle, although stated by the Supreme Court on numerous occasions,[36] is fundamentally weak, since it is founded on a principle of civil law, whereas expropriation, as previously discussed, is basically a public law matter. Moreover, the principle has been undercut in practice by permitting the expropriated party to show new facts or circumstances after the original claim was submitted.[37]

3. Criteria for Just Compensation

The Starting Figure. As a practical matter, compensation is nearly always determined by the Appraisal Tribunal, an agency of the Executive Branch. The composition and functions of the Appraisal Tribunal are described in Section V (3) below. For present purposes, it is necessary only to know how the Appraisal Tribunal begins its valuation. Generally, with respect to immovable property, the point of departure is the assessed value for tax purposes plus 30 per cent. This figure is the limit on which, according to Article 13 of the Expropriation Law, the government and the private property owner may agree in an out-of-court completion of an expropriation. Since assessed value for tax purposes is nearly always much lower than actual value—often in the range of 50 per cent of the actual value--the procedure for out-of-court settlement is virtually never used. Nevertheless, the assessed value will be taken into consideration by the Appraisal Tribunal. It is also this sum (again increased by 30 per cent) which forms the amount required to be deposited by the State as a condition of obtaining possession while the ultimate compensation is being litigated. However, it is recognized by the courts that assessment for tax purposes is not a fair basis for determining the value of a piece of property. [38]

"Fair Value". The concept of "fair value" as developed in the United States and particularly in the case of Smyth v. Ames[39] has been essentially adopted in Argentina. Thus, to calculate the value of a piece of property it would be important in the first instance to discover its original cost, then the cost of reproduction, then the capitalized value of income derived therefrom, and in certain circumstances, the value of services rendered by the property or, where a corporation owns the property, the going value of securities based on that property. The Appraisal Tribunal determines each of these amounts and will, on request, consider evidence or argument offered by the expropriated party. Where recent expropriation proceedings have fixed the value of adjacent properties, such valuation is typically taken into account in determining compensation for the remaining property.[40] Again, if there has recently been a sale of nearby similar property, such information may be presented to and will be considered by the Appraisal Tribunal.[41]

One interesting point peculiar to Argentine law is the so-called "coefficient of disposability" of property, which reflects an increase or decrease in value of a piece of property according to whether or not it is occupied by tenants. Typically, if property is occupied by tenants the value is less than it would otherwise be because rent control in the past has continuously extended the period of leases, thus reducing the effective yield on rental property. It has been held by the Supreme Court, however, that the coefficient of disposability is not to be taken into account in valuation in expropriation cases, on the ground that under Article 24 of the Expropriation Law[42] the state takes free of leasehold or similar interests, with a 30-day period for dispossession of tenants.[43]

Business Properties. Although the value of a business as a going concern is an essential part of the owner's assets, the courts in Argentina have considered that losses to a businessman apart from physical effects come under the heading of future profits, which under Article 11 of the Expropriation Law are excluded from compensation, and do not come under the heading of consequential damages, which are entitled to compensation.[44] In this writer's view, this distinction is unsound. It might be argued, however, that the opportunity of a businessman to continue his business has not been taken since he could set up again in another place.[45]

Damages and Expenses. Article 11 of the Expropriation Law (see Section IV (1)) contains a broad, clear formula: damages directly and immediately resulting from the expropriation are to be compensated. Thus, for example, fees incurred in drawing up plans and securing municipal clearances for construction of a building were included within the amount compensable when the building was subsequently expropriated.[46] Similarly, storage and shipping costs of merchandise were included within the compensable value of such merchandise.[47]

As for costs incurred in connection with defense by the expropriated party, the Expropriation Law provides in Article 28 that the costs of judicial proceedings are to be borne by the expropriating agency when the compensation awarded exceeds the initial offer by more than half of the difference between the original offer and the owner's demands; if the compensation awarded is greater than the initial offer by less than half the difference between initial offer and demand (or indeed is less than the initial offer), the costs of the proceedings are to be borne by the expropriated party. Thus the Expropriation Law establishes a special rule concerning costs of judicial proceedings different from the normal rule in Argentina.[48] It has been argued many times that this rule is contrary to the constitutional guarantee of private property, in that it diminishes the compensation received by the private owner.[49] But despite numerous attempts, the principle embodied in Article 28 has never been successfully challenged.

4. The Relevant Time for Purposes of Valuation

Theoretically, the relevant time for purposes of calculating value of expropriated property could be (i) the date of the declaration of public utility; (ii) the date of the out-of-court offer made to the owner; (iii) the commencement of the judicial proceedings; (iv) the date of transfer of possession to the expropriating agency; or (v) other dates such as the time when the owner lost effective use of the property.[50] Argentine law has chosen the moment of dispossession as the relevant time for fixing value of property.[51] However, if a lengthy period of negotiation or litigation followed this moment, rigid adherence to the date of dispossession would, in the context of the continuing inflation in Argentina, have served and in fact did serve to put a heavy and unfair burden on the expropriated party. This problem has, as previously mentioned, been solved by the recent Supreme Court decision authorizing the court to take the devaluation of money into account.[52]

The effect of an announcement of a particular project might be either to lower or to raise the value of the property in question, depending on the nature of the project and of the property to be taken. Article 11 of the Expropriation Law makes it clear that the value of the property is to be assessed as if the project in question had not been carried out or authorized. One court chose to disregard an allegation that the award had taken into account the incremental value produced by the announcement of the public project. However, the Supreme Court ruled that the provision was *"de orden público,"* that is, it could not be set aside by the parties or the court.[53]

5. The Requirement of Prior Compensation

As we have seen, Article 17 of the Argentine Constitution, which contains the guarantee of inviolability of property, also states that expropriation for reasons of public benefit must be authorized by law and previously compensated. In practice, it turns out, this requirement has been greatly weakened.

Under the 1866 Expropriation Law an expropriation could not be perfected until delivery or deposit with the court of the compensation judicially determined to be due to the property owner. Only in cases of urgency could the Executive Branch obtain possession of the property by depositing a tender amount with the court subject to subsequent adjudication. In such cases of urgency the State could take possession but title would remain with the property owner until final adjudication and payment of the sum awarded.[54]

The current Expropriation Law provides

> When there has been no out-of-court settlement, the Expropriating Agency shall, in the case of immovable property, deposit with the federal court where the property is located an amount determined according to the assessed value for tax purposes subject to an increase up to 30 percent . . . The pendency of the proceedings shall be entered in the Registry of Property, making the property untransferable thereafter. (Article 18).

The normal practice under the current Expropriation Law is that upon payment of the deposit called for in Article 18 the State gains possession of the property, whether or not the matter is one of urgency. Moreover, though commentators have criticized the principle, [55] Article 19 of the Expropriation Law provides that the court shall declare the passage of title and order its inscription in the Registry of Property when the deposit as computed above has been paid. The latter question—that is, the formal passage of title —seems relatively minor, since in any event the State has taken possession and the owner has been deprived of the use of the property. What seems more serious is that a long time may go by before a determination of just compensation occurs. Thus, even leaving aside the question of inflation, the principle of no expropriation without prior payment of an amount equal to the value of the property is severely undercut. A small amelioration is derived from the practice that the private party may withdraw the amount deposited with the court without awaiting or prejudicing the final judgment.

6. Payment

Argentine law does not provide for payment of compensation in anything other than cash. In practice, the National Treasury pays the sums judicially determined as compensation in chronological order, that is to say, with precedence from the time of judgment and according to availability of appropriated funds. As previously mentioned, nearly all Argentine writers on expropriation have criticized the effect of payment in cash and only on the date of final judicial determination, in the context of rapid inflation. On June 26, 1967, the new Supreme Court accepted the view of the critics, and for the first time allowed an award based on the value determined as of the date of dispossession, adjusted to the date of judgment, taking into account the effect of the intervening inflation.[56]

One additional issue that deserves mention is the question of tax on expropriation awards. As a matter of federal law, it has been held that amounts awarded as compensation for a state taking are not taxable;[57] on the other hand, provincial taxes—usually relating to transfers of real property—have been permitted where the provincial law expressly provided for tax on expropriation awards.[58]

V. Expropriation Procedure

1. Effort at Out-of-Court Settlement

In Argentine law the effort to reach an extrajudicial settlement between the Expropriating Agency and the property owner is considered the first alternative in arriving at the sum to be paid by the taking agency to the owner. Nevertheless, in practice, the procedure for out-of-court settlement has lost its significance, because under Article 13 of the Expropriation Law the state can only offer to pay the amount stated in the tax records plus 30 per cent, and with these limits few property owners take up the offer.[59] In turn, since the law apparently does not compel the state to go through the nonjudicial procedures, it sometimes happens that the taking agency skips the nonjudicial procedure altogether and immediately initiates judicial proceedings.

The reason for placing a limit on settlements between the state and private property owner was apparently to foreclose corruption on the part of public officials. The consequence, however, has been for practical purposes to eliminate the nonjudicial procedure. In the writer's view, either this procedure should be eliminated completely or another means should be found to permit realistic negotiations while safeguarding their integrity. According to Article 13 of the Expropriation Law, determination of the appropriate compensation shall be made by competent officials of the taking agency, based on the declared value for tax purposes plus 30 per cent already described. If the tax records do not include improvements, a 'sum shall be fixed for these separately by the "competent officials," and the same is true for property other than immovable property. If no agreement is reached in this manner between the expropriating agency and the property owner, application must be made to the court which will then appoint a panel of appraisers as described below.

2. Commencement of Judicial Proceedings

Preliminary Stage. Once a law or declaration of public utility has been issued and an out-of-court settlement has proved impossible (or the attempt has not been made) the normal procedure is for the national Executive to designate the Solicitor General or comparable official to initiate and prosecute an action looking to the expropriation of the property located at *X,* as called for by the relevant law. Usually, the same decree sets forth the amount to be deposited with the court by the expropriating agency, as well as the source of this deposit in the budget.

Pursuant to this decree, the Solicitor General (or the District Attorney) brings the action of expropriation before the Federal Judge with jurisdiction in the area where the property is located. Attached to his petition are: (i) a certified copy of the decree designating him; (ii) the tax receipts relating to the property, used to justify the value assigned to the property for purposes of the deposit; (iii) a voucher showing the deposit with the National Bank of the amount reflected in the tax assessment record, plus 30 per cent, subject to the order of the court. It is interesting to note that the law does not obligate the State to deposit this amount but only requires a deposit of the assessed value, which may be increased up to 30 per cent. In practice, however, the State always accompanies its petition by a certificate showing that the maximum permissible deposit has been made.

Typically, the form in which the deposit is made is as follows

I hereby deposit for purposes of compensation the [stated] sum, which may be withdrawn by the property owner upon delivery of good title to the property in question free of any encumbrances and with all taxes paid.

These precautions are designed to make sure that the deposit is paid to the true owner. There is no guarantee, on the other hand, concerning the possibility that the compensation fixed in the judicial proceedings might be less than the amount deposited, since this never happens. If the property owner cannot deliver good title or cannot, for example, furnish proof that all taxes have been paid, it is customary for the judge to decree that a small sum be left with the court until the tax question is cleared up, with the transfer of title meanwhile going ahead.

The same petition by the representative of the State also usually requests an order authorizing immediate possession of the property by the State, and an order authorizing the Registry of Property to record the pendency of the expropriation proceedings, which has the effect of preventing any transfer of ownership.

In accordance with the procedure authorized in Article 18 of the Expropriation Law, the court in response to the Government's petition simultaneously notifies the property owner of the petition and sets a date for reply and issues an order that possession be transferred to the State. Theoretically, the Appraisal Tribunal is to be notified of the order to transfer possession, so that it may send a representative to examine the condition of the property at the moment of transfer. In fact, however, the expropriating agency rarely asks for notification of the Appraisal Tribunal and the private owner rarely objects to omission of this step, so that this requirement in the law largely remains an empty formality.

If there is a law in effect declaring the property in question of public utility, and if no issue can be raised as to whether the particular piece of property is included within that declaration, a property owner in his answer often acquiesces in the demand for expropriation, while reserving the right to demand return of the property if it is not used for the purpose for which it was taken.

3. Determination of Just Price

Once the initial steps of petition, deposit, order to take possession, and answer have been taken, the court is ready to accept proof as to the value of the property. The principal proof on which the final judgment nearly always is based is the report of the Appraisal

Tribunal. This body, more an administrative body than a court, consists of one member appointed by the expropriating agency, one member appointed by the property owner and ten permanent members--three from private associations concerned with immovables (engineers, architects, and builders); two nominated by the Executive Branch to represent the taxpayer; and one representative each of the Army Engineers, the National Mortgage Bank, the Public Water Administration and the City of Buenos Aires. The chairman of the Appraisal Tribunal is the Under-Secretary of Public Works.

The Appraisal Tribunal can take testimony and make its own investigation. Two-thirds of the Appraisal Tribunal must be present to constitute a quorum, and a simple majority is required for its decisions.

While the report of the Appraisal Tribunal is technically not binding on the court, Article 14 of the Expropriation Law does call for the judge to decide the level of compensation on the basis of the record before and opinions of the Appraisal Tribunal. In fact, the opinion of the Appraisal Tribunal is nearly always accepted, except if it appears clearly that it was rendered on a basis other than the criteria established by the Supreme Court. It has been held that the court may not hear additional experts, since this is the function of the Appraisal Tribunal.[60] This view seems unsound, since the Expropriation Law does not prohibit such proof and it is expressly provided for in the Code of Civil Procedure. Moreover, if the Appraisal Tribunal does not submit its report on time, a practical solution would be for the court to hear from the experts itself. However, under present practice, the report of the Appraisal Tribunal is paramount. In order to determine the basis of the decision by the Appraisal Tribunal and thus to permit challenges to its report, the complete record of its proceedings, including testimony, technical data, actions taken and not taken, and reasoning must all be submitted with the report.[61] If the report of the Appraisal Tribunal is unanimous, or even without unanimity if the representative of the taking agency voted in favor of the report, then the government cannot challenge it. Correspondingly, the private owner cannot challenge the report if his nominee voted for it.[62]

The Expropriation Law of 1948 gave the Appraisal Tribunal 30 days in which to render its report. This has now been modified by Law 14,393 of December 7, 1954, which states that the period for preparation of the report shall be 90 days, plus an additional 90 days if permitted by the judge. In practice, the report of the Appraisal Tribunal is often delayed far beyond these deadlines. Thus far the courts have been lenient on this point, and have neither adopted new procedural techniques for arriving at a valuation nor tried very hard to compel the Appraisal Tribunals to meet their deadlines. The fault here appears to be not in the statutory provisions, but in the Courts' attitude toward them.

4. The Court Hearing

Following receipt of the report of the Appraisal Tribunal, the parties submit written briefs in support of or in opposition to the opinion of the Appraisal Tribunal. Thereafter the judge renders a judgment on the amount of compensation. Also, where appropriate, the judge awards the costs of the proceedings, determined according to the relation between the offer claimed and the award discussed in Section IV(3). Normally the State pays promptly after the judgment is rendered.

Under current practice, title is formally declared transferred to the State at this stage, the idea being that in this way the constitutional requirement of prior compensation is satisfied. Since the government has been in possession--possibly for years--and has had no disadvantage from not being listed as record titleholder until the final compensation has been determined and paid, it seems to this writer that only the form and not the substance of the constitutional guarantee has been preserved through this device.

5. Rights and Remedies of Third Parties

In principle, the rights of third parties in connection with expropriation proceedings are to be adjudicated in a separate trial under Article 23 of the Expropriation Law. This is confirmed also by Article 26 of the Expropriation Law, which states

> No action of third parties can prevent an expropriation or its effects. The rights of the third party are considered to be transferred from the property to its price or compensation, with the property itself left free of all encumbrances.

In spite of the definitive character of these provisions, this writer does not believe that an absolute principle can be derived from them to the effect that third party holders of rights in property, whether *in rem* or *in personam*, may not intervene in the expropriation proceedings.[63] The writer feels that an exception should be made for the case in which title to the property in question is itself in dispute; that is to say, when a third party maintains that the supposed expropriated party is not the real owner. On this point there is precedent under the former Expropriation Law, and the current text is unchanged.[64] Of course, the intervention of a third party will not have the effect of paralyzing the expropriation in any way, but it will guard the rights of a third party as against the person who claims to be the owner.

If there is a mortgage on property subject to expropriation, it would be absurd to cancel the mortgage without paying off the debt and without giving a hearing to the mortgagee. When such a situation arises in practice, it is usual that at the time the owner requests that a check be issued to him in payment of the compensation award he also presents a statement from the mortgagee consenting to payment of the award and to cancellation of the mortgage, presumably on the basis that the creditor has taken other steps to protect himself against the debtor's insolvency or default.

6. Failure To Use the Expropriated Property for Its Intended Purpose

Law 189 of 1866 contained an express article stating that

> If the expropriated property is not used for the purpose for which it was expropriated, the former owner may take it back in the state in which he transferred it by paying the price of the compensation which he received.

This provision was not, however, included in the 1948 Expropriation Law now in effect. In contrast, most of the provincial laws contain express provisions concerning the possibility of recovery by the former owner of his property if it was not used for the purpose of public utility on which the expropriation was based.[65]

So far as national law is concerned, the writers consider it firmly established that retrocession is lawful despite the omission of the quoted passage in the current law.[66] However, the Administration does not admit this, basing itself on the fact that there has been no authoritative pronouncement on the point by the Supreme Court, and also on the difficulty of estimating administratively the value of the property to be returned.[67] Actually, there are current precedents for recovery of the property by its former owner. The federal court in Tucuman in 1965 held that while the absence of a provision concerning the return of expropriated property in the Expropriation Law prevents the detailed regulation of retrocession, the right to restitution of expropriated property is of constitutional dimension and therefore can be decreed in appropriate cases by the court itself. Since the issue was raised while the question of determining the proper compensation was still *sub judice,* the court considered itself competent to order return of the property rather than to order a money award by way of compensation.[68] Recent decisions of the national Supreme Court have recognized, at least indirectly, the right of the former owner to recover his property if the requirements of the Constitution have not been complied with.

It is important to distinguish between the action to recover the property once it has passed into the possession of the State (whether during or after the judicial proceedings of expropriation), and abandonment of expropriation by the State. The latter occurs when the State does not commence an action of expropriation within the time indicated in the Expropriation Law. According to Article 29 of the Expropriation Law, expropriation will be considered abandoned if the action is not begun within two years when the property is itself mentioned in the law, within five years when the property in question is included within a fixed zone, and within ten years when the property is included in a generic description giving the expropriating agency the authority to postpone expropriation pending modification of the property by the owner.

7. Irregular Expropriation[69]

If the guarantee of private property expressed in Article 17 is to be secure from invasion by the State, it must persist even when the State does not go through the steps required in normal expropriation. One way to express this is to say that injury to private property by the State gives rise to liability for an unlawful act.[70] Damages, restitution, and even rental payments have been on occasion ordered by courts in actions of this kind. For example, the Supreme Court annulled a municipal law requiring 30 per cent of gate receipts from boxing to be paid to the state;[71] and declared contrary to Article 17 of the Constitution a federal law prohibiting the shipment of grapes to wineries located outside the place where the grapes were grown.[72] In some cases, particularly where restitution is not possible or would be contrary to the public interest, an unintended injury to property has been treated as giving rise to a claim for compensation under the Expropriation Law, with the typically higher provisions for compensation in light of the Constitutional guarantee.[73] The most common cases of this kind involve side effects of public works projects; for instance, diversion by the government of a stream in order to supply water to a town, to the detriment of the riparian owner. In such case, though none of the procedures for expropriation have been followed with respect to the private owner's water, he is entitled to initiate an action reclaiming compensation from the court, regardless of the issues of proper delegation, public utility, etc.[74]

VI. Rights of Aliens

There is no legal or Constitutional differentiation between aliens and citizens pertinent to the question of property ownership in Argentina. Aliens are entitled to all the rights and subjected to all the burdens described in the preceding pages (Articles 14, 20). There is, however, a tradition, going back to the earliest days of the republic, providing for special compensation to particular aliens--first (1857) to the French (Law 221), then to the British (Law 222), to the Scandinavians (Law 223), and to the Prussians (Law 87). Though in recent times there has been no special legislation favoring aliens, there is no doubt as to the privileged status which foreigners, especially the representatives of important capital, enjoy in terms of protection from state taking property. Intercession by foreign ambassadors with the State, though not always successful, has been common over the years. More than once the protection of private foreign capital has been linked by foreign diplomats to the chances for public debt rescheduling by the major creditor nations.

Insofar as there may be said to exist a common international law concerning taking of property, Argentine law would seem to comply with it in that Argentine law requires compensation for a taking, requires a public purpose, and affords minimum procedural safeguards. If Argentine practice does not always result in full "fairness" to property owners, this cannot be said to be due to its nationality or to any discrimination inherent in the system.

Attempts to raise the protection accorded to the property of foreigners through international agreements have not been successful. The Investment Guaranty Agreement between the United States and Argentina at first related only convertibility of currency.[75] The attempt by the United States to negotiate a protocol failed to secure approval by the Argentine Congress and is not considered by Argentina to be in force.[76]

Conclusion

While Argentina has had a number of political upheavals throughout its history, it has not undergone the kind of shift in social and political thought that some of the other Latin American states have experienced. The absolute concept of property of the nineteenth-century codes—never indeed as absolute as it seemed —has eroded gradually in response to changing conceptions of the proper scope of governmental regulation. Similarly, the concept of public utility has been broadened to the point that very few properties are beyond the reach of the government's powers of acquisition, and there are very few activities that the government cannot become involved in if, as a matter of political decision, it chooses to do so.

Argentine law endeavors to live up to the Constitutional guarantee of compensation, though it frequently happens that there is a considerable delay between the fact of state taking and payment to the private party. The 1967 decision of the Supreme Court concerning reference to an inflation index went a long way toward correcting this situation. As for determination of compensation, though the principle decision is usually made by an administrative tribunal, the criteria as spelled out in the expropriation law are on the whole reasonable, and the courts are able to supervise the process of valuation.

All things considered, it may be said that the Argentine expropriation system is fair and reasonable in its treatment of the expropriated party, but not efficient in arriving at prompt decisions.

How adaptable the system might be to a major program of rural or urban social reform is not yet known.

Notes

1. See Manuel María Diez, *Derecho Administrativo,* Vol. IV, p. 222 (1969); Rafael Bielsa, *Derecho Administrativo,* Vol. IV, p. 424 (1965); Benjamin Basavilbaso, *Derecho Administrativo,* Vol. VI, pp. 107-127 (1956); Agustín Gordillo, *Derecho Administrativo de la Economía,* pp. 392-395 (1967); Fernando Legón, *Tratado Integral de la Expropiación Pública,* p. 168 (1934); Héctor Lafaille, *Derecho Civil. Tratado de los Derechos Reales,* Vol. I, pp. 423-424 (1943).

2. See Villegas Basavilbaso, op. cit. (note No. 1), p. 530; Diez, op. cit. (note No. 1), p. 343. For amplification of the author's views concerning the so-called police power and its use see Agustín Gordillo, *Estudios de Derecho Administrativo,* pp. 11-31 (1963).

3. See Agustín Gordillo, *Introducción al Derecho Administrativo,* p. 201 (1966).

4. Nearly all the provincial constitutions provide for expropriation only for public utility and upon payment of prior compensation, with only slight variation in wording. See, e.g., Art. 27 of the Constitution of the Province of Buenos Aires, Art. 6 of the Constitution of Catamarca, Art. 83, Para. 21 of the Constitution of Córdoba, Art. 23 of the Constitution of Corrientes.

5. The material concerning colonial Buenos Aires is collected in *Acuerdos del Estinguido Cabildo de Buenos Aires,* V. F. López, ed., 6 Vols. (1883-99). For selected decisions see Vol. I, pp. 122-3, 387; Vol. II, pp. 29; Vol. III, pp. 258, 668; Vol. VI, p. 279.

6. See Fernando Legón, op. cit. (note No. 1), p. 111, for exact text.

7. Agustín Ercolano v. Julieta Lanteri Renshaw, 136 Fallos de la Corte Suprema de Justicia de la Nación (hereafter referred to as Fallos) 161 (4 / 28 / 1922).

8. Oscar Agustín Avico v. Saúl G. de la Pesa, 172 Fallos 21 (12 / 7 / 1934).

9. Provincia de Santa Fé v. Carlos Aurelio Necchi, 268 Fallos 112 (6 / 26 / 1967).

10. Bourdieu v. Municipalidad de la Capital, 145 Fallos 307 (12 / 16 / 1925).

11. See Villegas Basavilbaso, op. cit. (note No. 1), p. 371.

12. See, e.g., Municipalidad de la Capital v. Isabel A. de Elortondo, 33 Fallos 162 (4 / 14 / 1888).

13. In other words, not only the immovables "needed" for a public project, but also those merely "convenient" for it, are now subject to expropriation. This rule was previously established by the Supreme Court in Carlos Casado v. José Mario Bombal, 85 Fallos 303 (6 / 19 / 1900).

14. See Rafael Bielsa, op. cit. (note No. 1), Vol. IV, p. 474, note 67.

15. See Walter A. Villegas, *Expropiación por causa de Utilidad Pública*, p. 288 (1939).

16. Nac. Arg. v. Juan Luis Clucellas, 242 Fallos 35 (10 / 13 / 1958).

17. See, Julio Oyhanarte, *La Expropiación y los Servicios Públicos*, p. 24 (1957) and José Canasi, *El Justiprecio en la Expropiación Pública* (1952) See also José Canasi, *Tratado Teórico Práctico de la Expropiación Pública*, Vol. 1, p. 121 (1967).

18. Empresa del Ferrocarril del Sud v. Municipalidad de La Plata, 128 Fallos 74 (9 / 17 / 1918).

19. See Miguel S. Marienhoff, *Tratado del Dominio Público* pp. 262-3. (1960).

20. Argentine law makes it clear that the surface owner has no rights to mine the subsoil beneath his property if it is covered by a concession. See, e.g., Art. 41 of the Law of Hydrocarbons.

21. Provincia de Jujuy v. Ledesma Sugar Estates & Refining Co., 209 Fallos 632 (12 / 30 / 47).

22. Gobierno de la Nación v. Ingenio y Refinería San Martín del Tabacal, S.A., 209 Fallos 390 (12 / 3 / 47).

23. Nac. Arg. v. Jorge Ferrario, 251 Fallos 246 (11 / 10 / 61).

24. Germán J. Bidart Campos, *Derecho Constitucional* (1966), Vol. II, p.354.

25. For elaboration of the author's view on this point see Agustín Gordillo, *El Acto Administrativo* (1969), pp. 185-237.

26. See Fisco Nacional v. Giraldez, 142 Fallos 83 (10 / 20 / 24), and Estado Argentino v. Urguizú, 176 Fallos 306 (12 / 11 / 36).

27. Gobierno Nacional v. Bordeau Teófilo, Vol. I., Cámara Federal de La Plata, Jurisprudencia Argentina 1965-II p. 370 (3 / 1 / 65).

28. Compare Ferrocarriles del Estado v. Carmelo V. Vidal, 150 Fallos 354 (3 / 12 / 28), and Ferrocarril Gran Oeste Arg. v. Vidal Hermanos, 120 Fallos 332 (2 / 27 / 15) with the previous case. See also Villegas Basavilbaso, op. cit. (note No. 1), p. 359.

29. Compare Ferrocarril Gran Oeste Arg. v. Vidal Hermanos, 120 Fallos 332 (2 / 27 / 15), with these two cases: Estado Argentino v. Urguizú, 176 Fallos 306 (12 / 11 / 36) and Fisco Nacional v. Giraldez, 142 Fallos 83 (10 / 20 / 24).

30. See text at note No. 23.

31. See José Canasi, *El Justiprecio en la Expropiación Pública* (1952), p. 159; Villegas Basavilbaso, op. cit. (note No. 1), p. 390; and Prov. de Tucumán v. José Aráoz,, Supreme Court of Tucumán, 53 La Ley 415 (3 / 13 / 48) and Cirelo Juan Zanola v. Nac. Arg. 253 Fallos 307 (8 / 3 / 62).

32. Gobierno Nacional v. Dumas, Corte Sup. de la Nación, 47 La Ley 865

(8 / 20 / 47); Admin. Gen'l de Obras Sanitarias de la Nación v. Torquinst y Bernal, 241 Fallos 73 (7 / 7 / 58). Compare case cited in note No. 9.

33. See Canasi, op. cit. (note No. 31), p. 147, 151. Compare case cited in note No. 9.

34. See case cited, 241 Fallos 73 in note No. 32. This criterion was abandoned in the *Necchi* case cited in note No. 9.

35. See, among others, Germán J. Bidart Campos, "Indemnización Expropiatoria y Devaluación Monetaria," 8 *Revista El Derecho* 659 (1964); Trigo Represas, "Influencia de las Fluctuaciones Monetarias en los Procesos de Expropiación," 2 *Revista JUS 178 (1962); Miguel Marienhoff, "Expropiación. 'Justa' Indemnización:* Concepto y Fundamento Positivo," *IV Revista Jurisprudencia Argentina* 255 (1959); Atilio Alterini, "La Indemnización Expropiatoria como Obligación de Dar Sumas de Dinero," I / IV, *Revista Jurídica de Buenos Aires* 185 (1964).

36. See Fisco Nacional v. Bernasconi y Cía., 178 Fallos 381 (9 / 10 / 37); Cozzi de Manaut v. Municipalidad de Buenos Aires, 253 Fallos 412 (9 / 7 / 62); Nac. Arg. v. Puppo, 224 Fallos 106 (10 / 16 / 52).

37. See Sconfenza v. Municipalidad de la Ciudad de Buenos Aires, 250 Fallos 226 (7 / 21 / 61); Nac. Arg. v. Colombo, 249 Fallos 691 (5 / 31 / 61).

38. See Nac. Arg. v. Mijalovich, 242 Fallos 224 (11 / 10 / 58); Nac. Arg. v. S.A. Ingenio y Refinería San Martín del Tabacal, 247 Fallos 150 (6 / 24 / 60); Banco de la Nación Argentina v. Sorbet, 248 Fallos 452 (11 / 25 / 60).

39. 169 U.S. 466 (1898). This was not an expropriation case, but rather a case involving railroad rate regulation based on the "fair value" of the railroad's properties. The Supreme Court laid down the following criteria: 1) original cost of construction, 2) amount expended in permanent improvements, 3) amount and market value of bonds and stock, 4) present cost of construction, 5) probable earning capacity of the property under the particular rates prescribed by statute, 6) the sum required to meet operating expenses.

40. Nac. Arg. v. Compta, 246 Fallos 208 (4 / 22 / 60).

41. See Nac. Arg. v. Sarli, 242 Fallos 150 (10 / 29 / 58); Nac. Arg. v. Santos Capello, 247 Fallos 545 (8 / 31 / 60); Nac. Arg. v. Dominquez y Cía., 248 Fallos 146 (10 / 26 / 60). Different criteria may be adopted if the land in question is very extensive.

42. Article 24 provides that once legal possession of the property is decreed the leasehold interests lapse and the tenants have a thirty-day period in which to vacate, subject to the State's right to extend this period as it deems reasonable.

43. Nac. Arg. v. Ezra Tenbal y Cía., 237 Fallos 690 (5 / 22 / 57); Nac. Arg. v. S.A. Argal, 237 Fallos 707 (5 / 22 / 57).

44. See Musso v. Nac. Arg. 242 Fallos 254 (11 / 14 / 58).

45. Nac. Arg. v. Valdemar Diring Lansen, 237 Fallos 38 (2 / 15 / 57); Nac. Arg. v. Kaysser, 244 Fallos 499 (9 / 23 / 59).

46. Nac. Arg. v. Luis Soubié, 249 Fallos 651 (5 / 19 / 61).

47. See cases cited in note No. 45.

48. The normal rule in Argentina generally provides for the costs and legal fees to be borne by the losing party.

49. See Villegas Basavilbaso, op. cit. (note No. 1), pp. 449-50; Diez, op. cit. (note No. 1), pp. 299-300.

50. Compare Villegas Basavilbaso, op. cit. (note No. 1), p. 403.

51. See Canasi, *Justiprecio,* (note No. 31), p. 115-116, note 90, for numerous citations to judicial decisions.

52. See the *Necchi* case cited in note No. 9.

53. Fisco Nacional v. Salvador Di Rosa, 242 Fallos 11 (10 / 1 / 58).

54. Cía. General de Ferrocarriles de la Prov. de Buenos Aires v. Busto de Silva, 108 Fallos 240 (2 / 18 / 08).

55. See Villegas Basavilbaso, op. cit. (note No. 1), p. 395; Diez, op. cit. note No. 1, p. 282 and others cited in note No. 1.

56. See the *Necchi* case cited in note No. 9.

57. See Pasquini v. Dirección General Impositiva, Tribunal Fiscal de la Nación, "Sentencias del Tribunal Fiscal de la Nación" (1966), Fallo 201, p. 498 (9 / 26 / 61); see also the Supreme Court rulings in Cerilo Juan Zanola v. Nac. Arg., 253 Fallos 307 (8 / 3 / 62); Administración General de Parques Nacionales y Turismo v. Martínez, 248 Fallos 678 (12 / 16 / 60).

58. Degó, Félix Antonio s. / demanda de inconstitucionalidad, 242 Fallos 73 (10 / 20 / 58).

59. See Canasi, *Justiprecio,* (note No. 31), p. 62.

60. For the view that experts' testimony is not admissible see Administración Gen'l. de Vialidad Nacional v. Adolfo Passini, 247 Fallos 155 (6 / 24 / 60); Nac. Arg. v. Domínguez y Cía., 248 Fallos 146 (10 / 26 / 60).

61. See Nac. Arg. v. Juan Luis Clucellas, 242 Fallos 35 (10 / 13 / 58); Federación Gráfica Arg. v. Golinoosky, 244 Fallos 170 (7 / 8 / 59); and Nac. Arg. v. Montanegro, 248, Fallos 288 (11 / 11 / 60), regarding the exception to the usual practice of accepting the Appraisal Tribunal's decisions.

62. See Dirección Gen'l de Ingenieros v. Musto, 214 Fallos 439 (8 / 25 / 49); Prov. de Jujuy v. Ledesma Sugar States & Refining Co. Ltd., 215 Fallos 47 (10 / 10 / 49); Ministerio de Guerra v. Bronzes de Andrieu, 216 Fallos 296 (3 / 30 / 50).

63. For the opposite view, see Villegas Basavilbaso, op. cit., (note No. 1), p. 442; Diez, op. cit., (note No. 1) p. 295. Compare Canasi, *Tratado,* op. cit., (note No. 17), pp. 796-799.

64. Prov. de Buenos Aires v. Mathilde Alvarez de Toledo de Díaz Velez, 211 Fallos 1013 (7 / 30 / 48).

65. See the provincial laws cited in Villegas Basavilbaso, op. cit. (note No. 1), p. 454, note 9.

66. See, among others, José Canasi, *La Retrocesión en la Expropiación Pública* (1964), and Villegas Basavilbasco, op. cit. (note No. 1), p. 456.

67. The Attorney General stated that opinion (*Procuración del Tesoro de la Nación,* 98 *Dictámenes* 451 (9 / 29 / 66), based on an inconclusive decision of the Supreme Court (Horacio Bauzá y otro v. Administración General de Vialidad Nacional, 252 Fallos 310, (5 / 18 / 62), and even though the admissibility of retrocession seems assured after the decision rendered in Nac. Arg. v. Angel y José Tonello, 272 Fallos 88 (11 / 6 / 68), it seems unlikely that the Administration will modify its present criterion, unless some new legal provision authorizes it to reach an agreement as to the valuation of the immovable. It seems to us that the same kind of difficulties that hinder out-of-court settlements in expropriation cases will be present in retrocession cases.

68. See Gobierno Nacional v. Terán, Cámara Fed. de Tucumán, 122 La Ley 650 (12 / 17 / 65).

69. See the decisions mentioned in note 67; for other aspects of the problem see José Canasi, "La Retrocesión en la Expropiación Pública y la Ley Nacional 13.264," 113 *La Ley* 567 (1964) and "Doctrina y Jurisprudencia," a note by Nerva in 109 *La Ley* 892 (1963).

70. See María Graciela Reiriz, *Responsabilidad del Estado* p. 19 (1969).

71. Club Atlético River Plate v. Municipalidad de la Capital, 171 Fallos 142 (9 / 22 / 34).

72. See Emilio Cahiza, v. Gobierno Nacional, 177 Fallos 237 (4 / 7 / 37). See also Milberg v. Provincia de Buenos Aires, 216 Fallos 241 (3 / 23 / 50), involving the payment for a fence built in response to an irregular taking, and Delcasse v. Gobierno de la Nación y la Sociedad Puerto de Rosario, 145 Fallos 89 (11 / 6 / 25), regarding the payment of interest (rent) to the legitimate owners of an island for an "illegal occupation" by the State—a "bad faith tenant."

73. Zavaleta de Labrue v. Nac. Arg. y Parodi y Fegini, 211 Fallos 46 (6 / 4 / 48); Empresa Ferrocarriles de Entre Ríos v. Gobierno Nacional, 176 Fallos 363 (12 / 21 / 36).

74. Francisco Piria v. Prov. de Buenos Aires, 185 Fallos 105 (11 / 8 / 39); Zavaleta de Labrue v. Nac. Arg. y Parodi y Fegini, 211 Fallos 46 (6 / 4 / 48); Admin. Gen'l. de Obras Sanitarias de la Nación v. Prov. de Buenos Aires, 258 Fallos 345 (5 / 29 / 64).

75. See Cámara de Diputados, Diario de Sesiones de 1961, pp. 5986-6085; Cámara de Senadores, Diario de Sesiones de 1960, p. 978. See also agreement between United States and Argentina relating to Investment Guaranties, signed at Buenos Aires, December 22, 1959, 12UST955, 411 UNTS 41.

76. Signed at Washington, June 5, 1963, and entered into provisionally according to U.S. records on June 5, 1963.

Brazil

Miguel Seabra Fagundes

Contents

I. The Right To Own Property and Its Regulation   53
   1. The Concept of Property Under Brazilian Law   53
   2. The State and Private Property—The
      Portuguese Tradition   53
   3. The State and Private Property—The
      Constitutional Tradition   54

II. Restrictions on the Ownership and Use of Property   55
   1. Types of Restrictions on Enjoyment of Property   55
   2. Restrictions for Public Health and Safety   56
   3. Rent Control   56
   4. Restrictions on the Use of Agricultural Land   57
   5. Regulation of Business   57
   6. Direct Government Participation in Industry   57
   7. National Security and Extraordinary Legislation   58
   8. Rights of Aliens   59

III. The Power To Expropriate   59
   1. Evolution of the Institution of Expropriation   59
   2. Property Subject to Expropriation   60
   3. Purposes Justifying Expropriation   61
   4. Transfer to Private Parties   62

IV. Compensation and Valuation   62
   1. The Scope of Compensation   62
   2. Criteria of Just Value   63
   3. Determination of Just Value   64
   4. The Relevant Time for Purposes of Compensation   64
   5. Rights of Third Parties   66

V. Expropriation Procedure   66
   1. The Declaration of Public Utility or Social Interest   66
   2. Effect of the Declaration   67
   3. Judicial Proceedings   68
   4. Defenses Available to the Property Owner   69
   5. Judicial Review of Acts of Expropriation   70
   6. Irregular Expropriation   71

VI. Transfer and Use of Expropriated Property   72
    1. Transfer of the Expropriated Property   72
    2. Abandonment of Expropriation   72
    3. Failure To Use the Expropriated Property in
       Accordance with the Declaration of Expropriation   72
Conclusion   74
Notes   74

1. The Right To Own Property and Its Regulation

1. The Concept of Property Under Brazilian Law

The idea of property has the broadest of meanings under Brazilian law. It includes the totality of material objects (immovables, movables, livestock) and those deeds and other kinds of property having economic value. Only some personal rights within the realm of family relationships are not included. Thus, the concept of property goes beyond the concept of domain (*dominio*) which applies only to rights over material objects. This broad concept of property has its origins as far back as the Constitution of the Empire.[1]

The declaration in the 1967 Constitution of Brazil (as amended by Amendment 1 of Oct. 17, 1969) that "The right to own property is fully guaranteed, save in case of expropriation on account of public utility or necessity or in the common interest" (Article 150, Section 22) covers all types of property, regardless of the juridical acts or deeds from which the property derives, whether from civil or public law, from donations or purchase *inter vivos* or *causa mortis*, and regardless of the character of the property: tangible or intangible; or the nature of the property interest: full domain, rights in an object owned by another, contractual rights, or other rights.[2]

2. The State and Private Property—The Portuguese Tradition

Even in the absolutist kingdom of Portugal, where in theory the King was lord of all the land, legal texts suggest that the royal power was to be exercised sparingly. The so-called 'forced sale'—either the sale of immovables for the erection of churches, monasteries, and the like, or the sale of Moorish slaves to effect an exchange for Christians enslaved by Moors—was accepted as a regular procedure; but appraisal, carried out with the rigor of a quasi-judicial act, was always resorted to in order to determine the price to be paid.[3]

An example relevant to Brazil is the Decree of June 13, 1808, issued under the rule of Prince Regent John VI, then governing the entire Portuguese Empire from Brazil because of the Napoleonic invasion of Metropolitan Portugal. Faced with the need to acquire land on which to build a gunpowder and ordnance factory in Rio de Janeiro, the Regent decreed the expropriation of a farm on the outskirts of the city, but with the proviso that a "competent appraisal shall first be carried out, the resulting value of which, together with the increase established by my laws, shall be paid to the owners of property taken over for public service."[4]

The evolution of colonial law in this field culminated in the Decree of May 21, 1821:

> Whereas, the security of property is one of the bases of the social contract among men, and whereas, I know that the property of individuals is being taken from them against their will under the pretext of meeting the needs of the State or Royal Estate, and in complete violation of the sacred Right of Property; and further, that on many occasions the only purpose is personal gain, that in some cases is carried to the point where deeds or other documents necessary to claim compensation are denied to property owners;
>
> I hereby decree that from this date on no one shall be forcibly deprived of his property, regardless of the needs of the State, without prior agreement on the price which the Royal Estate must pay to the owner at the moment of transfer; since it could happen that on a given occasion the means to make prompt payment may be lacking, I order that in such cases the seller shall be given a suitable deed so that in due time he may collect compensation on the basis of consent freely given by the owner both to the transfer of his property to the State and to the form of payment. Those who would proceed otherwise shall be subject to the penalty of payment of double value to the injured party.[5]

3. The State and Private Property—The Constitutional Tradition

Though Brazil has had six different constitutions since its independence in 1822, the broad and full guarantee of the right of property has remained substantially unchanged. Thus, the political constitution of the Brazilian Empire, promulgated on March 25, 1824, declared:

> The right to own property is guaranteed in all its fullness (Article 173, Paragraph 22).

The first Republican constitution of February 24, 1891, stated:

> The right to own property is hereby maintained in full (Article 72, Paragraph 17).

Under the Constitution of July 16, 1934, the protection of property was reaffirmed, though it was coupled for the first time with a reference to the common or collective interest as a condition on the exercise of the right to own property:

The right to own property, which shall not be exercised against the common or collective interests, is hereby guaranteed (Article 113, Number 17).

The Constitution of November 10, 1937, contained the same guarantee but omitted the reference to the compatibility of property rights with social well being (Article 122, Number 14). Under the Constitution of September 18, 1946, and the Constitution of January 24, 1967, the social welfare clause reappears as a condition for the guarantee:

The Constitution guarantees to Brazilians and to foreigners residing in the country the inviolability of rights concerning life, liberty, personal safety, and property, subject to the following conditions: . . . (Article 150 of 1967 Constitution, Article 141 of 1946 Constitution)

The right of property is guaranteed, except in case of expropriation for public necessity or utility or social interest, in which case prior and just compensation must be paid in cash, subject to the provisions of Article 161 permitting the expropriated party to accept government bonds with a monetary correction clause. In case of imminent danger, such as war or internal disorder, the competent authorities may use private property if the public good so required, with assurance of the right of compensation at a later date.

. . . (Paragraph 22 of Article 153 of 1967 Constitution (Amendment 1), Paragraph 16 of Article 141 of 1946 Constitution)

II. Restrictions on the Ownership and Use of Property

1. Types of Restrictions on Enjoyment of Property

The right to own property may be restricted, either in its attributes (some people cannot own certain types of goods) or in relation to its exercise (some property cannot be used in conflict with certain protected interests, public or private). For example, the use of immovable property may be limited by considerations of the safety, quiet, and health of the neighborhood, or by the need to prevent interference with the use of adjacent property.[6]

Moreover, the need to build and maintain certain public services and facilities, such as electric power lines, sewers, airfields, and the like, imposes burdens on ownership of property—particularly immovable property. Finally, certain measures of a temporary nature, such as billeting troops or requisitioning warehouses for food depots, may interfere with private property, pending compensation. Such measures are only admissible during times of imminent public danger or during a state of siege. [7]

2. Restrictions for Public Health and Safety

By use of police powers, the State subordinates the exercise of the right to own property to its concept of the common good. Thus, the law provides that an owner may not threaten the life, health, peace, or comfort of the community through the use of certain goods. For instance, carrying firearms is prohibited without special permit; explosives may be produced only in certain areas; and there are special rules relating to the production or use of inflammable substances. Similarly, legislation and regulations apply with respect to control of noise, traffic flow, and similar aspects of public health and safety.

3. Rent Control

In addition to regulations based on public health and safety, there are other restrictions on the use of property in the nature of social legislation. For example, landlords of both residential and industrial property are restricted in their right to repossess property occupied by tenants, and are forbidden to refuse to renew leases if the lessee wishes to do so, except in certain conditions, such as the lessor's need to use the property himself or some default by the lessee. [8]

Moreover, owners are not free to increase rent at any time they see fit. In the case of residential property, periodic adjustments of the rent shall be made according to established legal criteria and official indices of monetary value. [9] In the case of commercial or industrial buildings, rent adjustments shall be made through legal arbitration, to be held whenever the lease has changed for renewal or every three years, if the value of the property has changed more than 20 percent since the previous fixing of the rent. [10]

4. Restrictions on the Use of Agricultural Land

Those tracts of land defined by law as *latifundio* or as *minifundio* are considered anti-social. The Constitution and the land statute contemplate the abolition of *latifundia* and *minifundia* by way of expropriation.[11] Moreover, land owners are subject to the agrarian policy laid down by the government, which may deal with the types of crops planted, farming methods, and conservation of natural resources.[12]

5. Regulation of Business

Other kinds of restrictions in the nature of economic regulation may be thought of as imposing limitations on the use of property. For example, Brazil has laws designed to prevent any action aimed at control of markets, elimination of competition, arbitrary raising of profits, and any other activity which may adversely affect the supply of goods and maintenance of necessary public services. Moreover, the production of certain non-essential goods such as alcoholic beverages, cigarettes, and perfumes is limited by law, and an individual person or firm is not permitted to participate, through stock ownership or otherwise, in more than one company engaged in the production of such articles.[13]

6. Direct Government Participation in Industry

The system of exploitation of property under Brazilian law is based primarily on free enterprise.[14] Accordingly, it is the role of private enterprise as a matter of preference and with the stimulus and support of the State to organize directly and to carry out economic activities.[15] Exploitation by the State of industrial or business activity is only justified when necessary to supplement private initiative, but whenever a given sector of the economy is unable to develop "in an efficient way in a competitive regime on the basis of free enterprise," the Government may by means of a specific law, intervene in such sector in order to take over exclusive exercise of certain activities.[16] In this way a private party may lose ownership in its goods, which may be expropriated by the State incidental to the exercise of monopoly. Alternatively, the private party may merely be deprived of use of the property in a given activity now committed to the State, being free to use it or dispose of it for other purposes. In either case, however, the private party is entitled to compensation.[17]

7. National Security and Extraordinary Legislation

In addition to the previously mentioned categories justifying state intervention in or interference with private property rights, the Brazilian Constitution makes provision for a number of extraordinary circumstances in which rights to property as well as other kinds of personal and civil rights are temporarily suspended. For example, Article 163 of the Brazilian Constitution of 1967 (Amendment 1), states that intervention in the economic domain and monopoly of a given industry or activity are permitted when essential for reasons of national security . . . individual rights and guarantees being assured. In that event, compensation may be paid to the owner at a later date. As in most Constitutions of Latin America, the Brazilian Constitutions have typically made express provision for the state of siege. Under the 1946 Constitution it was the Congress which could proclaim a state of siege (Article 66), under the 1967 Constitution (Amendment 1) that power is given to the President of the Republic (1) in case of serious disturbance of order or threat of the outbreak of such disturbance; or (2) in case of war (Article 155). The state of siege may apply to the entire nation or to particular regions. Under a state of siege designated government officials may search and arrest in private homes, and this power includes taking of property in the home; the designated government officials may use or occupy buildings, including buildings owned by private or public bodies; and they may take "other measures provided for by law," including expropriation without prior payment. Except in the event of war a state of siege shall not exceed sixty days, subject to extension by a new decree. When the state of siege ends, the restrictions and measures listed above end automatically, and affected persons are to be immediately restored to their status prior to the beginning of the state of siege. At that time they become entitled to return of their goods and compensation for their use during the state of siege, since the state of siege only authorizes suspension of rights and guarantees and not suppression of such rights and guarantees.[18]

8. Rights of Aliens

Under Article 153 of the 1967 Constitution (Amendment 1), Brazilians and aliens residing in the country are equally entitled to the guarantees of rights concerning life, liberty, security, and property. Nevertheless, the exercise of these rights is limited with respect to certain areas and certain kinds of property. For example, mines and mineral deposits are subject to authorization or concessions issued by the Federal Government only to nationals of Brazil.[19] However, aliens may be partners in Brazilian firms holding concessions if so authorized, except with respect to exploitation of oil, which is entrusted to a state monopoly, Petroleo Brasileiro, S.A. "Petrobras," a mixed firm whose shareholders are the national union, the states, municipalities, other public entities, and wholly Brazilian-owned firms.[20] A second important exception to the equality of Brazilian nationals, foreigners, and resident aliens in the use of property relates to the exploitation of hydroelectric power which, again, is limited to Brazilian nationals.[21] In addition, building and operating Brazilian flag ships and operation of journalistic enterprises, including radio and television, may be carried on only by Brazilians and corporations wholly owned by Brazilian nationals.[22]

III. The Power To Expropriate

1. Evolution of the Institution of Expropriation

The institution of expropriation grew up in Brazil as it did in many other countries in connection with undertaking of services typically performed by the State, such as the building of roads, schools, hospitals, sewers, military installations, and the like.[23] These objectives appear in the Republican Constitutions of 1891, 1934, and 1937.[24] From the first, however, certain additional objects of expropriation were recognized in Brazilian law. Thus in 1891 the Civil Code authorized expropriation of literary, artistic, or scientific works in cases where their owners would not consent to re-publication.[25] In 1941 (under the 1937 Constitution) the Expropriation Law added as authorized objectives the supply of provisions to centers of population, the operation of public transit, the preservation of historical and artistic monuments, and protection of natural resources of exceptional scenic or scientific value.[26] While these additions to the stated purposes of expropriation broadened the original categories, expropriation remained in essence a device for making use of private property needed in carrying out essential public services.

The 1946 Constitution made a major change. Under Article 141, Paragraph 16, the guarantee of property was qualified by the words "except in case of expropriation for public necessity or public utility, or social interest . . ." Again, Article 147 of the 1946 Constitution stated that "the use of property shall be conditioned upon social well-being. The law may, subject to the observance of the provisions of Article 141, Section 16, (including the right to compensation) promote a fair distribution of property, with equal opportunities for all." The 1967 Constitution (Amendment 1), as we saw above, reiterates the concept of public utility or social interest as a justification for expropriation. While it does not expressly retain the phrase "promote a fair distribution of property" from the 1946 Constitution, the 1967 Constitution (Amendment 1) does contain a list of principles of social justice, including freedom of initiative, appreciation of labor as a condition of human dignity, the social function of property, harmony and solidarity of the factors of production, and repression of abuse of economic power (Article 160). The new Constitution states that for the purposes contemplated (above) "the union may expropriate rural land."

2. Property Subject to Expropriation

In principle, any right or property having economic value is subject to expropriation. In practice, however, the laws implementing the provisions regarding expropriation in the successive Brazilian Constitutions have never permitted expropriation of movable property or of intangible rights, except for rights granted by the State such as patents and copyrights.[27] Recent legislation, however, states that all property may be subject to expropriation, thus including all things of value—movable or immovable, tangible or intangible.[28] One additional property right subject to expropriation is a franchise or public service concession. This may take the form of reassignment by the State to itself or to a third party of the right to operate the service in question, on the grounds that the present concession holder has proved unable to perform in a satisfactory manner. Another means of effecting expropriation of public service concessions is a taking by the State of the majority of shares in the firm holding the concession, followed of course by the Government's taking charge of the operations of the concession. In either case, compensation is due the prior owner.[29]

3. Purposes Justifying Expropriation

Recent Brazilian legislation has reduced the various bases set forth in the 1967 and prior Constitutions to two: public utility and social interest.[30] The Legislature has apparently reached the conclusion that the concept of utility, being broader than that of necessity, suffices for all cases—those in which it would be useful to expropriate a given property and those in which it would be necessary to do so.[31] Social interest is thought of as a different purpose, in that it implies an attempt to achieve social goals of the State through the use of expropriation such as "just distribution of property" under the 1946 Constitution (Article 147) or achievement of the "social function of property" under the 1967 Constitution (Amendment 1, Article 160). Typically, the traditional uses of expropriation, such as national defense, public health, construction of public works, achievement of state monopolies, and the like, are thought of as coming under public necessity or utility. Expropriation on the grounds of social interest may include, for instance, the taking of non-productive land with a view to redistribution and better exploitation, or the taking of property for resettlement of urban slum dwellers. To some extent, of course, the two purposes may blend—for example, in the area of conservation of natural resources, coupled with, say, an irrigation project. However, expropriation for purposes of social interest is generally pursuant to specific legislation, and that legislation—for example, the agrarian reform plan—establishes further criteria for the kinds of property that may be taken, typically property within a certain area found to be underproducing, overpopulated, or otherwise devoted to an uneconomic or undesirable use of the land.[32] In addition, the agrarian reform law authorizes expropriation of minifundia and latifundia; areas benefiting for large public works; and areas with large numbers of share-croppers, tenants, or squatters. In fact, as of 1970, no large-scale agrarian reform has taken place in Brazil.

4. Transfer to Private Parties

The fact that expropriation is undertaken on the grounds of social interest does not necessarily preclude the transfer of the expropriated property to private parties. The essential requirement for expropriation of private property is not that the transferee be a public entity, but only that the property to be expropriated shall be used in the common interest. Thus, for example, expropriation has been upheld where the land taken was transferred to a private firm which would erect a football stadium.[33] Again, the Federal Government was upheld in its expropriation of immovable property to be turned over to the Getulio Vargas Foundation, a foundation devoted to nonprofit educational and research activity. If, however, an expropriation was carried on only in the interest of the transferee, it should be disallowed.[34]

IV. Compensation and Valuation

1. The Scope of Compensation

Under Paragraph 22 of Article 153 of the 1967 Constitution (Amendment 1), compensation for expropriation must be just. The criterion of justice, literally, means economic equivalence between the value of the expropriated property and the value of the payment. Expropriation shall not be the cause of either impoverishment or enrichment of the expropriated party. The consequence of expropriation shall be only the replacement by cash (or in cases of taking of large agrarian holdings, special government bonds)[35] of the owner's former property, in such amount as may match as closely as possible the value of the property taken, including its economic significance. Compensation must cover not only the value of the expropriated object itself, but also the advantages and rights related to use of property. For example, when warehouses owned by certain coffee dealers were taken by the government, the Civil Chamber of Sao Paulo held that it was necessary for the coffee dealers to acquire or erect new warehouses, and accordingly the compensation award included the cost of acquiring new warehouses.[36] Again, in cases where the sum awarded is greater than the sum originally tendered by the expropriating agency, courts typically award attorneys' fees.[37] Similarly, interest is awarded from the date of transfer of property to the date of final determination of the just price. Consequential damages, such as loss of possible profits, are not awarded.[38] The principle is to reduce the specific sacrifice demanded of the individual property owner in the common interest as much as practicable and thus to distribute the sacrifice throughout the community as a whole.

2. Criteria of Just Value

Under the previous Law of Expropriation, the award of compensation with respect to taxable immovable property was limited to a range between ten and twenty times the rental value less tax.[39] It was thought, however, that such a standard might well conflict with the Constitutional principle that compensation must be just, and the provision was abolished in the Expropriation Law of 1956.[40]

The 1956 Expropriation Law directs the court in an expropriation case to consider the following factors in determining the compensation to be paid:

a. Assessed value for tax purposes
b. Acquisition cost of the property
c. Profits earned from the property
d. Location of the property
e. State of preservation of the property
f. Insured value of the property
g. Market value over the past five years of comparable property
h. Valuation or depreciation of the remaining property

Of these factors, the most important are the three elements most subject to variation—profits earned from the property, market value, and appreciation or depreciation of the property remaining in private ownership. Since by hypothesis the owner is not interested in selling his property, the attempt to make him whole through compensation must take into account the profits he has been earning or could earn from the property. Accordingly, profit yielded by the property is the most important element in determining the amount of compensation payable. Moreover, losses due to the unavailability of the property taken, including loss of profits due to interruption of business, must be taken into account. The period for which lost profits are compensated is that in which the former owner could reasonably be expected to acquire comparable income-producing property with the proceeds of the compensation award. The market value of the property at a given moment may not always suffice to make the former owner whole. Only when it is found that the former owner would not suffer other losses besides that of his property, and when there is no division of the property (since this always entails other damages), is it appropriate to rely on market value as the best way of determining price.[41]

In providing that any appreciation in value of the remaining property as a result of the expropriation may be taken into account, the law seeks to place the determination of compensation on an economically just basis, excluding unjust enrichment on the owner's part. But not all such increases in price are to be considered. General appreciation which includes also immovables not expropriated, and remote, barely probable increases are not to be included in any assessment. Only immediate and special increase in values shall be deductible from the amount of the price.[42] To take generic increases into account would be to treat unequally persons in identical situations. This is prohibited by the Constitution.[43] Moreover, it would infringe indirectly upon the principle of just compensation.

3. Determination of Just Value

As can be seen from the above list of criteria, determination of compensation is in part a technical matter. Accordingly, the judge before whom the expropriation proceedings are brought must appoint an expert, and both the State and the private owner may appoint assistants to the expert. The expert's report is only advisory and the judge may reject some or all of it, but he must consider the report and explain any differences.

4. The Relevant Time for Purposes of Compensation

The value of expropriated goods is, basically, to be determined as of the date of appraisal.[44] However, in the event that more than one year elapses between such appraisal and judicial determination of the amount of compensation—whether by the court of first instance or on appeal—the court shall also determine the appropriate adjustment to be made to take account of changes in monetary value. This principle, only recently added to Brazilian expropriation law after some doubt as to its consistency with the Constitutional principle of just compensation, now provides a measure of realization of the large devaluation from year to year that has in recent times been affecting the Brazilian *cruzeiro*.[45]

A related problem is the consequence of failure by the expropriating authority to make the requisite payment or deposit. Typically, this comes about when the original declaration by the expropriating authority is found insufficient by a court. Normally the law does not make provision for this contingency, aside from a requirement of six per cent interest on unpaid debts.[46] Recently, however, some courts have considered that the circumstances of rapid inflation unforeseen in either the Civil Code or the Constitution require provision to be made for adjustment to take account of large-scale currency devaluation. For example, the Fourth Civil Chamber in São Paulo wrote in 1959:

> The loss in value of purchasing power of currency suffered by the expropriated party upon receipt several years after transfer of the tendered compensation is contrary to explicit Constitutional guarantee of full prior compensation. This damage is greater than mere delay and amounts to a deprivation of compensation due. It could be objected that to make allowance for loss of purchasing power of the currency runs counter to the official value given by the State to its currency and denies the legal tender. However, in a case such as the present one, it is not possible to ignore the real value of the currency. This case is not a simple case of a money debt, but rather is a case of money being used to make whole a person deprived of his property in the interest of the State, and accordingly entitled to an equivalent between the money award and his property.[47]

Again, the Civil Chamber in Guanabara wrote in 1965:

> ...Jurisprudence is an instrument which must move together with social conditions. There is no other economic phenomenon which so affects the country at present as the constant devaluation of currency...The criteria [calling for adjustment of compensation on the basis of changes in the value of the currency] are thus better adapted to the aims of the Constitution and avoid the flagrant injustice which would occur if the expropriated party had to pay accumulated back taxes up-dated in accordance with the most recent indices of monetary adjustment.[48]

The Federal Court of Appeals has expressed itself along similar lines.[49] The Brazilian Supreme Court, however, has not formally departed from the former rule—that the legal rate of interest is the only means of adjustment arising from delay in making the appropriate payment for rights of third parties.[50]

5. Rights of Third Parties

As we have seen, the Constitutional principle of just compensation applies to all those who have proprietary interest in property subject to expropriation. If third parties—for example, tenants in houses—had to look to the expropriated party for compensation they would either lose rights without compensation or, if they recovered, would deprive the expropriated party of some of the compensation paid to him by the State. However, the current expropriation law adopts the principle of unity of compensation coupled with "subrogation," whereby subordinate holders of interests in the property expropriated (for example, lessees) may proceed against the primary party and claim a share in the compensation award (Article 26). In practice, where the rights of two or more persons in a given piece of property are clearly established (for example, in case of a mortgagee), subrogation operates without difficulty.[51] Where the rights of the property owner and others are not so easily assessed—for example, in the case of a lessee or the holder of a right other than ownership such as an easement—the principle of subrogation does not provide adequate protection for the third party. A court might hold that the provision limiting compensation to the value of the rights of the actual owner is unconstitutional, and accordingly include the value of third party's rights in the basic award. Alternatively, a third party might proceed directly against the State, alleging that he had been deprived of property contrary to the Constitutional guarantee. Some instances of both of these procedures have occurred.[52] Neither one, however, is fully established in the decisions of the Supreme Court or other higher courts of Brazil.

V. Expropriation Procedure

1. The Declaration of Public Utility or Social Interest

The declaration of public utility or social interest is usually made by decree, issued by the Executive Branch. The competence to delegate the authority to issue the declaration depends on the governmental unit for whose benefit the expropriation is made; thus, for example, if the expropriation is made for the benefit of the National Government, the declaration of public utility or social interest is issued by the President of the Republic or his delegee; if the expropriation is for the benefit of a state or territory, the declaration is issued by or on behalf of the government of that state or territory; if the expropriation is for the benefit of a municipality or of the Federal District, the declaration is made by or on behalf of the relevant prefect.[53]

In certain cases, such as those concerning highway construction for the Federal Government, it is not necessary to issue the declaration of public utility, since that declaration is deemed made by approval of the project by the competent administrative body.[54] Whenever the property to be expropriated is already in the public domain—for example, property of a state to be expropriated by the National Government, or property of a municipality to be expropriated by a state or by the National Government—the declaration of public utility or social interest requires the assent of the Legislative Branch, as well as of the Executive.[55] In other cases, it is possible, though unusual, for the declaration to be issued by the Legislative Branch. A legislative declaration is, in effect, a law requiring the Executive to act.[56]

In addition to the normal course of expropriation on the initiative of a governmental entity, holders of public service concessions have the right to initiate expropriation procedures in the courts.[57] Upon good cause shown, the courts may direct the Executive Branch to issue to a declaration of public utility with respect to property required, for example, by a telephone company, electric utility, or waterworks.[58]

2. Effect of the Declaration

According to the Expropriation Law of June 21, 1941, the declaration of public utility or social interest has the following effects:

1. It provides for a beginning and final date for the expropriation (Article 10).

2. It authorizes the officials named in the declaration to take possession of the property, and, in the case of immovable property, to enter onto that property (Article 7).

3. It authorizes an inventory on the physical conditions of the

property and an evaluation of the property as a basis for compensation (Article 10).

4. It puts a freeze on the value of the property, so that improvements after the effective date of the declaration are not compensable by the expropriating agency, except if made by authorization of that agency (Article 26).

5. It restricts removal of the property. Transfer of movable property as to which a declaration of public utility or social interest has been issued is a fraudulent transfer.[59]

Subject to the above, the owner continues to be free to make use of his property as he chooses, including building on it, leasing it, transferring it, or using it until the expropriation has been consummated by payment of compensation for the property.[60]

In the case of expropriation for public utility, the declaration lapses if the expropriation is not carried out or if the transfer of property does not take place voluntarily within a five-year period from the date the declaration is published. In case of expropriation for social interest, the period is two years from date of publication of the declaration. Once a declaration has lapsed, a full year must elapse before a new declaration may be issued concerning the same property.[61]

3. Judicial Proceedings

If, following the declaration of public utility or social interest, the expropriating authority and the property owner fail to agree on the price, either party (or in certain cases a beneficiary of the expropriation) may bring the case before a court with a view to determining the value of the property through judicial procedure and effecting the transfer of the property following the deposit of the requisite sum by the expropriating authority. Action on this petition follows ordinary civil procedure, subject to certain modifications, such as simplification of service of summons, prohibitions of delay, and with provision for appointment of experts by the judge.[62]

Once the case has been brought before the court, the expropriating authority (or the beneficiary of the expropriation) may, on the basis of urgency, request that the court issue a provisional decree, authorizing the expropriating authority to take possession.[63] Normally, such a request is filed with the original petition; however, if the need for possession becomes urgent after the original filing of the petition, a request for possession may be made subsequently.

Approval of the request for possession is subject to provisional deposit of the value of the property. This value is set for most property in accordance with the summary procedure prescribed in the Code of Civil Procedure concerning hearings on preventive or provisional measures.[64] In the case of immovables subject to building or land taxes, the amount to be deposited is fixed on the basis of data already in existence. In the case of property subject to building taxes, the deposit shall be equal to the price tendered if that sum is equal to at least twenty times the rental value. If the price tendered was less than this value, the deposit shall equal twenty times the rental value. In the case of an immovable residence, if the value offered by the expropriating authority (Union, States, etc.) is challenged by the owner, the provisional value to be deposited will be determined by the judge within 48 hours.[65] Before fixing the value the judge may hear the expert but is not obliged to accept his report. In the case of property subject to land taxes, the amount of the deposit shall equal the value stated in the official land registry (*cadastre*) for taxation purposes in the proceeding fiscal year. If no current assessment is available, it is up to the judge to fix the amount of deposit, taking into account the time when the assessed value was originally established and estimates of subsequent increases or decreases in value of the property.[66]

As a rule, the fixing of the amount to be deposited may be done only upon notice to the property owner. However, this rule may be waived on request of the expropriating party in cases where it is not necessary to have a judicial decision on the amount to be deposited.

Whenever the declaration of public utility or social interest suggests an urgent need for the property, the request for provisional transfer of possession must be made within 120 days from publication of the declaration. Since the law forbids the repetition of an allegation of urgency, only facts occurring subsequently can create a second opportunity for a petition of urgency once this period has expired.[67]

4. Defenses Available to the Property Owner

The defense in expropriation hearings is limited to contesting the price offered and to raising objections of a procedural nature. The question of whether possession of a given piece of property is, in fact, a matter of public utility or social interest is not subject to judicial review in the expropriation proceeding. This point is made clear by Article 9 of the Expropriation Law of 1956, which on this issue repeats the substance of earlier laws.

The reason for this limitation, of course, is based on the need to simplify the process of expropriation and to protect it from delays which could postpone definitive transfer from private to public possession of property declared to be of public utility or social interest. However, judicial consideration of procedural defects, such as those concerning competence, form, motivation, or object of the expropriation is not precluded. This is guaranteed by Article 153, Paragraph 4 of the Constitution, which provides that the law shall not exclude any injury to individual rights from consideration by the Judicial Branch.

5. Judicial Review of Acts of Expropriation

Perhaps the most important question concerning the act of expropriation concerns the legitimacy and truthfulness of the stated motives and purposes - in other words, whether or not the expropriation is truly based on public utility or the social interest. Writers from the time of the first Brazilian Constitution up to today have, for the most part, been of the view that judicial control of the motives and purposes of the declaration of expropriation must be admissible.[68] Their view has been that a contrary conclusion would go against the Constitution. The present writer does not share the majority view. In his view, the basic principle that all Constitutional guarantees are subject to judicial control is not violated by eliminating judicial review over the assertions made in the declaration of expropriation. This is so because a direct challenge is possible subsequently; thus the choice of remedies prior or subsequent to the act of expropriation is a matter of procedural methods which may be decided upon by the Legislative Branch.[69]

Case law has gone in different directions on the issue of judicial review. Some courts have permitted consideration of the question of public necessity;[70] others have rejected this possibility, and have limited the scope of judicial hearings to the establishment of the price, the method of payment, and the issue and transfer of ownership.[71] Today, however, it can be stated that the position of the courts, including the Supreme Court, is the restrictive one. In expropriation proceedings, the courts today exclude any examination of the existence of public utility or social interest.[72]

With respect to all those elements in the action of expropriation not committed to the discretion of the expropriating agency, judicial control of the administrative act is possible. Thus, for example, in addition to questions of form and procedure, the judiciary may examine expropriations decreed for the benefit of private persons to see whether such expropriations fit within the cases specified by law.[73] The judiciary may review, and, if necessary, cancel expropriations asserted to conflict with positive law—as in the case where the property is destined for a use other than the one stated in the declaration, or where the allegation of extended public use is a pretext for seizing property of a particular owner.[74] The courts are careful, however, not to go beyond the function of the judiciary and not to substitute their judgment or discretion for those of the executive branches. Accordingly, the issue of whether a particular piece of property is the most desirable or useful for a public project, or whether that project is best designed to advance the public good, or whether the public good will be served by a particular social or economic policy with which the expropriation is connected, are all questions beyond the scope of inquiry of the courts.

6. Irregular Expropriation

Brazilian law does not know so-called "inverse condemnation" or indirect expropriation, whereby in case a state or other expropriating authority "takes" privately owned property without going through the procedures of expropriation, the property owner asks a court to restore the property or award damages on the ground that the state has been guilty of illicit action. Since the state could frustrate such a proceeding by issuing a declaration of public utility or social interest and thus beginning the formal process of expropriation, the practice in Brazil is that owners affected by an irregular expropriation accept the *fait accompli* and sue simply for the value for the property taken plus damages resulting from the unlawful action. In such cases the Supreme Court has considered it well settled that the value of the property must be taken as of the date of unlawful occupation, with compensatory interest and damages from that date to the date of judgment.[75]

VI. Transfer and Use of Expropriated Property

1. Transfer of the Expropriated Property

The effect of the Constitutional requirement for prior compensation is that transfer of property cannot take place without deposit by the expropriating agency of the compensation due.[76] Normally the transfer is completed and in case of immovable property the new ownership is recorded in the Public Registry upon receipt by the expropriated party of the amount deposited. In the event the owner does not appear in order to claim the amount deposited, or in case title to the property is in dispute so that it is impossible to collect the award immediately, the expropriating agency, having done all it was required to do, may treat the transaction as completed and take final title.[77] It is clear that a different solution would lead to the result that transfer of property to the State in accordance with public utility or social interest could be frustrated at the will of one or more private parties.[78]

2. Abandonment of Expropriation

Expropriation may be abandoned at the bequest of the expropriating authority at any time during the judicial proceedings for expropriation or even after a compensation award has been rendered. Since the justification of expropriation is advantage to the State, or rather to public utility or social interest, there is no reason why the State should take over private property or pay compensation therefor if the public interest would not be served by such action. However, if the State does abandon an expropriation, it is liable to the owner for damages which the declaration and proceedings of expropriation may have caused him.[79]

3. Failure To Use the Expropriated Property in Accordance with the Declaration of Expropriation

It may happen that property expropriated as set forth above is not used for the purposes set forth in the declaration of public utility or social interest. In the event that the property is not used at all, it must be tendered to the former owner for the compensation paid. This follows from Article 1150 of the Civil Code, which provides:

> In cases in which the property is not used in accordance with the purpose for which it was expropriated, the Union, the States or the Municipality shall offer to return an expropriated immovable to the former owner for the price paid.

Literally, this provision would apply not only where the property was not used at all, but also where it was used for a purpose other than the one stated in the declaration of expropriation. However, case law distinguishes between nonuse, or nonuse in the public interest, and a different use from the one stated. As the Civil Chamber of São Paulo has stated, "As long as the property is used for public utility or social interest, the alteration of the original project does not constitute reason for the invalidation of the act of expropriation and does not create a right in favor of the con-demnee."[80] This result is reconciled with Article 1150 on the basis that to invalidate an expropriation in such cases would be simply a formality since the State could, through a second declaration, render the new use legitimate, thus negating any claims the former owner might have had.

In the event the property is not used at all or is transferred to a third party not entitled to it, the former owner may bring suit for return of his property. Again, this conclusion might be thought to conflict with Article 35 of the Expropriation Law, which states that expropriated goods "once appropriated to the public treasury may not be returned except in case of nullity of the expropriation." Whether the state has the option of returning the property or responding in damages is not clear. Some cases have held that the right guaranteed by Article 1150 of the Civil Code is a personal right, convertible into a claim for damages.[81] Other cases, however, consider the owner's right as a real right giving him a claim for return of the property.[32] This writer believes the latter view is the more consistent with the Constitutional nature of expropriation, since if the basic justification of expropriation fails—because the property is not used or is transferred to a third party without legal justification—the act of expropriation becomes invalid and should be reversible.[83] Conversion of the owner's claim into a claim for money damages may well render the

Constitutional guarantee ineffectual in practice, thus permitting circumvention of the Constitution by an act of mere force cloaked in legitimacy.[84]

Conclusion

Brazil in the second half of the 1960's took a sharp turn from the direction in which it seemed to be heading in the first part of the decade. Emphasis has been placed on economic growth and industrialization, rather than on redistribution of land and urban renewal. Accordingly, expropriation as a tool of social reform with political overtones has not played the role it has in other countries. Land reform with compensation in 20-year government bonds instead of cash was authorized in 1964, but no significant use has been made of this power. While controls have been imposed in other areas of individual rights, the protection of property has not been significantly impaired.

Nevertheless, the State's right of eminent domain remains predominant. Any degree of public purpose or use will today support expropriation, whether because the state chooses to assume a monopoly position in an industry or requires particular property for a public facility. But the guarantee of compensation in cash and in full value remains in effect, and to the extent any exchange of real property for cash can be considered fair, Brazil today maintains its traditional position.

Notes

1. See Augusto Teixeira de Freitas, *Consolidação das Leis Civis*, p. 74 (1876); Laforate Rodrigues Pereira, *Direito das Coisas*, p. 24 (1877); J. M. de Carvalho Santos, *Código Civil Interpretado*, Vol. VII, p. 314 (2nd ed., 1945).

2. See Ruy Barbosa, *Comentários à Constituição Federal*, Vol. V, pp. 399-414 (M. Peres ed., 1933) for a series of opeinions and comments on the question concerning the content of the property laws.

3. *Ordenações do Reino*, Book 4, Tit. XI, Sec. 4, as quoted by Ildefonso Mascarenhas Silva, "Desapropriação por Utilidade Social," 82 *Revista de Direito Administrativo* 2-3 (1965).

4. Ibid., p. 3.

5. Ibid., pp. 3-4.

6. Civil Code of Brazil, Tit. II, Chap. 2, Sec. V.

7. Federal Constitution, Amendment No. 1, Art. 153, Sec. 22.

8. Law No. 4494 of Nov. 25, 1964, Arts. 8-11; Decree No. 24, 150 of April 20, 1934, Arts. 1, 3, 8.

9. Law No. 4494 of Nov. 25, 1964, Arts. 3-5; Law No. 5334 of Oct. 12, 1967, Arts. 1-3.

10. Decree No. 24, 150 of April 20, 1934, Arts. 8, 13, 16, 31.

11. Federal Constitution (Amendment No. 1), Art. 160, Sec. 4; Law No. 4504 of Nov. 30, 1964 (Land Statute), Arts. 4, 18, 19, 20.

12. Law No. 4504 of Nov. 30, 1964, Arts. 1, 2, 18, 34, 35, 42.

13. Federal Constitution (Amendment No. 1), Art. 160, Sec. VI; Law No. 4132 of Sept. 26, 1962, Arts. 1, 2, 6.

14. Federal Constitution (Amendment No. 1), Art. 157, Sec. I.

15. Ibid., Art. 170.

16. Ibid., Art. 163.

17. Ibid., Art. 153, Sec. 22.

18. Ibid., Art. 155.

19. Ibid., Art. 161, Sec. 1; Mining Code, Arts. 15, 38, 80.

20. See Law No. 2004 of Oct. 3, 1933, Art. 18.

21. See Decree Law No. 852 of Nov. 11, 1938, Art. 6.

22. Federal Constitution (Amendment No. 1) Arts. 173 and 174.

23. Law No. 422 of Sept. 9, 1826, Art. 1; Decree No. 353 of July 12, 1845, Arts. 1-35.

24. Federal Constitution of 1891, Art. 72, Sec. 17; Federal Constitution of 1934, Art. 113, Sec. 17; Federal Constitution of 1937, Art. 122, Sec. 14.

25. Civil Code of Brazil, Art. 660.

26. Decree Law No. 3365 of June 21, 1941 (Expropriation Law), Art. 5.

27. Civil Code of Brazil 660; Regulation approved by Decree No. 16, 264 of Dec. 19, 1923, Art. 66.

28. Expropriation Law of 1941, Art. 2.

29. Synesio Rangel Pestana v. Estado de São Paulo, Tribunal de Justica de São

Paulo, 81 RQA 210 (1962); Cia. Paulista de Estradas de Ferro v. Estado de São Paulo; Supremo Tribunal Federal, 76 RQA 217 (1962).

30. Expropriation Law of 1941, Arts. 1, 2, 5-7, 9; Law No. 4132 of Sept. 26, 1962, Arts. 1 and 2.

31. Prefeitura Municipal de Guarujá v. Condomínio Sítio Pai Cará; T. J. de Sao Paulo, 58 RQA 232 (1959).

32. Law No. 4504 of Nov. 30, 1964 (Land Statute), Art. 48.

33. Luis Hermany Filho e Cia., Ltda. v. Prefeitura do Distrito Federal, T. J. de Guanabara, 146 *Revista Forense* 273 (1951).

34. Laura Rocha Guimarães v. Fundação Getúlio Vargas, S.T.F., FFRQA 238 (1964).

35. Federal Constitution (Amendment No. 1); Art. 161, Par. 1, relating to Expropriations of Rural Lands.

36. Luis Ferreira, S.A. v. Prefeitura Municipal de Santos, T. J. de São Paulo, 58 R.D.A. 237 (1959).

37. Prefeitura Municipal de São Paulo v. Expolio de Oscar Cazzoli, S.T.F., 26 R.D.A. 225 (1949).

38. Municipal de São Paulo v. Humberto Vitale, T. J. de São Paulo, 146 R.T. 135 (1942); Municipal de São Paulo v. Horacio Cardelli, T. J. de São Paulo, 152 R.T. 600 (1944); Aças Roechling Buderus Ltda. v. Municipal de São Paulo (1942).

39. Expropriation Law of 1941, Art. 27.

40. Expropriation Law No. 2786 of March 21, 1956, Art. 4.

41. See Miguel Seabra Fagundes, *Da Desapropriação no Direito Brasileiro,* p. 351 (1942), for a more general discussion.

42. In the case arising out of the expropriation of ITT's subsidiary in Rio Grande do Sul in 1962, the State argued that costs of wages and fringe benefits should not be included in calculating the rate base upon which the value of the assets was to be determined. The notion was not accepted and the question was not presented on appeal because of settlement.

43. An opposite stand was taken by the courts of the States of São Paulo—Juvenal Serapião do Prado v. Prefeitura de São Paulo, T. J. de São Paulo, 27 R.D.A. 201 (1950)—and Guanabara—José Martins de Amaral v. Prefeitura do Distrito Federal, T. J. de Distrito Federal, 53 R.D.A. 149 (1957).

44. Expropriation Law No. 2786 of March 21, 1956, Art. 3 (amending Art. 26 of the Expropriation Law of 1941).

45. Expropriation Law of 1941, Art. 26(2) (as amended by Law No. 4686 of June 21, 1965).

46. Civil Code of Brazil, Arts. 1062-64.

47. Município de Araraquara v. Mário Vitório Dosualdo; T. J. de São Paulo, 63 R.D.A. 161 (1959).

48. Antônio Peres Casanova v. Estado da Guanabara, T. J. da Guanabara, 10 Revista de Jurisprudencia do Tribunal de Justiça do Estado da Guanabara 283 (1965).

49. *Aureleano Barbosa e outros v. Central Elétrica de Furnas, S.A.,* Tribunal Federal de Recursos, Diário da Justiça, p. 2758 (8 / 9 / 67).

50. Sumula No. 416: "There is no reason for complementary compensation due to delays in the payment of the price."

51. Expropriation Law of 1941, Art. 31.

52. Fumo Pinto Corrêa v. Prefeitura Municipal de São Paulo, T. J. de São Paulo, 81 R.D.A. 222 (1962); Elias Juliano Bonnard v. Prefeitura Muncipal de São Paulo, T. J. de São Paulo, 36 R.D.A. 233 (1953).

53. Expropriation Law of 1941, Art. 6.

54. Law No. 302 of July 13, 1948, Art. 24 (dealing with highways and public roads); Law No. 4102 of July 20, 1962, Art. 25 (dealing with railroad companies); Law No. 4089 of July 13, 1962, Art. 37 (dealing with the Sanitation Dept.); Law No. 3995 of Dec. 14, 1961, Art. 14 (dealing with transportation and electrical energy).

55. Expropriation Law of 1941, Art. 2, Sec. 2. See also Augusta Amália Becker v. Prefeitura Municipal de Itanhaén, S.T.F., 58RQA 227 (1958).

56. Expropriation Law of 1941, Art. 8.

57. Expropriation Law of 1941, Art. 3.

58. Francisco Matarazzo Jr. v. José Ribeiro de Almeida, T. J. de São Paulo, 18RQA80 (1948); Olímpio Garcia Figueiredo v. Francisco Matarazzo Jr.; S.T.F., 48RQA 226 (1953).

59. Code of Civil Procedure of Brazil, Art. 675, II, Art. 676, II and III.

60. See Haydée de Melo Zarvos v. Prefeito Municipal de São Paulo, 53 RQA 143 (1957).

61. Expropriation Law of 1941, Art. 10; Law No. 4132 of Sept. 26, 1962, Art. 5.

62. Expropriation Law of 1941, Arts. 3, 10, 13, 16-19, 21.

63. Expropriation Law of 1941, Art. 15 (as modified by Law No. 2786 of May 12, 1956). See Cia. de Carres, Luz e Força do Rio de Janeiro v. Alcides Alves Pereira, T. J. de São Paulo, 54RQA 128 (1958).

64. Code of Civil Procedure of Brazil, Art. 685. Under this procedure, the hearing

opens 48 hours following the filing of the petition, whether or not an answer has been received from the respondent. The judge holds an open hearing lasting no more than 3 days, followed by an immediate decision. The provision for immediate decision does not release the judge from the duty to base his decision on proof and on reasoning, which must be stated as a basis for his decision.

65. Decree Law No. 1075 of Jan. 22, 1970.

66. Law No. 2786 of May 21, 1956 (Expropriation Law), Art. 15 (1) c and d.

67. Ibid., Art. 15 (2).

68. Ruy Barbosa, *Comentários à Constituição Federal,* Vol. II, pp. 415-416 (H. Pires ed., 1933); Leite, Soledôneo, *Desapropriação por Utilidade Publica,* p. 58 (1902).

69. Compare Miguel Seabra Fagundes, *Da Desapropriação no Direito Brasileiro,* pp. 166-167 (1942).

70. Marin Feydet Ribeiro v. Fazenda Muncipal, T. J. de Guanabara, 1RQ163 (1905); Ambrosio Crespo de Oliveira v. Cia. Française du Port do Rio Grande do Sul, S.T.F., 51RQ537 (1915).

71. Gabriel Neto Amarante v. Estado de Minas Gerais, T. J. de Minas Gerais, FFRF326 (1938); Banco da Bahia v. Companhia Concessionária das Docas do Porto da Bahia e União Federal, S.T.F., 16 A.J. 215 (1930).

72. Isabel Sampaio de Almeida Prado v. Cia. Paulista de Estradas de Ferro, S.T.F. 27RQA193 (1949); Chadler S. A. v. Estado da Bahia, S.T.F. 21RQA144 (1948).

73. Luis Herman y Filho & Cia. Ltda. v. Prefeitura do Distrito Federal, T. J. do Distrito Federal, 58RQA230 (1958); Prefeitura Municipal de Guarujá v. Condomino Selio Pai Cará, T. J. de São Paulo, 56RQA241 (1957).

74. Law No. 4717 of June 29, 1965, Art. 2(e).

75. Turano Emílio Cesário v. Depto. Nacional de Estradas de Rodagem, S.T.F. 72 R.D.A. 187 (1962).

76. José Katelian v. Prefeitura Municipal de Uberoba, S.T.F., 84 A. J. 230 (1947); Manuel Joaquim Pereira Ramos v. Fazenda do Distrito Federal, T. J. de Guanabara, 61 A.J. 120 (1941); Banco do Brazil e Empresa Auto-Omnibus Vista Santa Maria Ltda. v. Prefeitura Municipal de São Paulo, T. J. de São Paulo, 224 R.T. 323 (1954).

77. Expropriation Law of 1941, Art. 34.

78. The Law of Expropriation provides in Art. 33 that "the deposit with the judge of the price fixed by the decision shall be considered prior payment of compensation." In order to reconcile this text with the constitutional requirement of prior compensation, it must be understood that in accordance with Art. 29 (which conditions the taking of possession either on payment or appropriation of the funds) and Art. 34 (which provides that in case of reasonable doubt about

ownership, the owner is required to furnish proof before the judge, with the deposit meanwhile remaining in court) the deposit only assumes the force of payment in exceptional circumstances; that is, when the owner does not appear in due time in order to claim it, or when he does not furnish satisfactory title.

79. José Katelian v. Prefeitura Municipal de Uberaba, S.T.F., 17 R.D.A. 108 (1947); Geraldo Majela Muanda v. Dept. de Aguas e Energia Elétrica, T. J. de São Paulo, 58 R.D.A. 247 (1959).

80. Pompeu Augusto dos Santos v. Prefeitura Municipal de Santos, T. J. de São Paulo, 54 R.D.A. 122 (1957).

81. Gertrudes Schaumann Heyck v. Prefeitura Municipal de São Paulo, T. J. de São Paulo, 32 R.D.A. 223 (1952); Américo Georgetti v. Estado de São Paulo, T.J. de São Paulo, 54 R.D.A. 138 (1957).

82. Paulo Prado do Amaral v. Prefeitura Municipal de São Paulo, S.T.F., 51 R.D.A. 284 (1957); Thomaz Paladino v. Fazenda do Estado de São Paulo, T.J. de São Paulo, 59 R.D.A. 281 (1958).

83. Transfers to third parties shall be legitimate in cases of entities working for a common interest recognized by the Public Administration, of persons affected by a redistribution of land for social purposes, and of buyers of land which is destined for resale as a result of urban planning.

84. Miguel Seabra Fagundes, "Da Contribução do Codigo Civil para o Direito Administrativo," 78 R.D.A. 1 (1964). See also Fermino da Silva Whitaker, Desapropriacao, p. 73 (2nd ed; 1926). For a contrary view see Eurico Sodie, *A Desapropriação por necesidade ou Utilidade Publica* (2nd ed., 1945) and Macario Peçaneo, *A Desapropriação* (Zelio Valverde ed., 1941).

Chile

Alamiro de Avila Martel
with
Manuel Salvat Monguillot

Contents

I. The Concept of Property in Chilean Law   85
  1. The Civil Code and the Individualistic Concept
    of Property   85
  2. Development of the Provision for Expropriation
    in the Constitutions of Chile   86
  3. The 1963 Amendment of the Guarantee of Property   88
  4. The 1967 Amendment of the Guarantee of Property   90
II. The Elements of Expropriation   92
  1. The Legal Nature of Expropriation   92
  2. The Expropriating Agency   93
  3. Property Subject to Expropriation   94
  4. Legal Effects of Expropriation   95
III. Compensation   95
  1. The Concept of Compensation   95
  2. Form of Payment and the Question of Deferred
    Compensation   95
  3. The Effect of the Expropriation Itself on the
    Value of the Property Taken   97
  4. Determination of the Amount of Compensation   98
IV. Expropriation Procedure   98
  1. The Judicial Proceedings   98
  2. Transfer of the Property   98
  3. Scope of Judicial Review   99
  4. Rights of Third Parties   99
V. Special Laws Including Expropriation Provisions   100
  1. Public Service Activities   101
  2. Housing and Urban Renewal   103
  3. Agrarian Reform   104
Conclusion   109
Notes   110

I. The Concept of Property in Chilean Law

1. The Civil Code and the Individualistic Concept of Property

The Civil Code of Chile went into effect in 1857, at the height of the "liberal," individualistic, nineteenth-century intellectual tradition. Article 582 of the Code provides that

> Property *(dominio)* is a real right over a tangible object to enjoy and dispose of it arbitrarily, provided such enjoyment or disposition is not contrary to law or the rights of others.

Article 583 adds that comparable rights over intangibles, such as usufruct, may also be considered property.

This absolutist formulation of the concept of property was never literally true or, to put it another way, the phrase "contrary to law" always had substantial content. A host of restrictions upon the enjoyment or use of property has existed in Chile since the time of the Civil Code—indeed in some of the other parts of the Code itself. Some restrictions on property rights relate to specific types of property such as mining property;[1] some restraints relate to the impact of various laws of a tax or regulatory character.[2] A number of what might be considered restraints on property rights have been challenged as contrary to the guarantee of the inviolability of property which was contained in the Constitution of Chile until 1967. With the exception of those laws that were sought to be applied retroactively, the Supreme Court had generally sustained laws such as those providing for a rise in wages pursuant to a cost-of-living adjustment, prolonging leases, or imposing ceilings on rents, as well as laws imposing restrictions on the construction of buildings or on uses to which certain lands could be put.[3]

Essentially such restrictions—and there were many others—have been considered not violations of the right to property, but limitations on the exercise of that right, as expressly provided by the Constitution of 1925 (see Section I (2)). Another exception to the principle of inviolability of property has always been expropriation for public use (or similar phrase); that is, the actual transfer and possession of title from an individual to the State in return for payment of compensation. While the character and level of restrictions on property—as on all forms of economic activity—have been increasing steadily in the twentieth century, the basic guarantee of property did not change until 1967.

85

2. Development of the Provision for Expropriation in the Constitutions of Chile

Since the earliest time of its independence, Chile has regulated expropriation in its Constitution, probably as a liberal safeguard of the right to property. Thus Article 9 of the Constitution of 1818 stated

> The State may not deprive any person of the possession and free use of his property except if this is required by the nation's defense, and even in that case with the indispensible condition of an apportionment based on the abilities of each individual, and never with insults or abuse.

The Constitution of 1822 introduced the concepts of "common utility or necessity." Article 115 of the Constitution of 1822 provided

> [The Executive] shall deprive no one of his possessions and properties; and when some rare case of common utility or necessity should demand it, the value [of the property] shall be compensated on the basis of just evaluation of good men.

The possibility of expropriation was expanded in the Constitution of 1823, which provided (in Article 117)

> No person may be deprived of his property except because of public necessity determined by the State to be exceptionally grave, and with prior compensation.

The liberal Constitution of 1828 limited the basis for expropriation to the need for public service, and introduced the new concept of considering separately under compensation the "value" of the property and the "damages" caused to the owner. Article 17 of the Constitution of 1828 provided

> No citizen may be deprived of the property that he possesses or to which he is legally entitled, or any part thereof however small, except pursuant to judicial sentence. When public service requires a person's property, he shall be paid for its just value, and, if the property is retained, also for damages.

The next Constitution, that of 1833, which remained in force for almost a century, stated (in Article 12 (5)):

The Constitution assures to all inhabitants of the Republic . . . the inviolability of all their properties whether they belong to private persons or communities, and [it assures] that no one may be deprived of his property or a part thereof however small, except pursuant to a judicial sentence, or in case where the utility of the state, determined by a law, requires the use or seizure of such property, which may only be done through prior payment to the owner of compensation, either as agreed with the owner or as assessed in the judgment of good men.

Though the 1833 Constitution, like the Civil Code, embodied the nineteenth-century liberal tradition, the 1833 text was in several respects an expansion of previous versions of the power to expropriate. In particular, the phrase "utility of the state" was thought to comprise not only what the state itself needed, but anything that was included within the "utility" of public agencies, including towns, and including private firms engaged in public services such as transportation and communication. Moreover, the use of the word "utility," in place of the previous words "need" or "necessity," was interpreted to give the public welfare priority over private welfare, without the need of proving the narrow concept of necessity. However, this priority had to be determined by a law; that is, not by a resolution of the Executive Branch or by delegation, nor for that matter by a resolution of the Congress alone or one of its chambers, nor by court decision.

The question of how specific the law authorizing an expropriation had to be was much debated under the 1833 Constitution. One view was that the Constitution required specific enumeration of the property to be taken in the authorizing law.[4] The other view, which gradually prevailed for reasons of practical necessity, was that if the use of the property was defined with reasonable specificity, for example, construction of streets, plazas, railroads, etc., it would not be necessary to name each property owner in the area to be so used.[5] Nevertheless, the ideal was the maximum specificity or at least the most precise definition of the criteria by which the executive agency would determine the properties to be taken under a general authorization.

The question of the guarantee of property was among the most debated issues in the Constitutional Convention which produced the Constitution of 1925. Some delegates, fearful that any amendment of the 1833 text would weaken property rights in Chile, sought to maintain the previous language unchanged.

Others, reflecting the dissatisfaction with Chilean society and development in the years following World War I, wanted a change, emphasizing the needs of society. At least one delegate, seeking to introduce the ideals of communism into Chile, demanded the outright abolition of the principle of private property. President Arturo Alessandri personally intervened in the debates on this subject, and called for a compromise that would on the one hand restate the inviolability of private property, but would on the other hand write into the Constitution the concept of the social function of property.[6] The outcome was substantially along the lines of President Alessandri's compromise proposal. Article 10 of the Constitution of 1925 read

> The Constitution assures to all the inhabitants of the Republic:
>
> . . .
>
> (10) The inviolability of all property without any distinction.
>
> No one may be deprived of property under his control, nor of any part thereof, nor of the right he may have therein except by virtue of a judicial decree or by expropriation, on account of public utility, determined by a law. In such case, compensation shall be paid to the owner in advance, either by agreement with the owner or as decided in appropriate judicial proceedings.
>
> The exercise of the right of property is subject to the limitations or rules demanded by the maintenance and advancement of the social order and, to that end, the law may impose obligations or servitudes of public utility in favor of the general interest of the State, the health of the citizens, and the public welfare.

Thus several of the problems that had arisen under the earlier Constitution were settled. For example, property was defined as "of all kinds without any distinction." "Public utility" was substituted for "utility of the State," possibly broadening and certainly clarifying the bases for state taking. But the essential features of the nineteenth-century concept were preserved—the reason for a taking in favor of the community must be established not by administrative action but by a law; compensation must be paid prior to transfer of the property; and absent agreement, payment must be in cash, not in bonds or other method of deferred payment.

3. The 1963 Amendment of the Guarantee of Property

The 1925 restatement of the guarantee of property worked well enough so long as the State limited itself to building streets, roads, and public facilities. But with the quest for economic development that swept all over Latin America in the early 1960's, the government of President Jorge Alessandri (son of President Arturo Alessandri referred to earlier) considered the institution of large-scale programs of land reform and urban renewal. For such programs the requirements of Article 10(10) of the Constitution of 1925, and particularly the requirement of prior payment of the full amount of compensation in cash, would be a serious obstacle. Accordingly, the government introduced and the Congress passed Law 15,295, amending Article 10(10) by adding the following:

> The judge may authorize the taking of material possession of the property expropriated once the judgment of first instance has been handed down in the case of expropriation for public works which are urgently required or of rural lands, provided that the only issue before the court is the amount of compensation and provided the owner has been paid some or all of the amount as ordered in accordance with the following paragraph.
>
> Nevertheless, if abandoned rural properties or agricultural properties which are plainly poorly exploited or are cultivated at a level below the normal level prevailing in the region in question having comparable soil are expropriated for reasons of public utility with the objective of encouraging appropriate distribution of agrarian property, the proprietor shall be given prior compensation of 10 per cent and the remainder in equal annual installments for a period not to exceed fifteen years, with interest as established by law.
>
> This form of compensation may only be utilized in conformity with the law which permits protests of expropriation before a special tribunal whose decision is appealable to the appropriate Court of Appeals, and which establishes a system of annual readjustment of the balance of compensation for the purpose of preserving its value. No new expropriations may be initiated calling for deferred compensation if any delay exists in the payment of installments as provided for in previous expropriations pursuant to the preceding paragraph.
>
> The budget law will always be understood to include the necessary authorization for the service of such debts, and installments of such debts shall upon coming due, serve to extinguish all kinds of obligations to the Treasury. The General Treasury of the Republic shall pay the installments due plus any readjustments and interest against presentation of the appropriate certificates.

The 1963 amendment applied only to abandoned or insufficiently exploited rural properties, and to cases of expropriation for public works of urgent necessity. In the case of agrarian properties, the state could take over by paying only ten per cent of the compensation due, leaving the balance to be paid in installments of up to fifteen years. In the case of urgent public works, while the full amount of compensation must still be paid in cash, the property could be taken before a final decision by the courts had been arrived at.

4. The 1967 Amendment of the Guarantee of Property

The Alessandri government did not achieve much success in its agrarian reform program. When Eduardo Frei campaigned successfully for the presidency in 1964, one of the chief items in his program (along with gaining control of the foreign-owned copper industry) was creation of an effective nationwide agrarian reform program. Even before Frei assumed office, he appointed a commission to study amendment of the National Constitution with a view to achieving the following goals related to property:

a) emphasis on the concept of the social function of property;
b) facilitation of the distribution of property;
c) encouragement of much greater intensity in the agrarian reform program; and
d) authorization for the State to carry out public works expeditiously, particularly in connection with urban renewal.

The purpose of the commission, as the message from the President-elect stated, was

To stimulate social function of the right of property and to provide the state with the tools necessary to carry out, with legislative authorization, the great reforms required to make property accessible to the majority of the citizens of Chile.[7]

The revised version of Article 10(10) of the Chilean Constitution went into effect on January, 20, 1967. It is worth quoting in its entirety, since it not only amplifies the permissible scope of agrarian reform, but changes in many respects the law that had grown up under the 1833 and 1925 Constitutions as interpreted by the Supreme Court of Chile:

The Constitution assures to all the inhabitants of the Republic:
. . .
(10) *The Right of Property in its Diverse Aspects*

90

The law shall establish the method of acquiring, using, enjoying and disposing of property and those limitations and obligations which will assure its social function and make it accessible to everyone. The social function of property includes, when the general interests of the state require, public utility and welfare, the best utilization of the productive sources and energies in the service of the community, and the elevation of the conditions of life of the population as a whole.

When the interest of the national community requires, the law may reserve to the state the exclusive dominion of natural resources, means of production and other property which it declares to be of preeminent importance for the economic, social or cultural life of the country. The law, similarly, shall aim for the appropriate distribution of property and for the constitution of family property.

No one may be deprived of his property except by virtue of a general or special law which authorizes expropriation for reason of public utility or social interest determined by the legislature. The expropriated party shall always have the right to compensation, the amount and conditions of payment of which are to be equitably determined, taking into consideration the interests of the collectivity and of the expropriated parties. The law shall determine norms for fixing compensation, the tribunal which shall hear claims concerning the amount of compensation according to law, the form of satisfying the obligation to compensate, and the opportunities and manner in which the expropriating agency shall take material possession of the expropriated property.

In case of expropriation of rural properties, compensation shall be equivalent to the assessment in effect for the payment of territorial taxes, plus the value of improvements not included in such assessment, and may be paid partly in cash and the balance over a period not to exceed thirty years, all of the above in the form and under conditions to be determined by law.

The law may reserve for the national domain of public use all waters in the national territory and may expropriate any such waters in private ownership for the purposes of incorporating them in the public domain. In such case the owners of expropriated waters may continue to use them in the capacity of concessionaires of a right to use and shall only have a right to compensation when, because of the total partial extinction of such right they are deprived effectively of waters sufficient to satisfy their prior needs on the basis of a rational and beneficial use.

Small rural property worked by its owner and homes inhabited by their proprietors may not be expropriated without prior payment of compensation.

It is evident that the 1967 amendment to Article 10 of the Constitution accomplishes, at least on paper, a substantial change in the relation of private property to the State. Indeed, the amendment reflects in many respects a conscious determination to reverse the law that had developed in Chile as a result of the Constitutional texts, the decisions of the Supreme Court, and the writings of the leading commentators. This point will become clearer in the following sections of this paper. Just to highlight here the major changes specifically related to expropriation: 1) to the concept of public utility as a basis for expropriation was added the concept of social interest; 2) expropriation which previously was thought to be possible only pursuant to a specific law (see Section I (2)) now is authorized pursuant to a general or special law; 3) the requirement that compensation must be paid before the property can be taken by the State is eliminated completely; under the amended version, all the owner receives upon transfer of property to the state is a claim, under norms to be established by law; 4) the norms for compensation are to be determined "equitably," taking into consideration the interest of the collectivity as well as of the expropriated party; 5) the substantive elements of compensation, the procedures for fixing the amount, and even the tribunal itself are to be established by statute, in contrast to the previous system in which, as discussed below, substance, procedure, and form were all considered to be contained within the Constitutional guarantee of inviolability of property; 6) new Article 10 speaks of a number of situations in which there will be no compensation or only partial compensation; 7) new Article 10 distinguishes among different owners in some cases according to the size of their holdings, with the smallest apparently being entitled to the guarantees previously available to all property holders.

II. The Elements of Expropriation

1. The Legal Nature of Expropriation

Until 1915, expropriation was thought in Chile to be of the nature of a compulsory sale. This concept, sounding in private law, was based on a Decree with Force of Law (DFL) of 1838 that referred to the expropriating authority as purchaser, and it was reinforced by the language of the Code of Civil Procedure, which refers (in Article 919) to the expropriated party as seller and the amount of expropriation as "price" and also uses the word *"justiprecio"* (literally, just price) to characterize the compensation to be determined by the experts (see Section III (4)). On the basis of these texts, the Court of Appeals of Valparaiso in a judgment of 1907 had stated:

Expropriation signifies in law a forced sale for purposes of public utility; except as they are contrary to the special character of expropriation and the provisions which regulate it, the general provisions of the law of contracts and of sales are applicable to expropriation.[8]

This view was, however, rejected by the Supreme Court of Chile in 1915, which said:

Expropriation for cause of utility of the state based on considerations of general interest, belongs fully in the domain of public law and is governed by the provisions which the Constitution itself has set out.[9]

Subsequent case law has unanimously confirmed this view. Though expropriation is not a sale in the ordinary meaning of that term, it is conceived of as the replacement of one right—the right to possession of property—by another right—the right to compensation. Thus expropriation is distinct from confiscation, which is penal in nature and does not result in creation of a right to compensation; and is distinct from attachment and sale to satisfy a pre-existing debt.

2. The Expropriating Agency

Since expropriation is, as we have seen, an institution of public law, only the State is the holder of the power to expropriate. However, in practice the State is assisted by other agencies and even by private persons (concession holders) in executing works of general benefit. In this sense, the expropriating agency must not be confused with the beneficiary of the expropriation. The former—i.e., the State—has the power to decide unilaterally upon the expropriation. The beneficiary may be the State itself, an administrative person, or even a private person, for instance the holder of a concession to provide a public service such as the Chilean Electric Company.

Private persons cannot have the power to expropriate; that is, they cannot initiate the action of expropriation for their own benefit, since obviously the Legislature cannot grant to a private person the right to deprive another of his property. There is one case in Chilean law, Decree-law 219 of May 30, 1931, which authorized industrialists to expropriate immovable property necessary to establish industries or expand existing ones. This precedent, which appears to contradict the principle set forth above, serves, on the contrary, to confirm it, since the objective pursued by the law maker was not to increase the property of one private person at the expense of another, but to promote the greater development or improvement of industry as a means of strengthening the national economy. In any event, it is not actually the industrialist who expropriates, but the State that does so in his favor.

3. Property Subject to Expropriation

Subject to the requirement of suitability for a work of public utility or social interest, any kind of property can be the subject of expropriation. Thus goods and chattels, immovable property, tangible or intangible things, and also intellectual or artistic property may be expropriated. With respect to the latter, Article 10 (11) of the Constitution makes it clear that intellectual property is subject to expropriation:

> The Constitution assures to all inhabitants of the republic:
> (11) exclusive property in every discovery or creation, for such period of time as the law shall provide. If the law requires expropriation thereof, the author or inventor shall be given appropriate [competente] compensation.

A condition precedent for an expropriation is a law, whether generic or specific, declaring that public utility or social interest justifies the expropriation. The Legislature, in making this determination, takes into account the intended use of the property to be expropriated, since this is what determines the satisfaction of the public need that justifies the expropriation. In the past there have been differences of opinion whether expropriated property may only be utilized for the purpose specified by the Legislature in the Declaration of Public Utility or whether, on the other hand, once property has been incorporated into the national patrimony, the State may use it for whatever purposes it chooses.[10] To some extent this debate is less important since the 1967 amendment to the Constitution, which expressly states that the law authorizing an expropriation may be either special or general. Nevertheless, it is common that such law declares with some specificity the intended use of the property to be taken.[11]

4. Legal Effects of Expropriation

Apart from the transfer of possession and ownership of the property already referred to, expropriation has a number of other legal effects. The most important effect is that expropriation grants to the State a free and clear title to the property expropriated, so that all rights of third parties over the property are extinguished. Thus, for example, the interest of a mortgagee may be satisfied from the compensation award, and the law makes provision to this end (see Section IV (4)). But the security interest that the mortgagee or other creditor may have had in the expropriated property disappears, or rather is merged in the property itself upon passage to the State. Correspondingly, though there is no general provision of law on the subject, a number of special laws have now established the rule that expropriation clears property titles of any clouds or defects that might have affected them.

III. Compensation

1. The Concept of Compensation

As we have seen in defining the nature of expropriation, compensation is in Chile an integral component of the institution of expropriation. What distinguishes expropriation from, for example, unlawful confiscation is that in expropriation, compensation is substituted for possession of the property in question. Compensation is not, as already mentioned, a purchase price, but is designed as well to make the expropriated party whole; that is, to make reparation for damages suffered as a result of the taking.

2. Form of Payment and the Question of Deferred Compensation

Until the Constitutional reform of 1967, it was clear that payment of compensation had to be prior and had to be made in cash, not in bonds or other property. As recently as 1952 the Supreme Court had reiterated its previous pronouncement on this point in holding unconstitutional Article 82 of DFL 345 issued in 1931, which obliged property owners to accept bonds equivalent in par value to the value of the property to be taken.[12] Again in 1956 the Supreme Court held unconstitutional a portion of DFL 224, a new text of the General Construction Ordinance, which authorized municipalities to defer payment for expropriations, although the ordinance stated that the municipality would not take possession until the price had been paid.[13] On both of these points it is clear that the 1967 Constitution has effected a major change. Only the last paragraph of Article 10 (10), dealing with small landholders, provides for prior payment in cash, whereas the general provision on compensation specifically omits the requirement of prior compensation that had been in the Constitution of 1925, and provides instead that the amount and conditions of payment will be determined "equitably." With regard to rural property, moreover, the Constitution specifically provides, as we have seen (Section I (4)), for part cash payment and the balance in installments up to thirty years.

The new Constitution retains, however, the requirement that compensation must be established fairly. Though the norms for compensation, the form and conditions of payment, and the court which will hear the suit for compensation are all subject to provisions in the law authorizing the expropriation, the amount of compensation must still be determined by a court in the manner spelled out in Section III (4). Prior to the 1967 Constitution there were various attempts to modify or weaken the effect of the requirement of judicial determination of the amount of compensation. For example, provisions in various laws provided for compensation of immovable property in amounts corresponding to the assessed value of the property on the tax rolls plus 10 per cent. At least three times the Supreme Court struck down such provisions.[14] An attempt in the 1953 version of the General Construction Ordinance referred to above to use the tax value simply as the basis of administrative determination of the amount tendered as compensation was likewise struck down by the Supreme Court.[15] How much of this Constitutional law as established by the Supreme Court remains operative following the 1967 amendment is not yet clear. But the Constitutional requirements of judicial determination and of fairness suggest that the conditions of payment which the 1967 amendment of Article 10 commits to the Legislature are still subject to judicial scrutiny. In deciding a case seeking to have an expropriation law declared "inapplicable" on the ground of unfairness, the Supreme Court will have to interpret the phrase "taking into consideration the interests of the collectivity and of the expropriated persons."

3. The Effect of the Expropriation Itself on the Value of the Property Taken

One issue that has troubled Chilean courts and legislatures for a long time is the effect of an expropriation, or rather of the project for which the expropriated property will be used, on the value of that property. The typical case involves construction of a railroad or highway which, once built, quickly increases the value of the adjacent and neighboring land, often including land still owned by the expropriated party. Article 917 of the Code of Civil Procedure provides that, for purposes of determining the value of expropriated property, the consequence of the project for which the expropriation was carried out shall not be taken into consideration. Similar provisions are contained in other laws. In contrast, the Law on Construction and Urbanization of 1960 states that "whenever property acquires greater value in consequence of its partial expropriation, such increase in value of the part not expropriated shall be deducted from the price of the expropriation."[16] When the constitutionality of this provision was challenged, the Supreme Court held that "the reduction of compensation by the amount of increase in the value of the property not expropriated does not in any way deprive the expropriated party of the guarantee provided by the Constitution."[17] More recently the Supreme Court put the matter affirmatively:

> In order to determine the value required to be paid for expropriation of land required for a road it is appropriate to reduce from the sum representing the value of the expropriated land an amount corresponding to the increase in value acquired by the land remaining in the hands of the expropriated party attributable to the works for which the expropriation was carried out.[18]

4. Determination of the Amount of Compensation

Aside from the above limitations, there are few substantive guidelines for determining the amount of compensation to be paid. Chile has no general expropriation law, and the guidelines appearing in Articles 915-925 of the Code of Civil Procedure are essentially procedural and not substantive. These Articles provide only that when an expropriation is commenced, the judge sitting where the property is located shall call upon both parties to appoint experts for the purpose of making the appraisal called for by Article 10 (10) of the Constitution. If the two experts agree, their determination is accepted; if they disagree, they must appoint a third expert; and if they fail to agree on such third expert, the judge will appoint him. If thereafter all three experts disagree substantially, the amount of compensation is fixed by adding the amounts determined by each of the experts and dividing the sum by three, subject to modification by the court on the basis of conformity to applicable norms.

IV. Expropriation Procedure

1. The Judical Proceedings

Article 925 of the Code of Civil Procedure requires that the expropriating agency must commence the action to expropriate within six months of the time of the issuance of the law authorizing the expropriation, unless that law itself establishes a different time period. The proceedings are begun by a petition to the judge, asking that he name experts to establish the value of the property to be taken as described in Section III (4). The Court of first instance has, as we saw above, a very limited role, which comes into play only when the three experts appointed arrive at three different determinations and the court is authorized to adjust the average of these three.

2. Transfer of the Property

According to Article 919 of the Code of Civil Procedure, once the decision on the award has been made, it is published five times in a local newspaper; thereafter, if no objection is raised by third parties, the judge will order payment and at the same time will order the transfer of the property to the State. Presumably, under the new Constitutional provision, transfer will take place upon delivery of the down payment called for in the particular law authorizing the expropriation.

3. Scope of Judicial Review

It is possible to appeal a determination of compensation, but such appeal may not hold up the expropriation proceedings; that is, the transfer of the property to the taking agency. Neither the trial court nor the court of appeals has any other jurisdiction in expropriation cases. No court, in other words, can review the issue of whether a particular activity is for the public benefit or social interest, nor whether the particular property in question is suitable for the stated purpose.[19]

All courts of Chile are obligated to carry out the laws of the nation, and therefore they cannot consider contentions that any law violates the Constitution. Only the Supreme Court can consider constitutionality of a law and in particular cases declare a law "inapplicable" as violating the Constitution. A party can raise the question of inapplicability of the law at any time during a case, provided the case has not become final. Resort to the Supreme Court does not stay the regular course of the case through the courts. As regards expropriation, the Supreme Court declined in one case to hear a challenge to the constitutionality of an expropriation where the private owner went through with the appointment of experts and only sought to bring a Constitutional challenge after the experts' award came down. The court said that the Constitutional challenge in expropriation cases could not be used to impugn the appraisal of the property, but only to resist the expropriation on the grounds that there had been no prior payment.[20]

4. Rights of Third Parties

It has already been noted that rights in the property expropriated by persons other than the record owner are extinguished by an expropriation. Thus neither mortgagees nor tenants, nor others claiming any interest in the property, can retain these interests after the expropriation, although the expropriation was not directed against them. Such third parties are, however, entitled to notice, in order that they may secure their interests in the compensation award, which is considered to have taken the place of the property. Article 919 of the Code of Civil Procedure provides that within three days of the announcement by the judge of the amount of compensation to be awarded, five notices must be inserted in a local newspaper at three-day intervals. The appearance of third parties in response to this notice cannot stay the expropriation. However, if title to the property itself was in dispute at the time of the expropriation, the compensation is to be paid into court, to be distributed as the rights of the claimants may emerge. Similarly, mortgagees may assert the claims or interests they had in the expropriated property against the compensation award, and for this purpose they can ask the court to take conservatory measures. The Council for the Defense of the State (a group of lawyers designated by the President as counsel to the State, and also authorized to give advisory opinions of law) [21] stated in 1939 that if it appears to the judge that the expropriated property is mortgaged, payment of the compensation award must be made to the public treasury, so that once the mortgage comes due or a judgment has been rendered in favor of the creditor, payment can be made to the creditor up to the amount of the loan, with the remainder going to the owner. [22]

The rights of tenants or lessees of expropriated property are provided for in the Civil Code. Tenants are to be given time to finish projects or to harvest standing crops. Under Article 1960 of the Civil Code, if a tenant has paid in advance for a lease in excess of two years, he may claim damages from the State—the only exception in Chilean law to the provision previously referred to that third parties can have no rights against the State arising from an expropriation. In case of a partial expropriation, if the tenant is left with a portion of the property so small that he can show he would not have entered into the lease for that portion alone, he is entitled to cancel the lease.

V. Special Laws Including Expropriation Provisions

We have seen that, apart from a few articles in the Code of Civil Procedure, there is no general expropriation law in Chile. There have been, however, a large number of laws providing for expropriation for particular purposes. Many of these embody variations from the norms described in the preceding pages though all, of course, are subject to the Constitutional guarantees. Some examples of laws providing for particular types of public activities are briefly mentioned below. The more recent innovations looking to major social transformations in the cities and in rural areas are dealt with in the succeeding sections.

1. Public Service Activities

The General Law of Construction and Urbanization promulgated by Supreme Decree in 1963 provided for urban plans in major cities and authorized (in Article 100) expropriation of buildings located where streets, parks, or public structures were contemplated under the plan. Two kinds of expropriations were authorized. "Ordinary expropriations," referring to buildings that were to be demolished because they were in poor condition, entitled the owner only to the value of the land transferred to the municipality, without any compensation for the demolished building, except that he could dispose of the remains. "Extraordinary expropriation," referring to property in good condition but inconsistent with the plan, required a special resolution of the appropriate town or city council approved by a two-thirds majority of the councilmen. Compensation in theory must include full value of the land and buildings plus damages resulting from lost profits. However, the compensation for the real property itself may not under the law exceed the value declared for tax purposes (adjusted annually by reference to the cost of living index) plus 10 per cent. If there is no agreement on the amount of compensation within 60 days of the resolution by the Town Council, any party may request the court to fix the amount. The court will follow the procedure established by the Code of Civil Procedure (see Section III (4)) except that the judge is not bound by the report of the experts, which is deemed only "informative." In expropriation under this procedure the municipality may not take possession until compensation has been paid.

Again, expropriation in aid of projects under the supervision of the Director General of Public Works—including the Bureaus of Architecture, Sanitary Engineering, Irrigation, Streets, Harbors, and Airports—are governed by a special law which permits expropriations on the basis of decrees issued by the Minister of Public Works "by order of the President." The procedure follows the pattern described in the preceding pages except that in the first instance "good men" (i.e., laymen of good reputation residing in the vicinity of the property) are appointed by the President to perform the appraisal function, rather than experts designated by the court, and that the good men are limited as to the amount they can award by the assessment placed on the property in question by the Bureau of Internal Revenue. However, it is possible for either side to contest the appraisal of the "good men," in which case the court does appoint experts to act in advisory capacity.

A number of similar laws govern the details of expropriation for the needs of railroads, electric power transmission lines, sewers, roads, telegraph poles, and similar facilities. All these laws have in common the feature that the property in question is to be transferred to the State or other taking agency as soon as the first assessment is made, usually by "good men" designated by a local or national official. As in the case of national public works, it is possible to appeal the assessment of the "good men" to the court, but meanwhile transfer of the property is permitted to take place when the amount determined by the good men has been paid into court.

A very different regime applies in case an electric company itself is to be expropriated. In such event the President must, under DFL 4 of August 31, 1959, request the Congress to enact a specific law declaring the public utility of taking the enterprise in question and appropriating adequate funds for payment of compensation. A commission of experts must be established to assess the value of the electric company's installations, properties and rights of all kinds associated with the public service which it has been providing. The commercial value of the enterprise must be taken into account, less the value of the capital previously amortized. The commission is made up of three expert engineers, one appointed by the President of the Republic, one by the electric company, and a third by the President of the Supreme Court. The parties may accept the assessment arrived at by this commission or they may request the courts to fix the amount of compensation. One interesting feature of this law is that if expropriation is carried out before ten years have passed from the date of the original concession, the value of the assessment must be increased by a surcharge of 20 per cent; if the expropriation is carried out in the following 10 years, the surcharge over the amount established by the commission of experts is to be 10 per cent.

2. Housing and Urban Renewal

From Chile's earliest days, the Government has been concerned with the need to provide urban housing. As early as 1892 a Council of Sanitation was established to oversee workers' dwellings, and in 1906 a Council on Construction of Workers' Housing was created with authority to provide mortgage financing for low-cost housing.

These first initiatives failed for lack of funds, but numerous laws and decrees were passed on housing or social welfare, all designed at least in part to acquire land and either construct or finance the construction of housing for low-income urban residents. In 1953, DFL 285 created the Corporation for Housing (Corporación de la Vivienda or CORVI) entrusted with, among other functions, the study and promotion of low-cost housing, the building of such housing, and the formulation of an overall housing plan.[23]

Among CORVI's powers is the power to expropriate lands when needed to implement the housing plan. Again, the procedure for expropriation calls for an attempt at agreement between CORVI and the private owner regarding compensation; failing agreement, the President of the Republic is to appoint a commission of three experts to make an appraisal. As soon as the experts have rendered their report, CORVI can take possession, with either party having twenty days thereafter within which to protest the award to the court. The difference in expropriation procedures carried on by CORVI is that that agency is authorized, if the expropriated party agrees, to pay some or all of the award in kind; that is, in housing or in commercial facilities.[24]

One of the major initiatives of the administration of President Frei was the creation in 1965 of a Ministry of Housing and Urbanism charged with establishing a coordinated program of urban housing and including CORVI as one of its components.[25] Expropriation authority was continued, and indeed expanded to include the land on which apartment houses had been built, for the purpose of straightening out and in some cases financing individual ownership of apartments in multiple dwelling units. One additional modification of the expropriation procedures was assignment to the Ministry itself of the appraisal function carried out under other laws by "good men" or by panels of experts.

Law 16,741 of August 4, 1968 expanded the power of the Ministry of Housing and Urbanism to clear titles where prior partitions had left ownership and conformity to the urban plan unclear. For example, it often occurred that construction pursuant to a town or village development plan had resulted in title to buildings or individual apartments being in persons other than the record title holder of the land. One of the ways of removing such "irregularity" would be through expropriation of the land and resale in corresponding shares to the owners of the residential units. Law 16,741 states that in cases of this kind compensation to the owner of the land is not to include any increase in the value of the land due to the residential development, unless the landholder proves he financed the development. Further, any sums paid by the residents of the development to the landholder as payment for the land, or as payment for public services not performed, must be deducted from the amount due to the landholder as compensation. Once the expropriation has been completed, the expropriating agency must sell the land back to the original residents, often on installment sales which are in effect government-financed purchases.

3. Agrarian Reform

Background. In the past decade, Chile has had two major Agrarian Reform Laws, one in 1962 in the administration of President Jorge Alessandri, the other in 1967 in the administration of President Eduardo Frei. Both laws were designed to meet the dual objective of increasing Chile's agricultural output and improving the lot of the rural residents of Chile, many of whom still lived a kind of plantation existence depending on the large landholder.

For various reasons the 1962 law was not really implemented, though a number of its institutions were taken over and expanded in the later law. President Frei contended that the main reason for the ineffectiveness of the Alessandri agrarian reform was that it was designed to maintain the existing social structure of the nation without adequately recognizing the social function of property. To analyze this charge would require economic and sociological discussion far beyond the scope of this paper. It is highly pertinent to the present discussion, however, to note the other explanation given by President Frei for the failure of his predecessor's land reform program. For one thing, as President Frei pointed out, under the 1962 law all compensation for expropriation of agrarian property had to be paid in cash; for another transfer of property under the Agrarian Reform Law had to await the judgment of a court, and even the judgments of the special Agrarian Tribunals created by the 1962 law were appealable through the ordinary courts of law. On both of these points the 1962 law had followed the guarantee in the 1925 Constitution, though (as we saw in Section I(3)) a partial amendment authorizing deferred compensation was put into effect in 1963. But the Frei government was determined to remove what it regarded as Constitutional obstacles to effective agrarian reform, and it was for this purpose that the amendment to Article 10 (10) of the Constitution discussed in Section I (4) of this paper was enacted.[26]

Outline of the 1967 Law. The 1967 Agrarian Reform Law established as the basic unit of agrarian property a standard unit of 80 hectares of irrigated land, subject to various adjustments depending on the geography, the fertility of the soil, and the irrigation of particular areas. Larger properties are denominated *latifundia* and are in principle to be taken by the State through the agrarian reform agency and redistributed. Smaller properties are denominated *minifundia* and are similarly to be taken by the State and consolidated for redistribution. The operating agency for the land reform is the Corporación de la Reforma Agraria (CORA). Law 16,640, the Agrarian Reform Law, contains 333 articles plus another 24 transitional articles, and no attempt will be made here to give a thorough explanation of its operations. In brief, however, the following types of rural property are declared to be expropriable:

a) land owned by a natural person having an extension of more than 80 hectares of basic irrigable land;

b) rural lands considered abandoned or inadequately exploited;

c) rural properties resulting from the division of property of more than 80 hectares, when such division occured after November 4, 1964 (the date of the inauguration of President Frei);

d) rural lands with certain exceptions owned by corporations or other juridical persons;

e) land operated under lease or partnership contrary to the governing law or contracts;

f) rural properties belonging jointly to two more more persons;

g) lands located in the zone of the so-called Propiedad Austral (Southern property) where questions have arisen concerning ownership or possession of the lands;

h) rural lands necessary to acquire for implementation of agrarian reform plans if the owner has offered to transfer them;

i) rural lands in small farms, for purposes of consolidation and redistribution;

j) rural lands located in certain areas where the State will carry out land improvement;

k) rural lands located in an area where the State is carrying out or plans to carry out irrigation projects.

Under the Agrarian Reform Law, land owned by a natural person prior to November 4, 1964 not in excess of 80 hectares of irrigated land is exempt from expropriation, provided it is neither abandoned nor insufficiently exploited, nor is a *minifundio,* nor is located in an area in which the State is carrying out irrigation works. Moreover, under Article 16 of the Agrarian Reform Law, the reserve for each proprietor may be increased by ten hectares for every son beyond five sons up to a total of 100 hectares.

The law contains numerous exemptions and qualifications, and when CORA notifies a proprietor of an expropriation, he may allege within thirty days that he is covered by one of these exemptions in the law or that a particular definition does not apply to him. For example, under Article 21, the owner may contend that he meets *all* of the following conditions: a) 95 percent of the usable land is subject to cultivation (80 percent in case of nonirrigated land); b) the exploitation of the land is carried out under conditions of production as established by the Ministry of Agriculture for comparable lands; c) the soil and other natural resources are being maintained in good state of conservation; d) payment for salaries, wages and participation is equal to at least twice the minimum rural salary in the department (province) in question with benefits such as housing and food estimated at a maximum of 25 percent of the wage or salary; e) workers are granted a share of the gross proceeds in a proportion to be established by the President of the Republic; f) all legal provisions are complied with in regard to rural housing, education, and sanitation, and no judicial or administrative sanction has been imposed for serious violation of social or labor laws. Even if all these conditions are complied with, an exemption is good for only twenty years.

Compensation. Compensation for land taken pursuant to the Agrarian Reform Law shall be equivalent to the value as stated on the rolls for the territorial tax plus any improvement not included in that listing. Payment of this amount is to be made partly in cash and the remainder in Agrarian Reform bonds. The ratio of cash to bonds depends on the reason for the expropriation, or more precisely, on whether the land is abandoned, in which case the cash may be 1 per cent; whether the land is by law declared inexpropriable, in which case the cash payment will be 33 per cent; or whether the property comes within the normal rule, in which case 10 per cent will be paid in cash. The provision for compensation discriminates according to the category of the property not only in respect to the proportion of cash to bonds, but also in respect to the different classes of bonds available. Article 132 of the Agrarian Reform Law establishes three classes of bonds, each of which carries 3 per cent interest but each of which has a different period of amortization. Class A are 25-year bonds, Class B are 5-year bonds, and Class C are 30-year bonds. Thus, for example, a property owner who has property declared inexpropriable but which is nevertheless taken may be entitled to a 33 per cent cash payment and the remainder in Class B (5-year) bonds. In contrast, a large landholder with badly exploited agrarian land may receive as little as 1 per cent in cash and the remainder in Class C (30-year) bonds.

An interesting feature of all of the bonds is that it was recognized that deferred compensation contained an element of penalty in the context of rising prices and lower value for the individual monetary unit. On the other hand, a one-for-one adjustment to a price index would itself have had inflationary effects. The compromise adopted in the Agrarian Reform Law is that each bond is issued in two series—70 percent in the first series, which is annually adjustable on the basis of the increase in the cost of living index, and 30 per cent in the second series, which is not adjustable. All of the Agrarian Reform Bonds are considered bonds of the State and bear the guarantee of the Republic. They may be used to satisfy obligations to the State or state corporations.

Expropriation Procedure and Judicial Review. When CORA has decided on an expropriation, it notifies the persons affected by sending an authenticated copy of the resolution by hand to the proprietor or an adult at the principal house of the agrarian property. At the same time the notice is published in the Official

Bulletin and is registered with the Registrar of Immovable Property. Any claims of the expropriated person on the basis of the exemptions in the Agrarian Reform Law must be made within 30 days before the Provincial Agricultural Tribunal, a special court created just to hear such claims. At the same time the property owner must state whether he chooses to exercise his right to a reserve of 80 hectares, and if so, in which part of his property.

The Agricultural Tribunal is an interesting institution in that, unlike other courts of Chile, it is not made up entirely of law professionals. In accordance with Article 136 of the Agrarian Reform Law, a Provincial Agricultural Tribunal shall consist of one senior judge of the provincial capital sitting by designation of the appropriate court of appeals, two "agrarian professionals," one designated by the President of the Republic from among public officials and one designated by the President of the Republic from among nonpublic officials upon nomination of the appropriate professional association. A lawyer is to act as secretary of the court.

The Agrarian Reform Law also creates Agricultural Courts of Appeal to decide certain issues that may be taken up from the Provincial Agricultural Tribunal. No appeal to the ordinary civil courts may be taken from the agrarian courts, and even the "*orden de no innovar*," which the Supreme Court can issue in other cases for exceptional reasons to stay proceedings pending further appeal, may not be issued in matters coming from the agrarian courts except if the Supreme Court is unanimous and if the appeal is based on serious presumptions of fault or abuse, in which case it must be heard within ten days. Thus for practical purposes it appears that agrarian reform has been insulated from the normal judicial procedures, and from a judiciary brought up on earlier concepts of the Constitution and the Civil Codes. In other words, provision is made for relief from arbitrary actions by individual government officials, but the regime of agrarian reform is not subject, as were prior efforts at agrarian reform, to either delay or substantive intervention by the ordinary judiciary.

A Provisional Assessment. Between 1965 and 1970, 1,373 farms with a total of 3.47 million hectares have been expropriated—roughly 23 per cent of the arable land of Chile.[27]   It is too early to tell whether agrarian reform can really be completed in Chile and whether (if it is completed) the lot of the rural worker and the agricultural output of the nation will in fact be improved. It can, however, be said that Chile under President Frei made the decision—and without any kind of revolution—that the classical principles of Constitutional and civil law were too great an obstacle for the needed social change. The rule of law would be preserved, but the content of the law would, as regards rural Chile, be very drastically changed.

Conclusion

As this paper goes to press (September 1970), Chile stands once more before a major social transformation, the extent of which is not yet known. Insofar as the incoming administration builds upon Chile's legal and Constitutional tradition, it can contemplate in the field of property a fairly steady evolution from the Constitution of 1833 guarantee of the inviolability of private property through the use of the concept of public utility in the 1925 Constitution to the Constitutional Amendments of 1963 and 1967. In the process, the requirement of showing the State's need for particular property, the requirement of express Legislative authorization for a taking, the requirement of implementation of legal procedures before a taking, the requirement (in many laws) of compensation prior to actual occupation, and the requirement of payment in cash all disappeared or were substantially eroded. Also, as we saw, the resort to the regular judiciary in defense of private owners' rights was eliminated in cases of agrarian reform, and the definition of "social function" of property was expanded so far as to contain no practical limits. The standard for compensation today is "equity," "taking into consideration the interests of the collectivity and of the expropriated parties," and the norms giving content to this phrase are contained not in the Constitution but in the law authorizing the expropriation.

In short, property ownership in Chile today is precarious in the face of agrarian reform in the countryside and urban reform in the cities. Limits on the size of homes or properties have not yet been enforced; and, for example, newspapers or factories have not been expropriated, as they have been, for instance, in Peru. But the Constitutional shields for the individual against the State have, in the area of property, all but disappeared.

Notes

1. For reasons of national security, deposits of liquid and gaseous oil (Law 9618 of June 19, 1950) and of uranium and calcium phosphates, potassium salts, and others (Law 6482 of Oct. 23, 1960) are reserved to the State. For the same reason Law 16.319 of Oct. 16, 1965, declared to be of public interest for purposes of expropriation, the natural atomic materials contained in holdings as of June 30, 1964 or which should be constituted by virtue of declarations made prior to that date.

2. The tax on real estate is progressive if the proprietor does not build within a specific time. As regards rural lands, the State requires a certain degree of exploitation. Persons who pass or have passed goods through the coasts, frontiers, or airports, or from zones subject to special provisions (free ports) are subject to the power of the Customs in accordance with the norms of its Ordinance (DFL 213 of July 22, 1953, amended by Treasury Decree No. 8 of September 12, 1963 and by Law 16.127). Also some restraints to the right of property are to be found in the Sanitary Code DFL 226 of May 15, 1931, amended by DS 725 of the Ministry of Health, published in *Boletín Oficial* of January 31, 1968 and in the Regulations of the General Commentary established by DS 1382 of July 28, 1929, etc. Law 6071 of August 16, 1937, on horizontal property, establishes limitations on the use of apartments.

3. See Alejandro Silva Bascuñán, *Tratado de Derecho Constitucional,* Vol. II, pp. 277-8 (1963)

4. See Jorge Huneeus, *La Constitución ante el Congreso,* Vol. I, pp. 112-14 (2d ed. 1890).

5. See See Bascuñán, op. cit. (note No. 3), Vol. II, p. 280 (1963).

6. Id. at 272-274.

7. Message of President-elect Eduardo Frei Montalvao.

8. Sentence of the First Court of Appeals of Valparaíso of May 7, 1907 in Riesco v. Municipalidad de Valparaíso 15 *Revista de Derecho, Jurisprudencia y Ciencias Sociales* (hereafter referred to as *Rev. Der. Jur.*), Sec. 1, p. 522 (1918).

9. Undurraga v. Cabrera, Supreme Court, Nov. 11, 1915, 13 *Rev. Der. Jur.,* Sec. 1, p. 232 (1916).

10. *Memoria del Consejo de Defensa Fiscal,* p. 72 (1934).

11. Law 7209 of Oct. 31, 1942; DFL 206, April 5, 1960, Article 27.

12. *Arzobispado de Santiago,* Supreme Court, July 22, 1952, 49 *Rev. Der. Jur.,* Sec. 1, p. 259 (1952).

13. *Empresa de los Ferrocarriles,* Supreme Court, July 4, 1956, 53 *Rev. Der. Jur.,* Sec. 1, p. 127 (1956).

14. See Bascuñán, op. cit. (note No. 3), p. 283.

15. *Luis Lama Maloff*, Supreme Court, Dec. 3, 1958, 55 *Rev. Der. Jur.*, Sec. 1, p. 338 (1958).

16. DFL 224 of July 22, 1953, amended by DFL 192 of March 25, 1960, published in the *Boletín Oficial* of April 1, 1960.

17. *Rabi*, Supreme Court, May 8, 1945, 43 *Rev. Der. Jur.*, Sec. 1, p. 179 (1946).

18. Abraham Villanova Machado v. State (Fisco), 48 *Rev. Der. Jur.*, Sec. 1, p. 418 (1950).

19. State (Fisco) v. Guzmán Contreras, Supreme Court, May 24, 1960, 57 *Rev. Der. Jur.*, Sec. 1, p. 83 (1960).

20. See Bascuñán, op. cit. (note No. 3), Vol. III, p. 437.

21. The Organic Law of the Consejo de Defensa del Estado appears at DFL No. 1 of 1963, *Diario Oficial*, July 4, 1963.

22. See *Memoria del Consejo de Defensa Fiscal*, p. 148 (1939).

23. Final text of DFL 285 of July 25, 1953 is in DS 1100 of the Ministry of Public Works (*Boletín Oficial*, July 26, 1960).

24. DFL 2 of 1959, Art. 51.

25. Law 16.391 of Dec. 16, 1965.

26. Message of the Executive to the Congress proposing approval of the Agrarian Reform Law (Nov. 22, 1965), in *Ley de Reforma Agraria* (Editorial Nascimiento, 1967).

27. President's message to the Congress, May 21, 1970, *Boletín Oficial* (1970).

111

Mexico

Julio C. Treviño

Contents

I. Changing Concepts of the Right of Property   117
   1. Historical Evolution of Property Rights in Mexico   117
   2. The Social Function of Property   120
   3. Different Types of Property   121
   4. Nationalization, Expropriation, and *Modalidades*   122
II. The Elements of Expropriation   125
   1. Historical Background   125
   2. The Constitution of 1917   126
   3. Persons and Property Subject to Expropriation   127
   4. The Concept of Public Utility   128
   5. Scope of Judicial Review   130
III. Compensation   132
   1. The Question of Prior or Deferred Compensation   132
   2. The Amount of Compensation   136
   3. The Form of Payment   137
IV. Expropriation Procedure   138
   1. The Declaration of Expropriation   138
   2. Determination of Compensation   139
   3. Administrative Review—*Revocación*   140
   4. Judicial Review—The *Amparo*   140
   5. Transfer of the Property   141
   6. *Reversión*   141
V. Expropriation in Practice   142
   1. Current Scope of Expropriation   142
   2. Expropriation and Other Techniques for Acquiring Private Property   143
   3. Negotiation Between the State and Private Property Owner   144
   4. Formal Expropriation   145
VI. Property Rights of Aliens and "Mexicanization"   147
   1. The Place of Aliens in Mexican Law   147
   2. The Concept of Mexicanization   148
   3. The Scope of Mexicanization   149

4. Techniques of Mexicanization 150
5. Assessment 152
Conclusion 153
Notes 153

I. Changing Concepts of the Right of Property

Almost every observer of modern Mexico, whether from the point of view of politics, of economics, of sociology, or of law, comments on the simultaneous existence of two currents, the one directed to upholding individual liberties and to protecting private property and private enterprise; and the other directed to subordinating individual rights and liberties to a superior collective interest, including the socialization of law and a considerable intervention on the part of the government in activities of private parties. These twin currents have run throughout Mexico's history since 1917, with now the one and now the other cresting higher. Inevitably, the subject of expropriation, which represents one aspect of the State's dealings with its citizens, is constantly being affected by both these currents.

1. Historical Evolution of Property Rights in Mexico

Property in the Colonial Period. During the period of Spanish rule, the concept of property, in particular property in land, was based on the patrimony of the Spanish kings. The Spanish laws established several methods of land distribution, first through a system of royal graces or mercy, later through a system of public sales or auctions. In either case, ownership of land was based on a royal benefit to which certain conditions were attached, a violation of which could result in reversion to the Crown. Thus, for example, possession of land carried with it the obligation to live on the land, to cultivate it, and to care for it. Landholders had to obey, at least in theory, legislation designed to protect the life and property of the Indian villages. Mines were the exclusive property of the King of Spain; if ownership or possession of mines was transferred to a private person, such transfer was dependent on payment of taxes to the Sovereign and an actual working of the mine, with nonfulfillment resulting in reversion. Finally, the law put limits on the amount of land that any person could own. Thus, even in the Spanish colonial period of Mexico, the old Roman concepts of property, with their ideas that property ownership was absolute, exclusive, and perpetual, did not prevail.[1]

In addition to the conditional nature of property rights, Spanish colonial law also knew a form of expropriation designed to satisfy particular requirements of the Kingdom. Compensation was required prior to a taking on behalf of the Crown.[2]

The First Century of Independence. When Mexico's War of Independence ended in 1821, the distribution of land was initially assigned to the old *Intendencias*; that is, the regions or provinces into which the national territory had been divided under colonial law. When Mexico became a Federal Republic, the powers of the *Intendencias* passed to the state governments. However, placing the task of land distribution in local hands proved to be unsuccessful. The Constitution of 1857 federalized all uncultivated lands and then opened them to purchase by private persons, thus taking away from the states one of their principal powers.[3] The Constitution of 1857, consistent with its nineteenth-century liberal inspiration, established at least tentatively the inviolable character of private property, subject to cases of public utility, in which case prior compensation was required. On the other hand, the Law of 1863 Concerning Uncultivated Lands preserved the colonial pattern; that is, it provided for a reversionary right to the State quite apart from the power to expropriate for reasons of public utility.[4]

The first Civil Code of Mexico, issued in 1870, was markedly influenced by the French Declaration of the Rights of Man of 1789 and the Code Napoléon of 1804. As a result, Article 827 of the first Mexican Civil Code defined property as

the right to enjoy and dispose of something without any limitations other than those established by law.

Further, the 1870 Civil Code and its successor, the Civil Code of 1884, stated that

property cannot be taken except for reasons of public utility and on the basis of prior compensation (Article 828, 1870 Code, Article 730 of 1884 Code).

The Civil Code of 1884, issued during the reign of Porfírio Díaz and thus representing the high point of economic individualism in Mexican history, went even further, in that it provided (in Article 731) that the proprietor of a plot of land owned not only its surface but the subsoil as well. The Mining Code issued in the same year recognized the right of eminent domain by the State over mineral property (Article 3), but in the absence of the exercise of that right, the surface owner was stated to be the owner of mineral deposits which he could work without any need of prior permission or concession (Articles 2 and 10).[5]

The Constitution of 1917. Seven years after the end of the reign of Porfírio Díaz, and as the fighting stage of the Revolution was coming to a close, Mexico adopted its new Constitution, which is still in force today. As in so many other areas, the Constitution of 1917 was revolutionary in its approach to property, while at the same time retaining many of the elements of the prior system. Thus the 1917 Constitution departs completely from the theory that the right of property is a divine or natural right, and provides instead that property, particularly land and natural resources, is a right belonging to all of the nation. Accordingly, the right of private ownership, being derived from society, exists only as a function of society. At the same time, however, private ownership as such is not abolished.

One way to show the consequences of the change made in the 1917 Constitution is put side by side the corresponding provisions of the Civil Code of 1884 and the new Civil Code of 1928:

Civil Code of 1884	Civil Code of 1928
Article 729: Property is the right to enjoy and dispose of a thing without limitations other than those established by law. *Article 730:* Property is inviolable: it may not be taken except for causes of public utility and with prior compensation.	*Article 830:* The owner of a thing may enjoy and dispose of it subject to the limitations and modalities established by law. *Article 831:* Property may not be taken against the will of its owner, except for causes of public utility and with compensation.

The meaning of "modalities" *(modalidades)* will become clearer in the course of this paper (see especially Section I (4)). For the moment, at the risk of oversimplication, we may just say that a *modalidad* is a right of the state to impose restrictions on a property right through regulation, generally not entitling the property owner to compensation.

2. The Social Function of Property

As noted in the preceding section, one of the important concepts contained in the Constitution of 1917 is the concept of social function of property. Though the word does not appear in the Constitution itself, that document, and particularly the first three paragraphs of Article 27, are considered to contain the element, if not the definition, of the concept of social function:

> Ownership of the lands and waters included within the boundaries of national territory belongs originally to the Nation, which has had and continues to have the right to transmit ownership thereof to private parties, thereby constituting private property.
>
> Expropriations may only be made for reasons of public utility and by means of compensation.
>
> The Nation shall have at all times the right to impose on private property the modalities required by the public interest, as well as the right to regulate the exploitation of natural resources capable of appropriation, in order to conserve them and to make an equitable distribution of public wealth.

While there have been varying interpretations of the meaning of these paragraphs and of their origins, perhaps one of the best is the statement of Pastor Rouaix, one of the draftsmen of the Constitution, that the fundamental purpose of the delegates at the Constituent Assembly was to interpret a unanimous feeling born of the Revolution that began in 1910 "that Mexican law establish fully as a basic, solid, and unalterable principle that above the rights of individuals to property there were superior rights of society, represented by the State, to regulate its distribution as well as its use and conservation." [6]

The Supreme Court of Justice has said:

> [Article 27] sought to eliminate the classical concept which defined the right of property as an absolute untouchable right, and to replace it with a concept which recognizes private property as a social function. Thus, private property would not be the exclusive right of one individual, but a right subordinated to the common welfare. [7]

The third paragraph of Article 27 quoted above is understood to describe both the positive and the negative aspects of the social function of property: Negative in that the State can restrict the use of and even take property, positive in that it can impose obligations on the owner with respect to use of the property—the so-called "modality."[8]

3. Different Types of Property

Mexican law today classifies property not just into public and private, or movable and immovable, but into a series of categories depending on the owner and on the use to which the porperty may be put.

Original property, as we have seen, represents the concept that land and water derive from the State and that the State maintains a reversionary interest in such property regardless of current ownership.

National property comprises two classes of assets of the Federal Government—assets in the public domain and assets in the private domain but owned by the State. Among the former are all natural resources reserved to the State by the Constitution, as well as facilities such as factories and public buildings used for state services or enterprises. Temples open to the public for religious services also belong to this category. Properties in the public domain may be transferred to private owners only after being formally removed from the public domain. Other assets of the State are considered to belong to the private domain of the State and therefore may be transfered to private ownership.[9]

Agricultural property in Mexico is governed by an entirely separate legal regime based on Article 27 of the Constitution as well as a series of agrarian laws and the Agrarian Code of 1940. Without here going into a detailed discussion of a highly complicated subject, it is worth noting that there are two distinct systems of landholding in Mexico—collectively owned land held through the rural village or *ejido,* and individually owned land. *Ejidal* land is essentially state property assigned individually and collectively to certain farmers for private use. In practice, *ejidal* land is somewhere between state and private property, in that it is usually worked in individual plots by individual farmers, but title is vested in the village, the property cannot be mortgaged, and the rights of succession of members of the *ejido* depend on arrangements within the village and not on civil law. In contrast, individually held land is governed by civil law as regards transfer, mortgage, and inheritance, subject of course to the modalities and limitations that the State may impose on all properties. The chain of title of property held through the *ejido* is typically confused, being mixture of former Indian village titles, property "restored" during the Revolution and thereafter, and property acquired through an expropriatory proceeding known as *"dotación."* As we shall see below, small individual farmers—whose holdings constitute approximately one-half of Mexico's cultivated land—have the right in certain cases to resort to a special judicial proceeding (the *amparo*) to object if their holdings are sought to be incorporated in an *ejido*.[10]

Finally, *private property* is that property which is held by individuals (or firms) and is subject to the guarantees, both substantive and procedural, contained in the Mexican Constitution. In particular, Article 14 of the Constitution states:

> ...No one shall be deprived of life, liberty or properties, possessions or rights except through a trial before courts previously established in which the essential formalities of procedure shall be observed in conformity with laws existing prior to the act...

Article 16 of the Constitution states:

> No one may be molested in his person, family, home, papers or possessions, except pursuant to written order from competent authority stating the legal basis for the proceeding.

As procedural safeguards, these two constitutional guarantees are, in general, adequate to protect private property from arbitrary state seizure. The substantive safeguards will be discussed throughout this paper.

4. National, Expropriation, and *Modalidades*

Mexican law knows three methods by which the State affects the rights and activities that might be associated with private property: nationalization, expropriation, and *modalidades*. While the distinction between these three methods is sometimes blurred in borderline instances, it is possible to describe the general characteristics of each and to point out how each fits into the modern conception of the functions of the State and, correspondingly, of the social functions of property.

By *nationalization* is meant the assumption by the State through the Constitution or through a law of ownership of certain types of property or responsibility for an entire industry, such as petroleum, railroads, or electric power. Nationalization is not directed at a particular piece of property or person but aims to accomplish a general social goal. To put it in juridical terms, nationalization is thought of not as the transfer of property from one legal subject (the private owner) to another (the community or the State), but rather as transformation of the character of the property from private to collective property. *Expropriation*, in contrast, is directed to a specific property needed for a specific public activity.

A *modalidad* does not involve transfer of property at all, but involves the imposition by the State of duties or restrictions on the property for purposes of some national interest.[11] Thus, *modalidades* may include forced sharing of certain property with other parties or state organs; compulsory prolongation of leases for protection of tenants; requirements that the property owner erect facilities such as sewers or make their facilities available for processing mineral substances extracted by someone else under a state concession; restraints on exports or imports by private firms; restraints on prices that may be charged by private enterprises; and a large number of other manifestations of governmental policy.[12] The express authorization of *modalidades* in Article 27 of the Constitution (see Section I (2)) is the basis for the very active participation by the State in the economic life of Mexico, often without objective and impartial standards.

Modalidades do not call for compensation to the affected private property owner, though some commentators have urged that they should. As a general rule, nationalization likewise does not call for compensation, since, as noted above, it is not thought of as the transfer of property rights but as a change in the character of the property in question and the activities associated with it. Nevertheless, when nationalization is accompanied by an actual transfer of assets, it may be carried out through expropriation, calling for compensation, or through purchase by the State in accordance with the provisions of the Civil and Commercial Codes. A typical case of the latter technique was the purchase by the Mexican Government in 1960 of the stock of the largest electric power companies operating in Mexico. The underlying resources had been national property since the 1917

Constitution and the Government operated power plants and distribution systems, but some private companies had engaged in electric power manufacture and distribution under concessions from the State. When the Government decided that private electric companies would no longer be allowed, it first purchased the companies' assets, and then passed the legislation calling for the exclusive right of the government to engage in electric power production and distribution.[13]

When the Mexican oil industry was nationalized in 1938 it was done through the expropriation technique. The subsoil resources had been national property since the 1917 Constitution—although this was questioned by the oil companies—but the government decided to take over the production and distribution of oil products completely and, to that end, expropriated the machinery, installations, storage tanks and other assets of the oil companies which had been operating under government concessions.[14] From a juridical standpoint the legislation on oil matters that followed completed the nationalization process.

Expropriation does require compensation under the Mexican Constitution (Article 27), though unlike most of the Constitutions of Latin America, the Mexican Constitution of 1917 does not refer to "prior" compensation. We shall examine the question of compensation for expropriation in more detail in Section III. It is interesting, however, in seeking to differentiate among three forms of state intervention in the private economy, to read the following remarks of one of the members of the Supreme Court who passed on the claims of the oil companies in 1938:

> We must not conclude without reiterating that compensation is only an expression of the spirit of justice which inspires the laws, but not an indispensable condition of every expropriation or of all injury that may be suffered by private property. Compensation must always, in technical terms, be conditioned not to compensate 100 percent, but to serve as a means of regulating the equilibrium of economic forces, since compensation must, like property, fulfill a social function and must therefore be limited or restricted to what social needs and possibilities permit, lest economic disequilibria caused by free competition and liberal principles of property which do not recognize the mediating intervention of the State be emphasized or barred.[15]

It should be added immediately that this quotation, though authoritative, is not necessarily representative of the Mexico of today. While the Constitution remains in this respect unchanged and all of the principles of the Revolution begun in 1910 are still in full force, in fact the present economic strength of Mexico and its international prestige have to some extent changed the outlook of the country on matters of nationalization and on the means to carry it out.

Discussion of the complete scope of *modalidades* would require a complete description of the economic life of Mexico. Likewise, the extent of nationalization cannot be treated here in detail except to say that as of the end of the 1960's it includes the oil industry, the electric power industry, the railways, telecommunications and some important segments of banking, particularly for agricultural credits. Two final points in this introductory section, however, will conclude our differentiation of the three legal concepts. In expropriation, if the taking agency does not, within a certain time, use the property taken for the purpose set forth, the former owner has a right to reclaim his property. No such rule applies for *modalidades* or nationalization. More interesting, whereas expropriation may be carried out by the National Government or by the State Governments and in some cases by municipalities, only the National Government is entitled to impose *modalidades* and only the National Government can "nationalize."

II. The Elements of Expropriation

1. Historical Background

Nationalization and *modalidades*, at least as separate concepts are, as we have seen, products of the Mexican revolution; that is, products of the twentieth century. Expropriation, in contrast, dates back to the days of colonial rule and indeed can be traced to Spanish and even Roman law. Article 35 of the Constitution of Apartzingár of 1814, the first Constitutional document of independent Mexico, stated:

> No one shall be deprived of the smallest portion of what he possesses except when public necessity demands it; but in that case he shall have the right to just compensation.[16]

Similar provisions occur in nearly all the Constitutional documents of early Mexico, typically as a qualification on the guarantee of the right to property. Thus, for example, Article 112 (III) of the Constitution of 1824 says:

> The President shall not take the property of any private person or corporation nor disturb them in their possession, use, or enjoyment thereof, and if in any case it becomes necessary to take the property of a private person or corporation for an object of known general utility, he shall not do so without prior approval of the Senate or, if the Senate is in recess, of the Government Council, in any event compensating the interested party in accordance with the judgment of good men elected by the interested party and the Government.[17]

Very similar language appears also in the Constitutional Laws of 1836, and the *Bases Organicas* of 1843. The Constitution of 1857 stated, in Article 27:

> Property of persons may not be taken without their consent, except for reason of public utility and upon prior compensation. The law shall determine the authority which must make the expropriation and the conditions for such expropriation.[18]

Subsequently, a variety of laws met the requirement in Article 27 by defining certain projects as having the character of public utility, and by authorizing designated agencies to carry out the expropriation. For example, a law of May 31, 1882 authorized the municipal government of Mexico City and the Federal Government to take properties by way of expropriation for purposes of the concessions granted for construction of a railroad from Mexico City to the Pacific Ocean and to the northern boundary. Similarly, a law of July 3, 1901 authorized the Executive Branch to decree and carry out expropriations of potable water and land for purposes of municipal services in the federal territories.[19]

2. The Constitution of 1917

As we have seen, the Constitution of 1917 represents in many ways a discontinuity with prior Mexican history and an attempt to set forth the framework for a government of revolutionary Mexico. Thus, for example, the concept of *modalidades* and national enterprises is very different from the concept of property contained in the nineteenth-century civil codes and in the guarantees

126

contained in Article 27 of the Constitution of 1857 and its antecedents from 1814 on. Nevertheless, the provision concerning expropriation in the 1917 Constitution is, at least in terms, quite similar to the previous versions:

> Expropriations may only be made for a reason of public utility and by means of compensation [*mediante indemnización*].

It may be asked why the Constitution of 1917 retains the requirement of compensation, which may seem contrary to the general concept of the social function of property and the subordination of private to public interests. One answer may be that expropriation is a burden that falls entirely on the one person who is deprived of his property. If he were not compensated, the principle of equality of private persons before public institutions would be violated.[20]

The only substantive change, if it is one, between the 1917 verson and the 1857 version of the of the expropriation clause of the Constitution is the use of the word *mediante* (by means of) to modify *indemnización* in place of the word *previa* (prior). There has been much discussion among scholars as to whether this was in fact designed to establish a new juridical situation whereby compensation could be prior, simultaneous, or subsequent, depending on the needs and abilities of the State, or whether no change was intended, since in any event an expropriation is a forced sale and the use of *"mediante"* did not permit the inference that payment could be made after the transfer of the property.[21] We shall revert to this topic again in the discussion of compensation and forms of payment (see Section III (1) and (3)).

3. Persons and Property Subject to Expropriation

In principle, all property in Mexico is subject to expropriation, except property already owned by the National Government. Thus private property, property owned by states or municipalities, and agrarian property held by the *ejidos* are all subject to expropriation, provided the other conditions are met. It has been argued, on the basis of the text of Article 27 of the Constitution, that expropriation applies only to immovable property. However, the Supreme Court of Mexico, in agreement with the leading writers, has rejected this argument.[22]

In 1936 the State of Yucatan declared extraction and processing of henequen (hemp) a state-controlled activity, and ordered some private owners of tools and machinery to allow the farmers to use them. The private owners objected that this was either a *modalidad*, and hence illegal because it was not imposed by the Federal Government, or it was an expropriation, and illegal because it went beyond "lands and waters" as provided for in Article 27. The Supreme Court held that the act of the State of Yucatan was an expropriation, that it was lawfully carried out, and that it was subject to the requirement of compensation set forth in the second paragraph of Article 27.[23]

While in theory all kinds of property, movable as well as immovable, may be expropriated, it is not clear that intangibles such as patents, trademarks, stocks and bonds, and the like are subject to expropriation. Only cash itself may not be expropriated, and the reason for this appears to be not any special character of money as a kind of property, but simply the consideration that compensation is supposed to be paid in money. To expropriate money and pay compensation in installments would be forced compulsory borrowing, and this the State may not do.[24] The only other kind of property not subject to expropriation is certain property immune as a result of international law or treaty, as for example diplomatic property or property of international organizations lawfully established in Mexico (Article 14 of the Expropriation Law—GLNA).

4. The Concept of Public Utility

Article 27, Section VI, Paragraph 2 of the Constitution of 1917 provides:

> The laws of the Federation and of the States in their respective jurisdictions shall determine those cases in which taking of private property shall be of public utility, and in accordance with such laws the administrative authorities shall make the appropriate declaration.

Thus, some expropriations may be justified by objectives expressed in the Constitution itself, for example agrarian reform.[25] Others are spelled out in the national expropriation law as well as in the expropriation laws of the respective states. Article 1 of the Federal Expropriation Law of 1936 spells out the cases in which expropriation for public utility is in order: among them are establishment of public services; construction and maintenance of roads, bridges, tunnels, and transport facilities; expansion, cleaning up, and beautification of villages and harbors; construction of hospitals, schools, parks, gardens, sports fields, government office buildings and other structures to be used for the collective benefit; preservation of places of scenic beauty, historic, or artistic value, and other objects considered as notable characteristics of the national culture. Also, a number of the purposes have to do with national defense or public safety and measures of a public health character. One interesting item in Article 1 of the Expropriation Law is:

VIII. The equitable distribution of riches accumulated or monopolized through exclusive advantages of one or a number of persons with prejudice to the community in general or to a particular class.

Following eleven wide-ranging categories of statutory public purposes, the final clause of Article 1 reads:

XII. All other cases provided for by special laws.

The mining law, the communications law, and similar legislation contain additional causes of public utility, as do several Articles of the Federal Civil Code.[26] One interesting purpose, not commonly found in other countries, is in the Federal Law on Authors' Rights, which empowers the Federal Government to place specific limitations on the rights of authors in order to permit publication of intellectual or artistic works which are out of print or are sold at such prices as to prevent a general dissemination.[27]

The efforts of the judiciary to define the essential elements of public utility have not been very successful. In its first attempt at definition of the term following the Constitution of 1917, the Supreme Court described public utility as "that which satisfies a public need and rebounds to the benefit of the collectivity."[28] In the case from which this quotation was taken, the Supreme Court decided that an expropriation for the purpose of creating new population centers in Durango that did not follow the special rules in the Constitution regarding expropriation for agrarian purposes did not meet the requirement of public utility. Accordingly, the Supreme Court granted relief against the decrees of the state legislature in question. In 1936 in the henequen case previously cited, the Supreme Court rejected this concept of public utility as too narrow and "impossible to sustain under a correct interpretation of the Constitutional statute governing the matter."[29] The court defined public utility as embracing three concepts: public utility in the strict sense, when the property expropriated is used directly in a public service; social utility, characterized by the need to satisfy in a direct manner one social class and through such benefit the community as a whole (for instance, agricultural expropriation); and national utility, where the expropriation is required to enable the nation to confront national or international situations as a political entity.[30]

The Supreme Court itself recognized that this new definition of public utility is so broad that it includes anything that is not merely of private utility. In 1939 in a case arising out of the nationalization of the petroleum industry, the Supreme Court decided definitively that there is no essential difference between the concepts of public utility and public interest.[31]

It is clear that expropriation by executive determination alone, without a Constitutional or statutory basis, cannot be sustained. But can any expropriation coming within the purposes declared by the Constitution or by statute ever be unconstitutional as not for reasons of public utility? The decisions of the Supreme Court shed no clear light on this question (see Paragraph 5). As an important matter of procedure, however, it is still necessary for a correspondence to be established between the public purposes or public utility and the property to be taken. The determination of this correspondence is to be made by the executive authority designated in the law on which the expropriation is based. Thus, an expropriation must be founded both on a law defining the purpose of the expropriation and on a determination of need for a particular piece of property: if either of these factors is absent, the expropriation is illegal and can be struck down.

5. Scope of Judicial Review

Having stated that the basis for expropriation depends on two determinations, one by the Legislature and the other by the Executive, we may well ask what role, if any, is left to the Judiciary. The answer in Mexican law is far from clear.

Professor Gabino Fraga, one of the leading authorities on

administrative law, believes that the courts do have a significant role to play in creating substantive standards of public utility; that is, in determining whether a given expropriation involves a satisfaction of a need of the community entrusted to the State.[32] The decisions of the Supreme Court, however, are inconsistent on this point. In the case previously cited involving new population centers in Durango,[33] the Court appears to have taken a substantive stand on the components of public utility and on the powers of the Legislature to define that term. In a subsequent case, however, the Supreme Court decided it had no jurisdiction to review the constitutionality of causes of public utility established by the Legislature, since to do so would be to arrogate to itself the power granted by Article 27(VI) of the Constitution to the Legislative Branch—local or federal.[34] It is fair to say that while this was the rationale and holding of the Supreme Court, it reached its decision, after having carefully examined the statute in question and the public benefit from the challenged activity, which concerned the construction of low-income housing by the State of Veracruz.

If the Supreme Court is reluctant to challenge the public purpose as defined by the Legislature, it is apparently less hesitant to inquire whether a particular property is suited and necessary for that purpose, even where the Executive Branch has already formally made an affirmative determination on that issue.[35] Thus the Supreme Court has on occasion held that the Executive must prove the facts on which it bases taking of particular property for public purposes; absent such proof, the Court has struck down the expropriation.[36] For example, in a 1948 case, the State of Jalisco sought to take several pieces of land for purposes of construction of school buildings. While this was plainly a purpose within the law, the Government failed to show that it intended to put a school on each of the locations, or indeed that more than one school building in the area was needed. Accordingly, the Supreme Court granted an *amparo* (see Section IV(4)) against the expropriation.[37] Similarly, an expropriation under Mexico City's beautification program was disallowed in the absence of a showing of need for the properties in question in connection with the beautification program.[38] On the other hand, when land or buildings are taken for military installments, the Government is not put to comparable proof.[39]

Again, a challenge may be made under the rubric of public

utility on the grounds that the expropriation will benefit private more than public interests. For example, the Supreme Court granted suspension of the decree of expropriation on this ground in the case of a plot of land in the Federal District designed to be used to build a sports stadium. That purpose was expressly within the expropriation law, but the burden of proof on the Executive was not met once it was shown that the stadium would be owned and operated by private parties.[40]

Finally, the courts may intervene in a conflict between state and federal claims to carry out the same public activity, or to using the same public property for different public purposes.

In the first situation, the Supreme Court held unconstitutional an expropriation by the State of Nuevo León based on a state law that established as a cause of public activity the operation of airports. The Court held operation of air navigation facilities to be within the exclusive legislative competence of the Federal Congress, and therefore struck down the expropriation of plaintiff's land.[41]

The second situation, where no preemption of functions can be shown, is more difficult. For example, the State of Jalisco sought to extend a street in the city of Guadalajara, a purpose well within its competence, and stated that if needed it would take down a building belonging to the Mexican Telephone and Telegraph Company, a private enterprise operating under concession from the Federal Government. The Supreme Court resolved the conflict between the two public interests and two jurisdictions by recognizing the power of the State to carry out the expropriation for its local purposes, but conditioned the expropriation on confirmation by the federal authorities that new installations had been erected with their approval by the Telephone Company so that telephone services would not be interrupted.[42]

III. Compensation

1. The Question of Prior or Deferred Compensation

Practically all of the juridical works dealing with the subject of expropriation begin with the question referred to earlier (Section II (2)) concerning the meaning of the change in the present Constitution from *"previa indemnizacion"* (prior compensation) to *"mediante indemnizacion"* (by means of compensation).[43] It seems evident to this writer that the word *mediante* means something different from "prior," so that there can be no doubt that the draftsmen of the Constitution of 1917 intended to effect a change. The argument that the word *mediante* is used in other parts of the Constitution in a context where "subsequent to" or even "simultaneous with" would make no sense—for example, in Article 14 of the Constitution, which states that no one shall be deprived of life, liberty, possessions, or rights. . .*sino mediante judicio* (except through a trial)—is not persuasive in the context of the deliberate change from the 1857 Constitution. But what the word *mediante* means in the context of Article 27 still requires interpretation.[44]

Unfortunately, no notes were kept of the debates of the committee that drafted this Article. Some of the members of the Drafting Committee said that the use of the word *mediante* was designed to facilitate resolution of the agrarian problem. The fear, apparently, was that if compensation had to be prior and if the amount had to be fixed by the courts, then the large landholders could tie up and postpone agrarian reform indefinitely as they had done in the earlier attempts to break up the large land holdings amassed in the Porfirian era.[45] This fear could be an explanation for the use of the word *"mediante"* in place of the word *"previa."* A more direct response to that problem, however, was the provision in Article 27(XIV) discussed below, whereby for land given to villages the intervention of the Judiciary is practically eliminated.

The jurist Andrés Molina Enríquez, who participated in the drafting of the Article 27, though he was not a delegate, has contributed a personal interpretation which was accepted for some time. His interpretation is that compensation is in any case obligatory, but since there is no reason why it should be prior, it may be paid at any time from the moment when the declaration of expropriation is issued until the date when the owner loses the last appeal which the law gives him.[46] A current commentator, Mendieta y Nuñez, believes that the draftsmen actually wanted to give the State more freedom in matters of expropriation, but that this does not justify in all cases payment of compensation after the expropriation itself. According to Mendieta y Nuñez, three factors must be taken into account in determining the time for compensation: the public interest, the economic resources of the State, and the damages suffered by the former owner.[47]

The decisions of the Supreme Court on this issue have followed

133

an apparently contradictory course. Yet it seems to the present writer that three principles emerge from these decisions, reflecting the evolution since 1917 of the concept of property, of the idea of the social function of property, and of the concept of the public interest generally. The first group of decisions, handed down between 1917 and 1921, [48] established the proposition that compensation, being guaranteed by the Constitution, cannot be left uncertain. Though Article 27 does not state that compensation must be prior, neither does it say that compensation can be deferred, and accordingly it should be simultaneous, or at least guaranteed in a precise, real, and positive way.[49]

In the period of 1936 to 1938 [50], immediately before the great expropriations in Mexico, this principle was modified to say that the only delay permitted for payment of compensation is the time necessary for ascertaining the amount of compensation due. This was consistent with the argument mentioned above that mediante replaced previa in order not to hold up expropriation until the amount of compensation had been fixed. Moreover, the decisions of this period said that payment must be made in a manner that allows the recipient to have full enjoyment of the compensation to which he is entitled. Accordingly, payment over a period of twenty years as provided by the Expropriation Law of Veracruz was held to be contrary to the Constitutional guarantee.[51] A subsequent case made an important modification in this principle by relating the obligation of prompt payment to the purpose of the expropriation. Thus, where the expropriation was designed to accomplish an important social purpose, and achievement of that purpose could not be held up until the Government was able to provide full compensation, it was held that compensation could be deferred.[52]

The third phase of the development by the Supreme Court of the interpretation of the second paragraph of Article 27 dates from the cases arising out of the large-scale expropriations carried on by Mexico in 1938, notably in connection with the oil industry. [53] Article 20 of the Federal Expropriation Law of November 25, 1936 had made provision for payment of compensation in installments up to ten years. In the famous *El Aguila* case involving the taking of the oil refineries, the Supreme Court in 1939 upheld this provision against Constitutional challenge, again on the basis that not to have carried out the expropriation in question immediately would have greatly prejudiced the nation.[54]

134

The Supreme Court has not defined the degree of urgency required in order to sustain deferred compensation. In two cases contemporary to the *El Aguila* case, however, the Court seems to have laid down the principle that both urgency of expropriation and inability of the Government to make immediate payment must be present before deferral will be permitted as an exception to the general rule.[55] If either of these situations is not present, for example in the taking of a relatively small piece of private property, then compensation must be immediate.[56]

The result of these decisions is to place the laws on expropriation in a very indefinite situation in that the constitutionality of a state or federal law authorizing expropriation and providing for deferred compensation will depend on an act or situation subsequent to passage of the law. If a particular expropriation is carried out for an urgent cause of public benefit and if the economic capacity of the state does not permit immediate payment, the law will be considered Constitutional. If these circumstances are not present, the same law at least as applied will be deemed unconstitutional.

In the writer's view, what is needed is a legislative reform of the expropriation laws—both state and federal—to contain criteria for distinguishing between those cases that permit deferred compensation and those cases that do not.[57] Not only have the Mexican Legislatures so far not provided the definitions suggested above, but they have been careless in the way the expropriation laws are drafted. For example, Article 19 of the Federal Expropriation Law states:

> the amount of compensation shall be paid by the State when the property expropriated passes to its possession.

But Article 20, as we have seen, provides for installment payments up to ten years. Again, the Federal Code of Civil Procedure of 1943 provides in one of its chapters for the procedure to be followed for federal courts in cases when, according to the Constitution, compensation is to be established judicially, and Article 528 states that title passes to the government when the price is placed at the disposal of the private owner. Though the Code of Civil Procedure was enacted seven years after the Expropriation Law, it cannot be stated with confidence that it supersedes Article 20 of the Expropriation Law. Similar contradictions within the same statute or between expropriation laws and codes of procedure appear in many of the states of Mexico. [58]

2. The Amount of Compensation

Article 27 (VI) of the Constitution states, in pertinent part:

> The price to be fixed as compensation for expropriated property shall be based on the valuation of said property for tax purposes as registered in the census or revenue office, whether this valuation has been stated by the owner himself or simply accepted by him tacitly by having paid his taxes on that basis. Increases or decreases in value resulting from improvement or deterioration to the property subsequent to the assignment of a tax value shall be the only issue subject to expert decision or judicial determination . . .

Though in terms this provision relates only to immovables, now that it is clear that all kinds of property are subject to expropriation (see Section II (3)), it is established that Article 27 (VI) provides the governing principle for all valuations in expropriation cases. Movables are assimilated for this purpose to increases or decreases not reflected in the assessment records.

The principle of basing compensation on tax value has, it seems, the appeal that private property owners are, as it were, hoist by their own petard. But, as a number of writers in Mexico and elsewhere have pointed out, the tendency of property owners to assign as low a value as possible to their properties for tax purposes is taken into account by tax authorities in setting the rates, so that the result is in fact a vicious circle. [59] It is true that the method of valuation prescribed by the Constitution prevents fluctuation in the value of properties resulting from the news of the expropriation. However, the many instances of arbitrary and unfair results from this method of valuation seem to the present writer to argue for reform of the Constitutional system, looking to a system in which experts would establish the true value of all property expropriated, and not only of improvements or deteriorations after the last date of tax evaluation. [60] In the present condition of Mexico's economic development, the desirability of flexibility in administrative practice would seem to be balanced by considerations of fairness to private persons who may be affected by expropriation. Compensation on the basis of census or tax values is particularly unsatisfactory in regard to movable property

136

and also in regard to immovables in the many areas where new developments are going up, which are either not registered at all or whose registration is hopelessly out of date. This criticism is tempered somewhat by the fact that the Federal Government has largely abandoned the classical Constitutional model for expropriation (see Section V (2), (3) and (4)). Nevertheless, even in a negotiating process the Constitutional provision places private persons at a disadvantage in negotiating a fair price with expropriating authorities.

3. The Form of Payment

Discussion of forms of payment in a practical sense substantially overlaps discussion of the terms of payment. The alternative to cash is usually some form of evidence of public debt such as bonds which, of course, constitute deferred payment. Such payment is specifically provided for in Article 27 (XVII) of the Constitution with respect to agrarian properties; that is, with regard to land takings under the agrarian reform.

In addition to bonds for agricultural land, and in certain circumstances for other properties as well, Mexican law provides for payment other than in cash in several other circumstances. For example, Article 24 of the Federal Law of Irrigation of December 31, 1946, authorizes compensation in certain cases in other land, or part in land, part in cash, at the election of the private owner, provided he is in compliance with the provisions of the Agrarian Code covering small landholders. This law would probably be sustained against Constitutional attack, since it is an indirect way of regulating agriculture related to the land reform program. Nevertheless, the provision for election between land and cash on the part of the private property owner is certainly not foreseen in the Constitution.

The recent General Law on National Assets of January 30, 1969, cannot be sustained on the above analysis and is, in this writer's opinion, unconstitutional. Article 42 of this Law provides:

> When the Federal Government expropriates privately owned immovables for reasons of public utility, it may pay the compensation due through delivery of properties similar to those expropriated and may make a donation to the private owner of the resulting differences in value, provided that the private owners are persons of modest economic means and that the properties taken

were a family dwelling, a shop where they operated a small business or a family trade or industry.

In our view, even assuming compensation in kind is permitted by the Constitution, the option on the part of the Government is not. Moreover, the phrase "donation" seems to distort the obligation of the government into an act of grace. Finally, the idea that persons of modest means and those using their property for certain specified purposes are to be treated differently in regard to their rights to compensation, though consistent with the government's social policies, finds no support in the Constitution. However, at this writing, no challenge to the General Law on National Assets has yet been brought.

IV Expropriation Procedure

1. The Declaration of Expropriation

According to Article 27 (VI) of the Constitution (see Section II (4)), it is the administrative authorities who begin the procedure of expropriation by issuing a Declaration of Expropriation. This Declaration describes the particular property to be taken, sets a date for the taking, and recites the purpose for which the property is to be taken, often with reference to technical studies performed by the taking agency. Thus the Declaration serves to demonstrate the public need and the suitability of the property in question to that need. Further, the Declaration cites the legal authority under which the property is to be taken—either the Constitution itself, the Expropriation Law, or the numerous special laws authorizing the taking of private property for specified purposes. Often more than one law is cited as authority for the taking. In federal expropriations, the declaration or decree of expropriation is issued by the President of the Republic and is countersigned by the Head of the Ministry or Department entrusted with the function for which the property is to be used.

In federal practice, reference is invariably made to the fact that the property owners affected shall receive the compensation required by Article 27 of the Constitution. Some declarations indicate expressly when the compensation is to be paid, and some state the basis for establishing the amount of compensation, usually the census value of the property plus any increase in value due to improvements, as provided in Article 27 (VI) of the Constitution.[61]

Some declarations of expropriation, rather than specifying the basis for compensation, provide who will establish the compensation to be paid. If the project in question is to be carried out by a private person or a decentralized agency, the decree or declaration usually states who will be responsible for paying the compensation. Where the relevant legislation permits a choice, the declaration states whether the payment will be in cash or in kind.

The declaration of expropriation is always (in federal takings) published in the Official Gazette (*Diario Oficial*) of the Federation. If the address of the property owner is known, he must be notified personally; if his address is not known, publication suffices. Since this procedure is established by the Constitution itself, the Supreme Court has held that the hearing·requirement in the guarantee of due process provided by Article 14 of the Constitution (see Section I (3)) does not apply to the administrative procedure for issuing a declaration of expropriation.[62]

2. Determination of Compensation

Every property owner has the right to contest the compensation offered, subject to the constraints on valuation stated in Article 27 (VI) of the Constitution (see Section III (2)). The owner may ask the court in the district where the property is located to order the appointment of experts to complete an appraisal. The order will direct the owner and the taking agency each to appoint one expert, and upon failure of either party to do so, the judge may appoint the missing expert. If the two experts agree, the judge may fix the compensation in accordance with their recommendation. If they disagree, they must try to appoint a third expert who will fix the award; failing agreement on a third expert, the court appoints him. Either way the third expert must determine the compensation due within thirty days of his appointment. The establishment of compensation in this manner is not subject to appeal. If the property owner does not agree to sign the deed, Article 17 of the Expropriation Law authorizes the judge to do so in the owner's behalf.[63]

3. Administrative Review—*Revocación*

Article 5 of the Expropriation Law provides that the affected property owner may within fifteen days of notice of the Declaration of Expropriation, initiate an administrative proceeding for revocation of the Declaration. This proceeding is brought before the same agency or department which ordered the expropriation. While it is pending, all steps connected with the expropriation are suspended. [64] If no proceeding (*recurso*) for revocation is taken within the fifteen-day period, or if the proceeding is resolved adversely to the private property owner, the taking of the property proceeds forthwith (Article 6), unless an *amparo* is applied for as discussed below.

Neither the Constitution nor the Expropriation Law specifies what issues may be raised in the appeal for revocation. For example, it is doubtful that Constitutional issues may be raised, since only the federal courts are competent to judge such issues. But claims that the public utility relied on as a basis for the taking is not provided in law, or that the particular property is not suited to the purpose stated, or that that purpose could be accomplished better without resort to expropriation, or that the procedures for expropriation prescribed in the relevant law have not been followed, all appear to be proper subjects for the appeal for revocation. It should be noted, however, that the issue of compensation nowhere appears in the revocation proceeding.

4. Judicial Review—The *Amparo*

There is no regular jurisdiction in the civil courts of Mexico to review expropriation cases. It is, however, possible to raise certain fundamental issues of procedure or substance in an extraordinary proceeding known as *amparo* (literally, "shelter").

The *amparo* is peculiar to Mexico. It is subject to a Constitutional provision (Article 107) and an elaborate Amparo Law. *Amparo*, which must be brought in a federal court, is in some ways comparable to *habeas corpus* in the common law system in that it is a device whereby the judicial power may be invoked to protect individuals against actions by the State in violation of personal guarantees. The guaranty of property contained in Article 27 of the Constitution is considered a personal guarantee for this purpose. Accordingly, in certain cases it is possible, after the administrative remedy of revocation has been exhausted, to invoke judicial consideration of expropriation cases. The *amparo* may be used to challenge the constitutionality of the law under which the expropriation is proceeding, or to challenge the applicability of the law to a particular Declaration of Expropriation. Often both challenges are raised at the same time.

The proceeding for an *amparo*, like the proceeding for revocation, must be initiated in expropriation cases within fifteen days of the notice of the expropriation, since it is designed to prevent the taking from being consummated. However, the *amparo* will not be considered while a revocation proceeding is in progress.[65] The Supreme Court has said that in *amparo* proceedings growing out of expropriations, it will in the first instance examine any procedural challenges to the expropriation, and will go into substantive challenges only if no fault of procedure is shown.[66] If the court finds that the public interest would not be prejudiced but the injury to the claimant would be irreparable, the court can order suspension of the expropriation pending decision of the *amparo* proceeding. [67] If the court sustains the challenge to the expropriation, it can order the expropriation to be cancelled.

5. Transfer of the Property

Article 27 of the General Law on National Assets states that property subject to expropriation is transferred to the nation as soon as the decree of expropriation is published in the Official Gazette. This seems, however, to be contrary to the Constitutional guarantees of due process. At the very least, it would seem that transfer cannot take place sooner than fifteen days after notice of the declaration is published, or, in the event proceedings for revocation or *amparo* are initiated, before those proceedings are concluded. At all events, the General Law on National Assets seems to contemplate transfer of property to the nation or other taking agency without reference to the proceeding for determining the amount of compensation.

6. *Reversión*

Article 9 of the Expropriation Law provides that if the property taken by the State was not used for the purposes stated in the

Declaration of Expropriation, the former owner has the right within five years of the Declaration to institute an administrative proceeding for the return of his property, known as *reversión*. Similar provisions appear in other laws authorizing expropriation, such as the Mining Law and the Communications Law.[68] Some of these provisions provide for differing periods (a) within which the property taken must be put to the intended use; or (b) within which the former owner can claim *reversión*. The theory, however, is the same. If the property is not put to the use stated in the Declaration of Expropriation, the public utility justifying the expropriation was not present and therefore return or *reversión* is justified.[69]

As regards the Federal Government, successful claim for *reversión* results in a decree by the President published in the Official Gazette revoking the original decree of expropriation. The Mining and Communications Laws provide that in cases of *reversión*, the private owner must return all or part of the compensation he received. The General Expropriation Law and most of the other laws authorizing expropriation make no such provision.

V. Expropriation in Practice

As we have seen, expropriation in Mexico is in large measure a matter of administrative discretion, subject to certain Constitutional and legal requirements. In order, therefore, to obtain a true appraisal of how expropriation works in practice, it has seemed useful to examine in detail one series of recent expropriation decrees, and to consult informally with the public officials of the various departments charged with expropriation matters. This examination was directed to the practice of the Federal Government; the results, accordingly, may be somewhat different in detail from the practice of the various states.

1. Current Scope of Expropriation

In general, expropriation measures currently are reserved for certain works of infrastructure of large proportions, such as roads, dams, airports, and the like, and for projects of urban planning and renewal such as the new subway in Mexico City. Expropriation of commercial and industrial enterprises has not occurred in

Mexico for over twenty-five years. This does not mean that the Federal Government had not broadened the scope of its economic activities. But where the Government has taken over fields of economic activity such as the generation of electric power, it has done so by methods other than expropriation. In large measure, acquisition of previously private properties has been carried out by purchase, as part of the nationalization program described in Section I (4).

2. Expropriation and Other Techniques for Acquiring Private Property

The Federal Government, including the Department of the Federal District, has been pursuing a policy of resorting to expropriation only where no alternative is available. Even in such cases the Government has as far as possible attempted to avoid the rigidity of the expropriation laws, particularly as regards compensation.

Invariably expropriations on behalf of the Federal Government are today carried out on the basis of careful technical studies which take into account not only the "public utility" of a given project, but also the necessity and appropriateness of using particular properties for the project in question. Once the advisability or necessity of the public project has been decided upon, one of two methods for acquisition of private properties is used: for works of limited scope or size affecting only some specific properties, an effort is made to acquire the needed properties by way of private law; that is, by way of purchase or exchange through negotiation with the owners. For projects of great scope, such as roads or dams, which will affect a large number of property owners, the prevailing procedure is expropriation, since all the persons affected are rarely identified and since in any event it would be difficult to enter into individual negotiations with each of them.

The preparatory technical studies by the government agency in charge of the project generally include an analysis of the necessary costs and investments, including the cost of acquisition of private properties, and the prospects of recovery by the Government of its investment. In the latter regard a principal consideration is the increased tax revenue to be derived (except in rural areas) from the increase in value of immovable property of other owners who stand to benefit directly from the project to be carried out. However, there are certain cases of urban projects—for example, rapid transit roads for automobile traffic—where incremental taxes are not imposed, since it is considered that such projects do not benefit any particular property owners, but rather great sections of the urban population. Moreover, it is considered that there is no certainty whether any given project increases or decreases the value of property in the area.

In the case of major federal projects, attempts are sometimes made to obtain donations of land by private persons. This occurs in particular where the lands in question are located in remote rural areas and where the project in question may stimulate construction of roads or communication facilities that will result in an increase in the value of the remaining lands of the private owners. The basis of the donation is, essentially, a trade. The property owner donates a portion of his land to the State, and the State in turn imposes no additional taxes for the increased value of his remaining land. This practice was, for example, followed by the Secretariat of Communications and Transportation in the national program of improved telecommunications recently completed.

3. Negotiation Between the State and Private Property Owner

In those instances when it is possible to achieve the acquisition of property of private persons through purchase, the basis for negotiating a price is a prior valuation made by the department concerned with the acquisition. This valuation is made in ac- cordance with practices similar to appraisals by banks and commercial enterprises in connection with the private sale of real estate. The valuation includes: a) the direct value of the property, i.e., the value of the property considered in itself, estimated by an expert who takes into consideration such factors as the location of the property and the value of other properties similarly situated; and b) capitalized value, i.e., a value based on the productivity of the property in relation to its character and the purpose for which it is used. In rural real estate the quality of the land and the crops for which it is utilized are taken into account, whereas in the case of urban land or buildings the main factor is rental value. On the basis of valuation carried on within this framework a minimum and maximum value are established, and negotiation of the actual price is carried on within these limits. Generally the final price is chosen halfway between the maximum and the minimum.

If the negotiations for purchase result in agreement, another appraisal, this time an official one, is required before the purchase can be consummated. The official appraisal is carried out by the Commission on Valuation of National Property, which is an organ of the Secretariat of National Patrimony but includes representatives of the private sector as well.[70] The formal appraisal nearly always confirms the valuation made prior to the negotiation, since it is also based on direct value and capitalized value as discussed above.

Unless otherwise agreed, the purchase price is normally paid within the same year that the purchase was concluded. Normally no interest is paid on the purchase price if paid within the same year, although a number of months may have elapsed and the payment may not have been made all in one sum.

If the negotiations break down, of course, then the next step is to resort to the formal procedures of expropriation.

4. Formal Expropriation

In cases where it is known because of the scope of the project involved that it will be necessary to resort to the formal procedure of expropriation, the preparatory study referred to above must contain an analysis of the cost of compensation based on the area in question, the nature of the property, the yield or income from the property and some other factors. This analysis does not refer in detail to each property but is a global report included in the cost of the study of the project in question.

In some cases the expropriation decree will state only that the registered value plus any increment due to improvements shall be paid as compensation for the property to be taken, following literally the text of Article 27(VI) of the Constitution. It is interesting, however, that instead of resorting to the procedure for valuation provided for in Article 27(VI) and spelled out at length in the Expropriation Law and the Federal Code of Civil Procedure, (see Sections III(2) and IV(2)) the amount of compensation is usually established even in formal expropriation cases by agreement between the property owner and the expropriating authority. The procedure for reaching agreement is similar to the negotiating procedure described above; first the department decreeing the expropriation establishes a range of prices based on direct value and capitalized value, and then the parties negotiate within that range. Needless to say, such negotiation is carried on with the strict application of the Constitutional precepts in the background, which is always an element of pressure on the private owner. There is also the possibility that compensation will be ordered paid in installments of up to ten years, in accordance with the same legal provisions. In fact, the experience of the agencies consulted suggests that there are very few cases in which the compensation is not established by agreement. For example, the Secretariat of Public Works, which carries out a large volume of projects requiring the acquisition of private property, has not had to resort to the judicial procedure for determining compensation in the past ten years.

With respect to payment in a lump sum or installments there is no definite policy unless the expropriation decree in question has made a specific provision. In general, however, at least some of the agencies concerned endeavour to pay the compensation in a period not to exceed five years. If payment in installments is agreed on, the price will usually be somewhat higher than if payment were in a lump sum.

One interesting feature of the practical experience is that some government agencies have a policy of compensating third parties affected by expropriations, such as tenants of real estate. Since no requirement for the compensation of third parties exists in the law, this policy appears to depend on who the third parties are. Thus, for example, when certain lands were expropriated for construction of a federal highway, compensation was paid to the low-income tenant farmers on the property so that they could move to other lands.[71] This compensation was consistent with the policy of social benefit, and independent of the determination and payment of compensation to the property owners.

In sum, investigation into practical application of Mexico's expropriation laws reveals what is true with respect to much of Mexican law generally. The application of the legal norms to specific cases offers much greater flexibility and presents far greater possibilities of fairness to private persons than might be deduced at first glance from the legal norms set out to regulate these matters.

VI. Property Rights of Aliens and "Mexicanization"

1. The Place of Aliens in Mexican Law

Article 27(I) of the Mexican Constitution sets forth the basic limitations on the property rights of aliens in Mexican law:

> Only Mexicans by birth or naturalization and Mexican companies have the right to acquire ownership of land, waters and their appurtenances, or to obtain concessions for working mines, or utilizing waters or mineral fuels in the Republic of Mexico.
>
> The State may grant the same right to aliens, provided they agree before the Ministry of Foreign Affairs to consider themselves as Mexican nationals with respect to such property, and agree not to invoke the protection of their governments in matters relating to such property; under penalty in case of non-compliance, of forfeiture to the State of the properties so acquired.
>
> Under no circumstances may foreigners acquire direct ownership of lands and waters within a zone of 100 kilometers along the frontiers and of 50 kilometers from the seacoasts.

Numerous laws and regulations have been promulgated applying this paragraph of the Constitution. For purposes here relevant, aliens may own property (except real property within the forbidden zone) provided they agree before the Minister of Foreign Affairs to a so-called "Calvo Clause" whereby they renounce the right to protection by any government other than the Government of Mexico. However, since in all cases alien ownership of land requires an agreement with the Government, in fact acquisition of land by a foreign owner is a matter of discretion on the part of the Federal Government and not a right.[71a] The discretion is never exercised in favor of foreign companies, which may not own real property, but it may be exercised in favor of foreign-owned companies incorporated and established in Mexico, provided the foreign individual or corporate shareholders subscribe to the Calvo Clause.

Aside from these limitations, aliens in Mexico enjoy equality before the law with citizens, including all the rights and personal guarantees granted by the Constitution (see Articles 1 and 33 of the Constitution). The only important exceptions have to do with exercise of certain professions and with participation in the political life of the country. With regard to expropriation, nationalization, or imposition of modalidades, aliens stand on the same footing as Mexican citizens.

2. The Concept of Mexicanization

Mexicanization is not, strictly speaking, a juridical term or even a legal institution. It is not—as is sometimes thought by outsiders—a form of expropriation, and should not be confused with that term. But at least a brief discussion of Mexicanization seems in order here, in that Mexicanization does represent a form of interference by the State with the rights of private property ownership.

In simplest terms Mexicanization consists of a requirement, which may be expressly provided for in legislation or may be administratively imposed by the Government of Mexico, that at least 51 per cent of the capital of certain companies shall be owned by Mexican citizens. In some cases Mexicanization may also require that a majority of the management in such companies be Mexican. Sometimes Mexicanization is decreed according to the products produced or activities engaged in; at other times Mexicanization appears to be directed at specific companies singled out by the Government.

Mexicanization essentially is a manifestation of economic nationalism, which has been a significant force since the age of Porfirio Diaz, when two-thirds of the nonagricultural enterprise of Mexico was foreign-owned, including major portions of the petroleum, electric power, transport, and mining activity in the country.[72] But it is fair to suggest that Mexicanization represents not only the attitude of the Government toward foreign ownership as such. To some extent Mexicanization also represents a response to local businessmen seeking to put pressure on competitors backed from abroad by resources far larger than those available to themselves.

If Mexico were able to do so, it would probably endeavour to develop its economy entirely on the basis of domestic capital, making use of foreign resources only on a loan and not on an equity basis. Like other developing countries, however, Mexico has found that foreign resources available in the form of loans or through international organizations like the World Bank group or the Inter-American Development Bank are limited. Moreover, a typical feature of direct foreign investment not easily obtainable from alternative sources is the transfer of technology and management skills. Thus Mexican policy makers, particularly since the Second World War, have had a somewhat ambivalent attitude toward private foreign investment.[73] However, the trend to increasing participation by Mexicans in the development of their country has been a steady one, and in recent years this trend has been accompanied by increasing restrictions on foreign capital. An idea of the Mexican Government's attitude toward foreign investment may be suggested by the following excerpts from the acceptance speech of Luis Echeverria Alvarez as the Presidential candidate of the governing party of Mexico, the PRI, in November of 1969:

> Our development, in order to be independent, must be essentially financed with Mexican capital. We consider foreign credit as complementary to our own resources and usable for self-liquidating works and projects which expand the productive capacity of the nation. Foreign capital will be acceptable if it is applied to open new fields of activity and new enterprises for the enrichment of our technology; if it is associated with Mexican capital; if its proceeds are reinvested and its reserves are kept in Mexico; if it respects the laws and customs of the country, and if it is useful for improving the quality of our goods and services.[74]

3. The Scope of Mexicanization

As indicated above, there is no law of Mexicanization, and indeed there are a variety of techniques and definitions coming under the general rubric of Mexicanization. An idea of the extent of economic nationalism as it currently prevails in Mexico may, however, be gained from a brief cataloguing of industries committed in one way or another to control by Mexico or its citizens.

First, Mexican law reserves certain basic industries to the nation itself, to the exclusion of all private ownership. Among these industries are petroleum, basic petrochemicals, electricity, railroads, and telecommunications. Second, a number of industries, though not required to be State-owned, operate pursuant to concessions or franchises from the Government which are granted only to firms 100 per cent under control of Mexican citizens. Among these are radio and television broadcasting, distribution of gas, motor transport on federal highways, commercial forestry, banking and credit institutions, and insurance and bonding companies. Third, there are a number of industries which may by law be carried out only by enterprises 51 per cent of whose capital is owned by Mexican nationals. Among these are mining not otherwise covered, fabrication of products of the basic petrochemical industry, agriculture, and maritime transport. In addition to these industries Mexicanization may be applied to a number of other industries, or indeed particular concerns within industries, at the discretion of the Government through more or less direct means as suggested below.

4. Techniques of Mexicanization

Other than by statute, Mexicanization has proceeded generally through two separate devices, each in its own way subject to serious criticism on legal grounds. The most powerful device in the hands of the Mexican Government is the Decree of June 29, 1944, establishing the Temporary Necessity for Aliens to Obtain Permission to Acquire Property and Establish and Modify Mexican Companies That Have Alien Shareholders.[75] This decree was promulgated by President Avila Camacho during the Second World War pursuant to the extraordinary war-time powers granted to the President, which included suspension of individual guarantees for the duration of the war. The suspension of individual guarantees was lifted in September of 1945, but with a proviso that measures enacted during the war concerned with the economic life of the nation would remain in effect. Though numerous writers have questioned this proviso on Constitutional grounds and the Supreme Court has twice held it unconstitutional,[76] the Government has taken the position that the war-time decrees, including the decree concerning alien participation in the economy, remain in effect.[77]

The June 1944 decree was designed primarily to protect the Mexican economy against uncontrolled inflow of foreign capital fleeing from war-torn Europe. It provided, accordingly, that aliens or Mexican firms with alien shareholders had to obtain permission from the Foreign Ministry to acquire real property in Mexico, to acquire any kind of commercial or industrial business, to acquire control of any Mexican company, and to engage in a large variety of other kinds of transactions. The decree then granted to the Minister of Foreign Affairs the discretionary authority to permit any specified activities on such conditions as he might establish, including the condition that 51 per cent of the capital of the firm in question be held by Mexican nationals. Thus any firm with alien shareholders or seeking to have alien participation must come to the Foreign Ministry for permission to incorporate, and depending on the proposed corporate activity, such permission may be conditioned on attainment of 51 per cent Mexican ownership. (Articles 1, 2, and 3). A comparable condition may be imposed in case of Mexican-owned companies seeking alien participation or a change in their corporate structure. As of summer 1970, 51 per cent Mexican ownership is required for the steel, cement, glass, aluminum, and fertilizer industries.

Likewise, 51 per cent Mexican participation is required by the Minister of Foreign Affairs for companies to engage in any of the following industries: air, maritime and motor transport, motion pictures, fishing, publishing and advertising, rubber, soft drinks and soft-drink concentrates, packing and preservation of food products, and basic chemicals.

The penalty for noncompliance with the June 1944 Decree or the orders of the Foreign Minister thereunder is nullity of any act taken by the firm in question. In addition, the Decree provides that any property involved in unlicensed activity by firms coming under the decree is subject to forfeiture. However, this provision of the decree would seem to conflict with the guarantees of property (Article 27) and of due process (Articles 14 and 16) in the Constitution. No actual case of forfeiture of property under the decree is known.

The other technique of Mexicanization, though somewhat more subtle, is probably more widely used, in part because it is centered not in the Foreign Ministry but in the various centers of economic management within the Mexican Government. Rather than requiring a given percentage of Mexican ownership at the time of incorporation, the administrators of Mexico's economy may condition the granting (or continuation) of a series of privileges useful to the operation of the business on the agreement of the company that by a certain date a given portion of the shares of the enterprise will be offered for sale to Mexican nationals. For example, the Law Concerning Development of New and Necessary Industries[78] authorizes forgiveness of up to 100 per cent of import duties, export duties, stamp taxes, and up to 40 per cent of corporate income taxes for firms establishing new operations deemed to be consistent with the industrial development of the country.

Nothing is mentioned in this law about shareholding of Mexican companies applying for benefits under this law, but it is well known that such benefits are not granted to firms that do not have at least 51 per cent Mexican ownership. Similarly, a Presidential Resolution of September 27, 1961 authorizes exemption from certain federal taxes for firms engaged in the export of manufactured goods, and subsidies on the import of machinery designed for manufacture of export products. Again, neither this Presidential Decree nor the regulations of the Ministry of Economy thereunder say anything about shareholding of Mexican firms applying for the subsidies. Nevertheless, in practice, at least 51 per cent local ownership is required before the subsidies or exemptions are awarded.

To give just one more example of this technique, Article 131 of the Constitution, as amended in 1951, authorized the Congress to delegate to the Executive the power to raise or lower export or import duties, as well as to restrict or prohibit imports or exports when the President considers this to be in the national interest.[79] This power has been used for a variety of purposes, notably to decree import substitution and in effect to establish protected local industries. It has, however, also been used to put pressure on firms to engage in an immediate or gradual program of Mexicanization through transfer of ownership to Mexican nationals. Generally this requirement is accompanied by another requirement relative to local content of manufactured goods— typically 60 per cent of value added.

5. Assessment

The discussion of Mexicanization in this paper, being peripheral to the principal topic, has necessarily been somewhat impressionistic. To the extent it has given an idea of the administration of economic regulation in Mexico generally, the discussion is probably not far off from the attitude of the State toward private enterprise generally—for example, in the imposition of the modalidades referred to in Section I (4).

It should be stated that Mexicanization, though it has its aspects of arbitrariness, is generally carried out in a manner designed to minimize losses to the alien owners. Thus for instance, it is possible to negotiate with the government about the period for the transfer of shares to local owners so as not to dump them on the market all at once. Also, the majority of foreign investors find they can live satisfactorily with the Mexicanization and local content requirements, particularly when these are accompanied by tariff protection against external competition.

While alien firms doubtless have a somewhat more difficult time doing business in Mexico today than do Mexican nationals, foreign investment continues to flow into the country. Mexicanization appears to be a technique of gradualism offering a practical alternative to, and therefore protection against, the kind of expropriation of alien property that has taken place in other parts of the Hemisphere and indeed in the Mexico of thirty years ago.

Conclusion

Two generations have passed since the violent phase of Mexico's revolution, and the country has attained a level of economic advance and political stability unmatched in Latin America today. Causes and consequences are, of course, intermixed, but one important aspect of Mexico's maturity is that it has been able to find a series of viable compromises—between state and private ownership of industry, between local and foreign capital, between collective and individual agriculture, between a predominant party and political choice.

The same kind of compromise, not fully articulated but quite effective, can be seen in the area of expropriation: a fair amount of leeway for discretionary governmental action, but little evidence of abuse, and much evidence of negotiation and attempts to achieve fair results. If inquiry into the subject of expropriation is designed to shed light on the relation between the individual and the state, it can be said that for Mexico the reflection is fairly accurate. Mexico's legal regime in this area does not offer the kind of statute or Constitutional provision or Supreme Court decision that could serve as a model for use by other countries. Mexico does, however, offer to the Hemisphere a convincing illustration that it is possible to find a successful middle way.

Notes

1. See generally Jorge Olivera Toro, *Manual de Derecho Administrativo*, pp. 361-370 (2d. ed., 1967).

2. Villers, as cited by Ignacio Burgoa, in *Las Garantias Individuales*, pp. 457-58 (5th ed., 1968).

153

3. Andres Serra Rojas, *Derecho Administrativo,* p. 922 (4th ed., 1968).

4. See Lucio Mendieta y Nuñez, *El Problema Agrario de Mexico,* pp. 132-34 (8th ed., 1964).

5. See Serra Rojas, op. cit. (note No. 3), pp. 786-87, for the text of the 1884 Mining Code.

6. Pastor Rouaix, *Genesis of Articles 27 and 123 of the Political Constitution of 1917,* p. 135 (1945).

7. Castellanos Vda. de Zapata, Mercedes (hereafter referred to as the Zapata case), *Amparo Administrativo en Revisión,* 605 1932, Sec. 1A (Dec. 8, 1936). 50 *Semanario Judicial de la Federación* (5th Epoca) 2568, p. 2950.

8. See Rafael Rojina Villegas, *Introducción y Teoría Fundamental del Derecho y del Estado,* Vol. II (1944), p. 28.

9. Olivera, op. cit. (note No. 1), pp. 48 and 358.

10. See Lucio Mendieta y Nuñez, op. cit. (note No. 4), pp. 297-311.

11. See the Zapata case, op. cit. (note No. 7), p. 2583.

12. See Gabino Fraga, *Derecho Administrativo,* pp. 400-410 (12th ed., 1968).

13. The companies in question were the Compañía Impulsora de Empresas Electricas (a subsidiary of American & Foreign Power) and its affiliates and Compañía de Luz y Fuerza Motriz (a Canadian-owned company). See M.S. Wionczek, *El Nacionalismo Mexicano y la Inversion Extranjera* (1968).

14. See Cia. Mexicana de Petroleo "El Aguila" S.A. (hereafter referred to as the El Aguila case, *Amparo Administrativo en Revision* 2902 / 1939, Sec. 2a (12 / 2 / 39). 62 Semanario (5th Epoca) 3201, pp. 3026, 3029, 3033.

15. Agustín Aguirre Garza, "Las Modalidades de la Propiedad" (1938) as cited by Mendieta y Nuñez, Lucio, in *El Sistema Agrario Constitucional,* p. 73 (3d. ed., 1966). For the Zapata case, see Note No. 7.

16. Ignacio Burgoa, op. cit., (note No. 2), p. 458.

17. Ibid., p. 458.

18. See Andres Serra Rojas, op. cit. (note No. 3), pp. 995-996.

19. See Serra Rojas, op. cit. (note No. 3), pp. 995-6 and Fraga, op. cit. (note No. 12), pp. 403-4.

20. See the Zapata case (note No. 7), p. 2587 and *Teses de Jurisprudencia No. 91,* Jurisprudencia de la Suprema Corte de Justicia de la Nación 1917-1965, Tercera Parte, Segunda Sala, Apendice al *Semanario Judicial de la Federación* 115.

21. See, e.g., Serra Rojas, op. cit. (note No. 3), pp. 995-996, Fraga, op. cit. (note No. 12), pp. 403-404 and Burgoa, op. cit. (note No. 2), pp. 458-59.

22. See, e.g., Serra Rojas, op. cit. (note No. 3), pp. 1000-1001, Fraga, op. cit. (note No. 12), p. 411.

23. The Zapata case (note No. 7). In this writer's view, the better decision would have been to call the governmental activity a *modalidad.*

24. See Fraga, op. cit. (note No. 12), pp. 410-411, and the El Aguila case (note No. 14), p. 3036.

25. See the Constitution of Mexico of 1917, Art. 27, Secs. X, XVII.

26. Consult the Mining Law, Art. 3 (*Diario Oficial* of Feb. 6, 1961, as corrected on March 1, 1961), the Communications Law, Art. 21 (*Diario Oficial* of Feb. 19, 1940), the Law on Irrigation, Art. 2 (*Diario Oficial* of Dec. 31, 1946) and Articles 832, 833, and 836 of the Federal Civil Code (*Diario Oficial* of May 26, 1928, in force since Oct. 1, 1932) for more details.

27. See Art. 62 of the Federal Law on Authors' Rights (*Diario Oficial* of Dec. 31, 1956, as amended on Dec. 21, 1963).

28. Luján, Julio, *Amparo Administrativo en Revisión* (April 29, 1919) 4 *Semanario* (5th Epoca) 918.

29. The Zapata case (note No. 7), p. 2568.

30. Ibid., p. 2597.

31. The El Aguila case (note No. 14), p. 3026.

32. Fraga, op. cit. (note No. 12), pp. 406-410.

33. Lujan, op. cit. (note No. 28).

34. Pozos Petra, *Amparo Administrativo en Revisión* (June 19, 1926), 18 *Semanario* (5th Epoca) 1266.

35. *Tesis de Jurisprudencia No. 1117,* Jurisprudencia de la Suprema Corte de Justicia de la Nación (1954) 1997.

36. See Velasco, Cecilio, *Amparo Administrativo, Revisión del Incidente de Suspensión,* 286 / 1945, Sec. 22 (April 28, 1947) 92 *Semanario* (5th Epoca) 1031.

37. Rodriguez Casal, José, *Amparo Administrativo en Revisión* 1969 / 1948, Sec. 1a. (7 / 7 / 48), 97 *Semanario* (5th Epoca) 120.

38. Medina Osalde Claudeo, *Amparo Administrativo, Revisión del Incidente de Suspensión,* 8157 / 1941, Sec. 1a (Jan. 17, 1942), 71 *Semanario* (5th Epoca) 698.

39. Talavera, Enrique, *Amparo Administrativo en Revisión, 7127 / 1948,* Sec. 1a (2 / 7 / 51), 107 *Semanario* (5th Epoca) 866. This is consistent with other legal provisions. For instance, any authority or government department which erects a building for public services must send the site and building plans of the work in question to the Treasury Department, with the exception of the Defense Department or any other Department involved in constructions relating to military or national security matters.

155

40. Rueda Sotero, Alicia, *Amparo Administrativo en Revisión,* 8647 / 1946, Sec. 1a (10 / 24 / 47), 94 *Semanario* (5th Epoca) 647.

41. Villanueva Cisneros, Otilia, *Amparo Administrativo en Revisión,* 3350 / 1946, Sec. 2a (10 / 18 / 46), 90 *Semanario* (5th Epoca) 812.

42. Cía. Telefonica y Telgráfica Mexicana, *Amparo Administrativo en Revisión,* (Oct. 13, 1949) 102 *Semanario* (5th Epoca) 320.

43. See Fraga, op. cit. (note No. 12), p. 400.

44. Ibid., pp. 413-415; Serra Rojas, op. cit. (note No. 3), pp. 1004-1005, Burgoa, op. cit. (note No. 2), pp. 451-52; Mendieta y Nuñez, *El Sistema Agrario Constitucional,* pp. 71-74 (2d ed., 1940).

45. See Pastor Rouaix, *Genesis of Articles 27 and 123 of the Political Constitution of 1917,* pp. 135-37 (1945).

46. See Molina Enriquez, Andres, in a letter to the Justices de la Suprema Corte de Justicia de la Nación, *Boletín de la Secretaria de Gobernación,* pp. 85-86 (1 / 24 / 17).

47. Mendieta y Nuñez, *El Sistema Agrario Constitucional,* p. 75 (2d ed., 1940).

48. See, e.g., Olazcoaga, viuda de Barbosa, 3 *Semanario* (5th Epoca) 1180 (11 / 6 / 18); Vargas, viuda de Flores, Enriqueta, 6 *Semanario* (5th Epoca) 78 (1 / 9 / 20); Colin Enedino, 8 *Semanario* (5th Epoca) 696 (9 / 14 / 20); Pastor, Moncada, viuda de Blanco, Teodoro, 8 *Semanario* (5th Epoca) 508 (11 / 9 / 21); Caso, viuda de Rivero, Ramona, 9 *Semanario* (5th Epoca) 672 (12 / 7 / 21).

49. See the Pastor Moncada case.

50. See, e.g., Casa del Camino Cordobes, 49 *Semanario* (5th Epoca) 1804 (9 / 21 / 36); Llaguno, viuda de Lbarquengoitia Paz, 50 *Semanario* (5th Epoca) 553 (10 / 23 / 36). Terrazas, Pedro C., 53 *Semanario* (5th Epoca) 154 (7 / 3 / 37); Santibañez, Rafael, 53 *Semanario* (5th Epoca) 247 (7 / 7 / 37); Haas, Hnos. y Cia., 56 *Semanario* (5th Epoca) 1166 (5 / 6 / 38).

51. See Casa del Camino Cordobes case.

52. Gonzalez, Jacinto 58 *Semanario* 2287 (11 / 23 / 38) Thesis of Jurisprudencia 464, Jurisp. (1954) 893. Thesis of Jurisprudencia 93, Jurisp. (1965) 119.

53. See, e.g., Casa del Camino Cordobes, 49 *Semanario* (5th Epoca) 1804 (9 / 21 / 36); Santibañez, Rafael, 53 *Semanario* (5th Epoca) 247 (7 / 7 / 37); Coria Campos, Luis, 57 *Semanario* (5th Epoca) 875 (7 / 27 / 38); Gonzales, Jacinto, 58 *Semanario* (5th Epoca) 2287 (11 / 23 / 38); Cia. Mexicana de Petroleo "El Aguila" S.A., 62 *Semanario* (5th Epoca) 3021 (12 / 2 / 39).

54. See the El Aguila case, op. cit. (note No. 14).

55. See the Coria Campos, Luis, and Gonzalez, Jacinto cases, op. cit. (note No. 53).

56. See Velazquez, Santiago y Coags., *Amparo Administrativo en Jurisdicción,*

1868 / 1945, Sec. 2a (2 / 18 / 46), 87 *Semanario* (5th Epoca) 470 and Rosada Mijores, Pedro, *Amparo Administrativo en Revisión,* 2318 / 1942, Sec. 2a (9 / 19 / 46), 89 *Semanario* (5th Epoca) 2881.

57. See Fraga, op. cit. (note No. 12), p. 414.

58. See Regil y Peon, Alvaro de, *Amparo Administrativo en Revisión,* V 4652 / 1939, Sec. 2, 64 *Semanario* (5th Epoca) 3659 (6 / 29 / 40).

59. See Mendieta y Nuñez, op. cit. (note No. 47), p. 145.

60. Id., p. 147.

61. See Burgoa, op. cit. (note No. 2), p. 453; Fraga, op. cit. (note No. 12), p. 415; and Serra Rojas, op. cit. (note No. 3), p. 1006.

62. *Tesis de Jurisprudencia No. 468,* Jurisprudencia de la Suprema Corte de Justicia, Vol. II, p. 901 (1955).

63. Law of Expropriations of Nov. 23, 1936 (published in *Diario Oficial,* Nov. 25, 1936), Arts. 11-17.

64. The only exceptions are established in Art. 8 of the Law of Expropriation.

65. "Ley Orgánica de los Artículos 103 y 107 de la Constitución Federal" (Ley de Amparo) (published in the *Diario Oficial,* January 10, 1936), Art. 73 (XV).

66. Pozos Petra, op. cit. (note No. 34) and Teran Eloísa y Coaga, *Amparo Administrativo en Revisión,* 44 *Semanario* (5th Epoca) 3237 (5 / 20 / 35) 10584 / 1932, Sec. 3.

67. Ley de Amparo, op. cit. (note No. 65), Art. 124. See *Cia. Mexicana* "El Agua Caliente," S.A. 70 *Semanario* (5th Epoca) 904 (1941).

68. Mining Law, op. cit. (note No. 26), Art. 49, and Communications Law, op. cit. (note No. 26), Article 23.

69. Gonzalez de Cosio Ma. de los Angeles y coags, *Amparo Administrativo en Revisión* 9642 / 1946, Sec. 2 (April 17, 1947) 92 *Semanario* (5th Epoca) 614.

70. The commission is made up by a representative of the mentioned Secretariat, a representative of the National Bank of Public Works and Services, and a representative of the Association of Engineers of the Republic of Mexico.

71. Information obtained by author in informal consultations with officials of Department of Public Works.

71a. Special provision is made for acquisition of land by aliens through inheritance or succession.

72. Raymond Vernon, *The Dilemma of Mexico's Development,* pp. 42-3 (1965).

73. See, e.g., Raymond Vernon, op. cit., pp. 176-190 (1965).

157

74. See *Novedades* and *Exelsior* of November 16, 1969.

75. Decreto que Establece la Necesidad Transitoria de obtener Permisos para Adquirir Bienes por Extrangeros y para la Constitución o Modificación de Sociedades Mexicanas que tengan o tuvieren Socios Extrangeros, published in *Diario Oficial,* July 7, 1944.

76. Química Industrial de Monterrey, S.A. Sept. 20, 1962; Playtex de Mexico, S.A. Sept. 7, 1964.

77. See, e.g., Burgoa, op.cit. (note No. 2), pp. 226-228.

78. Decree of Dec. 30, 1950, amending Article 131 of the Constitution, *Diario Oficial,* March 28, 1951.

79. Actually, in the writer's opinion, the legal basis for the imposition of Mexicanization measures may be found in the constitutional concept of *modalidades.* (See Section I (4).)

Peru

Jorge Avendaño Valdés

with

Domingo García Belaunde

Contents

I. The Concepts of Property in Peru   163
   1. Property in the Civil Codes of Peru   163
   2. Property in the Peruvian Constitution   163
   3. Limitations on the Right of Property   164

II. The Elements Of Expropriation   165
   1. The Concept of Expropriation   165
   2. The Power to Expropriate   166
   3. Property Subject to Expropriation   167
   4. The Requirement of Prior Compensation   169
   5. Valuation   170

III. Expropriation Procedure   171
   1. Administrative Procedure   171
   2. Judicial Procedure   172
   3. Possibility for Judicial Review   173
   4. Rights of Third Parties   175

IV. Special Cases of Expropriation   176
   1. The Mining Code of 1950   176
   2. The Organic Petroleum Law of 1952   177
   3. The Law of Industrial Promotion of 1959   178
   4. The Electric Industry Law of 1955   178

**V. Laws Looking To Major Social Transformation—
Agrarian Reform and Urban Housing**   179
   1. Agrarian Reform   179
   2. Urban Housing   184

VI. Two Recent Cases   188
   1. Expropriation of the La Brea y Pariñas
     Petroleum Complex   188
   2. Expropriation of the Newspapers *Expreso* and *Extra*   192

Conclusion   194
Notes   195

I. The Concepts Of Property in Peru

1. Property in the Civil Codes of Peru

The nineteenth-century Peruvian Civil Code was copied with respect to property almost verbatim from Article 544 of the French Code Civil. The right to property was defined in Article 460 of the Civil Code of 1852 as "the right to enjoy and dispose of things." The Civil Code presently in force in Peru, dating from 1936, says substantially the same thing:

> Article 850: The owner of an object has the right to possess it, to collect its fruits, to recover possession or replevy it, and to dispose of it, within the limits of the law.

Thus ownership of property is thought of as a real right, in that it describes a relation between persons and things; an absolute right, in that it has none of the limitations attached to other interests like usufruct or mere possession. Ownership of property is exclusive, in that it leaves no room for ownership by others; and it is perpetual, that is it is not limited by any circumstance other than the owner's will.

The Civil Code recognizes, however, that the right to own property is not as absolute as the above language alone might indicate. Article 851 says:

> The legal restrictions on property established for the public interest cannot be modified or supressed by juridical act.

And Article 853 confirms that

> Expropriation is subject to its special laws.

2. Property in the Peruvian Constitution

Since its independence in 1821, Peru has had ten Constitutions, as well as a number of other Constitutional documents or provisional charters. The Constitution of 1828, which was the third Constitution of Peru, provided in Article 165:

> The right of property is inviolable. If the public good, legally

163

recognized, requires the property of any citizen, he shall be previously compensated for the value of said property. [1]

All subsequent Constitutions have contained a substantially similar provision.

The Peruvian Constitution of 1933 states in Article 29:

> Property is inviolable, whether it be material, intellectual, literary or artistic property. No one may be deprived of his property except for reason of public utility legally proved and upon prior payment of appraised compensation.

In addition to this basic article, Article 31 of the Peruvian Constitution confirms that property, regardless of the owner, is governed exclusively by the laws of Peru and is subject to the taxes, burdens, and limitations which those laws may establish. Further, the Constitution provides in Article 32 that aliens may hold property under the same conditions as Peruvians but that they may in no case invoke their special status or call upon diplomatic assistance. Article 34 of the Peruvian Constitution states:

> Property shall be used in harmony with social interest. The law shall provide the limits and conditions (*modalidades*) of the right to property.

The basic provision of Article 29 concerning the requirement for full and prior compensation became the subject of a sharp debate in 1963 when the first agrarian reform law was being formulated. Some thought that compensation must be paid in cash, while others thought that since the Constitution did not expressly prohibit it, the payment of compensation could be made in bonds or in installments. We shall come back to this point subsequently (see Section II (4)). At this point, it is worth noting only that the Constitution was amended in 1964 to add a second paragraph to Article 29 expressly authorizing payment of compensation over time or through bonds in cases of expropriation growing out of the agrarian reform program.

3. Limitations on the Right of Property

Peruvian law recognizes two types of limitations on property rights—contractual and legal. Contractual limitations—or more precisely, limitations arising out of juridical acts by the owner—include such limitations as usufructs, servitudes, and similar burdens imposed voluntarily by the owner on his property. In order to be effective, they must, according to Article 1042(5) of the Civil Code, be recorded in the Registry of Property. Legal restrictions; that is, restrictions resulting from legislation by the State, are effective without a requirement of registration.[2]

The "social interest" referred to in Article 34 of the Constitution quoted above has not been given a general definition in the law of Peru. What has happened is that a variety of laws relating to housing, subdivision of urban real estate, and comparable regulations have been based on the concept of social interest. One case in which the law has specified what is considered contrary to social interest is the Agrarian Reform Law of 1969,[3] which in Article 15 describes the following cases of rural property ownership as not in harmony with social interest:

a) Abandonment of the soil or deficient exploitation as well as poor management and deterioration of renewable natural resources;

b) prevalence of antisocial or feudal forms of exploitation of the soil;

c) conditions of work that are unjust or contrary to the law;

d) concentration of ownership in such a way as to constitute an obstacle for the growth of small and medium rural properties and as to bring about extreme or unjust dependence of the population on the landowner;

e) The *minifundio* or fragmentation of landholding in such a was as to result in poor use or destruction of natural resources as well al low return on the practice.

II. The Elements of Expropriation

1. The Concept of Expropriation

Expropriation is defined as the deprivation of private ownership by decision of the public power for the sake of collective interest.[4] Thus expressed in terms of a transfer of property, expropriation appears to be an institution of the civil law, whereas its purpose is derived from public law. Analysis will show, however, that though expropriation can be viewed as a limitation on the rights of property described in the previous section, in fact expropriation can be understood only from the point of view of public law.

Roman law commentators rested their explanation of expropriation on *"dominium eminens,"* or eminent domain; that is to say, on a superior right enjoyed by the State. But this concept confuses sovereignty and ownership. The State is not the owner of all property located in its territory, but only possesses sovereignty over such property. Modern thinking attempts to justify expropriation on the basis of the goals of the State, one of which is to promote the common good.[5] This goal could not be realized if the State could not depend on an instrument for acquiring property expressly required for the well-being of the community. That instrument, of course, is expropriation.

Notwithstanding the above, it may be useful to analyze the way the institution of expropriation affects the institution of private property. In this writer's view expropriation does not affect the absolute character of property ownership, since it does not curtail the owner's powers over his property; it does not affect the exclusive nature of property ownership because there is never more than one owner of the same piece of property. What expropriation does affect directly is the perpetuity of ownership, in that expropriation may extinguish the private right to ownership and replace that right with public ownership. Thus one might say that even as expropriation transfers a particular property from private to public ownership, so the institution of expropriation serves as a bridge between private and public law. The regulation of expropriation, however, is clearly one falling within public law. In particular, the institution of expropriation in Peru is governed by the Expropriation Law of 1940 (Law 9125) as amended a number of times since then and as modified also by laws dealing with particular public activities.[6]

2. The Power to Expropriate

The expropriating agency is the State. The State exercises the power to expropriate either through the Executive Branch or through the Legislative Branch. The Executive Branch may decree expropriation by means of a "governmental resolution" issued with the affirmative vote of the Council of Ministers. The Legislature may order an expropriation through a special law pursuant to which the Executive Branch issues the appropriate governmental resolution. When issued pursuant to an act of the Congress, the governmental resolution does not require the approval of the Council of Ministers.

Under either method the governmental resolution must designate the administrative agency in charge of the expropriation procedure. This agency may be a department of the national government, or it may be a subordinate body, for example a provincial council, a social service entity, a government corporation, or other public enterprise. But this only means that the procedures of the particular expropriation will be the responsibility of the designated entity, not that the power to expropriate is itself delegable.

Article 1 of the Expropriation Law states:

Compulsory expropriation shall be decreed by governmental resolution upon approval of the Council of Ministers *expressing the reasons which justify the public utility and need of the project* (emphasis added).

It will be noted that the underlined words are in two respects different from Article 29 of the Constitution quoted in Section I (2) above. The Constitution only mentions public utility and not public need. In this sense the statute would seem more restrictive than the Constitution. On the other hand, the Constitution speaks of legal proof of the public utility, whereas the statute seems to require only a statement approved by the Ministers justifying the public need or utility of the project in question. In practice, the proof of public need or utility is presented in the course of studies and proceedings leading to the issuance of the governmental resolution. In any event, inasmuch as no judicial action can obstruct, delay, or paralyze the process of expropriation, the lack of adequate proof of the public utility of a project could not prevent an expropriation from taking effect.

3. Property Subject to Expropriation

Two questions not settled either by the Constitution or by the Expropriation Law of Peru have been much discussed: 1) May property already owned by a public body be expropriated, if it is needed as part of a state project? 2) Does expropriation apply to movable as well as to immovable property? Not only have these

167

questions not been resolved by the Constitution and statutes of Peru but they have not been resolved judicially either. Both the examples given below were essentially political confrontations concerning a legal issue, ending in the one case in withdrawal of a proposed expropriation, in the other by completion of the expropriation essentially for political reasons.

In theory there would seem to be no reason why a state project cannot take any necessary property, regardless of its owner. Thus, for example, a national highway should not be legally denied the possibility of taking a portion of a municipal park needed for the right of way. But whether this kind of transfer of possession properly comes under the definition of expropriation as we have described it in Section II (1) is problematical.

In 1964 both Houses of the Congress passed a bill decreeing expropriation of the entire basement of the building called La Cabaña located in Lima and owned by that city's municipal government. The purpose of the expropriation as stated in the bill was to transfer the basement to the Peruvian Federation of Radio Broadcasting. Soon after the bill was passed by the Congress, the municipal authorities staged a major opposition, particularly in the press and over television. The mayor himself argued that municipal property could not be the subject of expropriation, since in any event it was state property. In view of the opposition created by this argument, the Congress preferred not to submit the bill to the President of the Republic for signature and promulgation. Thus although both Houses of the Congress passed the bill, it did not become law and the expropriation did not take place.

As to whether property other than immovable property can be expropriated, again there is no logical, philosophical, or Constitutional reason why not, except that under nineteenth-century French law this could not be done. The Expropriation Law of 1940 (Law 9125) does use illustrations in its articles on valuation and on transfer of the property expropriated which make it clear that the Legislature had immovable property in mind, but it is not difficult to adapt the statute to movable property; and, in fact, expropriation of movable property has taken place. [7]

One celebrated case concerned the effort by the government to take the shares and gain control of the Caja de Depósitos y Consignaciones (Bank of Deposits and Consignments). This institution was a private entity which the State had entrusted with the collection and custody of public rents and with the custody of funds deposited with courts. The national government was anxious to regain control of these functions, which the State considered an expression of its sovereignty. Accordingly, on August 9, 1963 a Supreme Decree was issued upon approval of the Council of Ministers, declaring the recovery by the State of these functions to be of great necessity and utility, and therefore declaring all the shares of the Caja de Depósitos to be expropriated, subject to the procedures to be established by the Ministry of Treasury and Commerce in accordance with the Expropriation Law. [8] A number of persons opposed this expropriation, on the ground that taking of shares of stocks was not permitted either by Law 9125 or by its subsequent amendments. Nevertheless, the expropriation was put into effect, including payment for the shares by the Government. The functions of the Caja de Depósitos were assumed by the Banco de la Nación which was created for this purpose, with the State holding all the shares and being responsible for the management.

4. The Requirement of Prior Compensation

Up to 1960 when the first agrarian reform law began to be discussed, the requirement of prior payment in cash for the full value of expropriated property was never questioned. But when the first draft of the agrarian reform legislation was made public, it appeared that payment for arable lands was to be made in bonds and debentures rather than in cash. This proposal seemed to many jurists to conflict both with Article 29 of the Constitution, which called for "prior payment of appraised compensation," and with Article 2 of Law 9125, which spelled out the Constitutional guarantee as follows:

> Expropriation shall be made through prior valuation and deposit in national currency of the value of the expropriated property . . .

The conflict between the agrarian reform proposals and the Constitutional requirement was accentuated by Article 1248 of the Civil Code, which stated that payment orders, bills of exchange, and other evidences of indebtedness have the effect of payment only upon discharge at the due date.

Some thought that the solution would be to modify Article 2 of the Expropriation Law, since the Constitution did not mention "payment" or "cash" but simply referred to prior compensation; others were of the view that that Article simply spelled out the requirement of Article 29 of the Constitution and thus could not be modified without violating the Constitution. In order to avert a major legal and Constitutional controversy that might impede the agrarian reform program, an amendment to the Constitution was proposed in the form of the following addition to Article 29:

> In cases of expropriation for purposes of agrarian reform, irrigation, urban growth and development, expropriation of power sources or in cases of war or public disaster, the law may provide that payment of compensation may be made in installments or through bonds of mandatory acceptance. The law shall determine the installments, type of interest, the amount of issue and other pertinent conditions; and it shall determine the maximum amount required to be paid in cash and prior to the expropriation.

Following approval by an absolute majority of both Houses of the Congress at two separate ordinary sessions, revised Article 29 became effective in November 1964.[9] Thus for agrarian reform, plus the other purposes specified in the new part of Article 29, deferred compensation through bonds or other means is permissible when authorized by statute. The inference is that for expropriations not coming within the enumerated categories, the requirement persists of payment in cash and in advance of the transfer of property to the expropriating agency.

5. Valuation

Article 2 of the Expropriation Law of 1940 provides:

> ... The valuation shall be made on the basis of the average between the direct and the indirect appraisal of the property. The appraisers shall take into account as concurrent data the declaration made by the owner for purposes of assessment of real property and industrial taxes and for purposes of income taxes.

Initially, the appraisal is made by the administrative agency charged with the expropriation. However, the owner has the right to name an expert to conduct an independent appraisal of the property in question. If the second appraisal is different from that made on behalf of the State, a procedure for settling the difference is provided for. Under Article 22 of the original Expropriation Law of 1940, the court of first instance in the district where the property was located was to select the impartial arbitrator by lot

170

from among a list of experts maintained by the Superior Courts, subject to a single challenge on behalf of the expropriated party before the drawing of lots. Under Article 3 of Law 12,063 of 1954, this procedure is abolished and the decision on valuation is to be made by two engineers designated by the Cuerpo Técnico de Tasaciones del Peru (Technical Organ of Appraisers of Peru) subject to approval by the Board of Directors of the Cuerpo Técnico.

Neither the Expropriation Law nor the commentators have shed any additional light on the process of appraisal—for example on the case of improvements made by the owner since the relevant tax declarations, the importance of going concern value or expected profits, or the effect of movements in the market on the compensation due. Since there is essentially no appellate review of the procedure for determining compensation (see Section III (3)), the Supreme Court of Peru has likewise failed to give any clarification on the subject of valuation.

One additional point related to compensation deserves mention. The increase in value of property remaining in the possession of the expropriated party as a result of the project for which the expropriation was designed is not, as in some countries, credited against the compensation due. Such increase is, however, subject to a one-time "improvements tax," comparable to the taxes imposed on other property owners when they benefit from a public project.[10]

III. Expropriation Procedure

The procedure for expropriation in Peru consists of two parts: the administrative stage; that is, the stage within the Executive Branch leading to issuance of the resolution of expropriation, and the judicial stage; that is, procedure leading to the actual transfer of the property to the State and delivery of compensation to the former owner.

1. Administrative Procedure

The procedure within the government includes technical studies which serve as the basis for the declaration of necessity or public utility, and an appraisal by experts on behalf of the government of the value of property, in accordance with the formula described in Section II (5). The administrative stage ends with the issuance of the governmental resolution decreeing the expropriation and explaining the public necessity and utility of the project for which the property in question is to be taken.

There is no requirement of notice or hearing in the administrative stage. Nevertheless, it appears from a decision of the Supreme Court that private parties do have certain opportunities to make objections at this stage and that if they miss these opportunities, they cannot be heard to complain later. According to Article 3 of Law 9125, expropriation in the case of urban property must cover the entire property except if the owner and the government agree otherwise. When the city of Arequipa expropriated a portion only of a private person's property in the city, the owner raised an objection before the court, citing Article 3 of the Expropriation Law. The court of first instance agreed with the owner and ordered expropriation of the entire property. However, the Superior Court reversed this decision and the Supreme Court sustained the reversal, on the ground that the owner had not raised the objection at the administrative stage." [11]

2. Judicial Procedure

According to Article 4 of the Expropriation Law, the governmental resolution of expropriation must be submitted to the court of first instance where the property in question is located, together with the appraisal made by the state's experts and the title record of the property or a certificate that title to the property is not recorded. Within 24 hours of receipt of these documents, the judge must notify the owner of the appraisal made by the State's experts, and the owner has three days thereafter to acquiesce in the appraisal or to appoint his own expert. If the owner appoints an expert of his own, the latter must conduct his appraisal within eight days of his appointment. Article 5 of the Expropriation Law expressly states that no extension of the period is permissible. If no appraisal on behalf of the owner is submitted within twenty days after the first notification to the owner of the State's appraisal, the State's appraisal is considered accepted. If the property in question is not registered, or if the owner is unknown or absent, notification is given pursuant to court order by publication for three consecutive days in the newspaper in the provincial capital that prints legal notices and by posting of notices on the property in question. If the owner has not appeared within three days of the last publication date, the State's appraisal is likewise considered accepted.

When the owner challenges the State's appraisal and there is a discrepancy between the appraisals submitted on behalf of the State and on behalf of the owner, the judge must, as we have seen, appoint a third expert, or rather two experts, from the Cuerpo Técnico de Tasaciones del Perú. Though the appraisal by the Cuerpo Técnico is submitted to the judge, the judge has no independent role to play in the appraisal. Once the amount of compensation due has been fixcd, the expropriating agency must deposit the amount within a three-day period. If the expropriating agency fails to proceed in accordance with this schedule, the expropriation proceeding is considered abandoned and the decree ordering the expropriation is considered to have lapsed.

´ As soon as the amount of the compensation award has been deposited, the court orders the owner to deliver a deed of transfer of title to the State. If the owner fails to comply or if he is absent or unknown, the judge is authorized to execute the deed of transfer on behalf of the owner. Thereafter the expropriating agency acquires full ownership and possession of the property in question. If the expropriated party was himself in possession, he must vacate the property forthwith. If the property was occupied by third parties, they have sixty days to vacate in case of residential property, and ninety days in case of commercial or industrial property.

3. Possibility for Judicial Review

The procedure described above involves the court of first instance at various stages, but essentially in a ministerial or nonjudicial role. The court examines neither the public utility or necessity of the project, nor the suitability or necessity of the particular property to the project, nor, except procedurally, the amount of compensation fixed. There are, however, some limited possibilities for judicial challenge to the expropriation proceeding, expressly set forth with respect to compensation, and available by implication in respect to the expropriation itself.

Under Article 13 of the Expropriation Law, the expropriated party has six months from the date of the deed of transfer to challenge the expert appraisal. Correspondingly, the expropriating agency has the right to challenge the appraisal made by the Cuerpo Técnico, in which case the former owner receives only the amount set by the appraisers designated by the State, with the balance remaining on deposit with the court. [12]

As to the expropriation itself, a legal challenge is more difficult.

Nevertheless, an expropriation may be illegal, in that all the requirements of the law may not have been followed or the actions were performed by unauthorized officials. In such situations there may be several ways to appeal to the judiciary—(i) the *acción popular*, (ii) the *recurso de inconstitucionalidad*, and (iii) *habeas corpus*.

(i) Article 133 of the Constitution of 1933 provides as follows:

> There is an *acción popular* before the judicial branch against regulations and against governmental resolutions and decrees of a general character which infringe the Constitution and / or laws, without prejudice to the political responsibility of the Ministers. The law shall establish the appropriate judicial procedure.

No implementing legislation corresponding to this Article was enacted until the Organic Law for the Judicial Branch of 1963.[13] Under Article 7 of that law, the *acción popular* may be brought as an ordinary civil action with the Solicitor General representing the State.

(ii) The Peruvian Constitution makes no provision for judicial review of legislative acts. However, Article XXII of the Preliminary Title of the Civil Code says:

> Whenever there is incompatability between a constitutional and a legal provision, the former is preferred.

Until 1963 this provision was unused, since there was no procedure to take advantage of it. When the Organic Law for the Judicial Branch was enacted, however, it included a provision for summary procedure to resolve conflicts of laws. The Supreme Court has held that this procedure coupled with Article XXII of the Preliminary Title to the Civil Code, provides a means to challenge the constitutionality of a law.[14] The challenge is limited to Constitutional questions; that is to say, for present purposes only the incompatability of the expropriation with the guarantee of Article 29 of the Constitution could be raised through this procedure. The proceeding is brought directly before the Supreme Court, again with the Solicitor General defending the state.

(iii) *Habeas corpus*, as derived from English and United States practice, is primarily an adjunct to criminal procedure, designed to protect individuals against arbitrary arrest or detention. But Article 69 of the Constitution states:

> All individual and social rights recognized by the Constitution support the action of habeas corpus.

The right of property has been considered an individual right for this purpose, and at least in the past the constitutionality of expropriation has been tested through this procedure.[15]   In 1968 Decree Law 17,083 limited penal procedure including *habeas corpus* in its penal law aspect to guarantees of personal liberty, inviolability of the home, and freedom to travel. A civil proceeding for *habeas corpus* remains, but in the cases arising out of the Statute concerning Freedom of the Press (see Section VI (2)), the Supreme Court has ruled that only specific acts against petitioners, and not laws of general application, could be considered in *habeas corpus* proceedings. The Court said that *habeas corpus* had been sustained in the past as a vehicle for Constitutional challenge of legislation because until passage in 1963 of the Organic Law of the Judicial Branch no other devices for challenging legislation had been available.

4. Rights of Third Parties

Peruvian expropriation law is designed above all to avoid delays of litigation and to secure needed property for the State free of any incumbrances. Thus while the law recognizes that third parties may have interests in property that may be affected by an expropriation, it gives neither tenants nor mortgagees or other creditors any rights either against the State or against the property itself. Under Article 16 of Law 9125, if occupants other than the owner claim to have a right to compensation for the taking of an immovable or a portion thereof, they may bring an action before the judge before whom the expropriation proceeding is pending, but such action may not interrupt or delay the expropriation proceeding itself. Article 8 of Law 12,063 of 1954 makes clear, moreover, that any such rights can be enforced only against the sum deposited with the court as compensation or against the former owner himself, without any liability on the part of the State. In other words, an owner and a tenant may in certain circumstances share in the compensation awarded. Separate awards for the value of the property, which might be measured in part by rent paid by the tenant, and for the value of the lease, which might be measured by the capitalized value of the difference between the rent paid according to the lease and the current rental for comparable property, are not permitted in Peru. By the same token, the history of a piece of property, once expropriated, is of no further importance. All liens, servitudes, clouds on title and similar interests are abolished: in return for a single payment to the record owner, the state takes free and clear title.

However, third party creditors receive a measure of protection from the fact, noted previously, that the expropriating agency pays the amount fixed as compensation into court, not directly to the expropriated party. Once the deed of transfer has been executed, the court calls for a record of incumbrances, if any, as filed in the local registry of property. If there are no outstanding liens or claims, the court orders payment of the award to the record owner. If there are mortgages or other liens outstanding, or if an action concerning title to the property is pending, the court orders the retention of the amount deposited until secured creditors have been paid or claims against the property have been disposed of.

IV. Special Cases of Expropriation

In addition to seeing the basic pattern of expropriation described in the preceding sections, it is necessary for an understanding of the law of expropriation in Peru to examine some of the special laws that make provision for expropriation. In this part we examine briefly some of the laws governing specific economic activity that authorize resort to expropriation. In the next part we look in somewhat greater detail at agrarian reform and urban renewal—in each of which the institution of expropriation plays a very major role. Finally, in the last part we examine two recent cases of expropriation that have received wide attention beyond the boundaries of Peru.

1. The Mining Code of 1950

The Mining Code currently in effect in Peru authorizes the holder of a mining concession to acquire or expropriate (both terms are used in the law) uncultivated land within the limits of his concession, surface land under cultivation within the concession, and even lands located outside the boundaries of the concession but which are indispensable to its proper operation. [16] The Code also allows the holder of the concession to expropriate the water resources necessary for mining operations and for household use by mining personnel, whether or not these resources are within the perimeter of the concession. Finally, the Mining Code permits concession holders to impose whatever easements may be essential to the rational utilization of the concession. Such easements may be established on any kind of land and over any extension necessary. Among the purposes of such easements may be construction of canals, tanks, pipes, railroads, roads, freight-handling equipment, railroad stations, shipping docks, and air-fields. Also, easements may be imposed for purposes of electric lines, lighting equipment, cable cars, maintenance operations of any kind, pasture for animals, and lumbering.

A holder of a concession who has the power to expropriate lands or to impose easements in aid of operation of the concession must bring such proposed action to the attention of the relevant regional mining judge, who is authorized to verify the need for the expropriation or easement and to evaluate the land or easement in question. The resolution concerning the expropriation proceeding and including the appraisal must be issued by the Director of Mining.[17]

2. The Organic Petroleum Law of 1952

The Organic Petroleum Law [18] permits any holders of oil or hydrocarbon concessions to request the expropriation of privately owned immovables and the establishment of easements on public or private immovables as necessary for the complete development and exploitation of their rights. This provision is spelled out in the regulation implementing the Petroleum Law, which states that the oil industry is of public utility and consequently enjoys preferential rights over any other use of surface land, subject to prior appraisal and payment of compensation. Expropriation is not in order if it would cause damage to the community as determined by the Minister of Development and Public Works.

One important difference between expropriation under the Petroleum Law and expropriation under the Mining Code should be noted. Expropriation in aid of mining concessions requires the approval only of the Bureau of Mining and the procedures set forth in the Mining Code and implementing regulation; in contrast, expropriations under the Petroleum Law are carried out pursuant to the Expropriation Law of 1940, Law 9125, with a governmental resolution issued by the Ministry of Development, the only difference being that instead of the State itself, the holder of the concession is designated as expropriating agency.

3. The Law of Industrial Promotion of 1959

The Industrial Promotion Law [19] distinguished two types of industrial activities: manufacture of articles characterized as basic, and all other manufacturing activity. Manufacture of basic products enjoyed benefits of various kinds under this law, including the right to request the application of the law providing for expropriation of unutilized rural properties when needed for manufacturing. A company which acquired property through expropriation under this authority was required to use it for the purposes stated. Until the property had been used for such purposes, the company could not transfer the property, under penalty of having the expropriation cancelled. The Industrial Promotion Law was repealed in July of 1970.

4. The Electric Industry Law of 1955

For the most part, production of electricity in Peru is in the hands of holders of concessions. Thus expropriation can affect the electric industry in two ways. The State may expropriate the property of a concession holder, and the concession holder may expropriate private property needed in operation of the concession.

As regards the rights of the State, it may under the Electric Industry Law [20] purchase directly or through the agency designated for the purpose, the properties utilized in connection with concessions for the supply of electricity. This right may be exercised by the State in cases where the concession period has expired, where the concession holder has renounced his rights, where the concession has lapsed, or in bankruptcy. In addition, the State may in cases of national emergency take over the use or control of any activity of the electric industry. If it exercises this latter power, the State must pay compensation to the concession holder, to be determined by taking as a base for valuation the average profit produced by the service in question over the preceding three years. When the national emergency passes, the concession holder is entitled to resume the exploitation of the operation of his services. As for expropriation by concession holders, the rights are comparable to those granted to holders of mining and petroleum concessions. Thus holders of electric service concessions have the right to impose servitudes, on the basis of plans approved by the Ministry of Energy and Mines. One interesting difference, however, is that a party whose property is sought to be expropriated may, in certain cases, oppose the establishment of the easements in question.

V. Laws Looking To Major Social Transformation—Agrarian Reform and Urban Housing

Perhaps the most interesting and important aspect of the Law of Expropriation is the resolution of conflict between state and private ownership in situations affecting not just individual persons or public projects, but great national programs found necessary for a nation's progress. Peru in the late 1960's and early 1970's offers two major cases which illustrate this clash of traditions, ideologies and laws. While neither program is far enough advanced to permit a full evaluation, it is pertinent to look at both in some detail.

1. Agrarian Reform

Development of the Drive for Agrarian Reform. Land holding and cultivation have existed ever since the conquest of Peru in the 16th century. As a social, economic, and legal problem, however, the question of land ownership emerged only in the 20th century. The first person to raise the problem in a significant way was the Marxist thinker José Carlos Mariátegui in a classic of Peruvian sociology published in 1928: *Seven Essays Interpreting the Peruvian Reality.* The Aprista party, through its leader and perennial candidate, Victor Raúl Haya de la Torre, adopted a program of agrarian reform as early as 1931, but neither the government then in office nor public opinion were as yet conscious of the need to look into the problem of ownership and cultivation of rural land.

The subject of land ownership first became a major political issue in the electoral campaign of 1956. The successful presidential candidate, Manuel Prado, subsequently appointed a study commission to prepare a draft agrarian reform law, and after three years of study the Commission submitted its report in 1960. Since then agrarian reform has been a principal subject for nearly all political leaders in Peru.

The military junta which governed the country during the

179

period 1962-63 promulgated a "Law of Bases" for Agrarian Reform.[21] This law created an Institute for Agrarian Reform and Colonization (IRAC) which took over the execution of seven important projects, including that of the valley of La Convención in the region of Cuzco. This area, stirred up by extremists and malcontents, was officially declared a "zone of application of Agrarian Reform by Decree Law 14,444.[22]

When Decree Law 14,444 was enforced, the Romainville family, proprietors of the rural estate Huadquiña in Cuzco, presented a petition for *habeas corpus* before the Superior Court of the District. Plaintiffs alleged that there had been no declaration of public utility, that the valuation of the property in question was ridiculously low compared with appraisals of similar property made only a few months previously by the same engineer, and that accordingly the right to property guaranteed in the national Constitution had been violated. The Superior Court decided in favor of the plaintiffs, and directed that the expropriation be stopped, since the law in question was not binding on plaintiffs. The Supreme Court, however, reversed and upheld the taking. The Court held: (a) the delcaration of public necessity and utility required for a lawful expropriation had in fact been made by Decree Law 14,444; (b) decree laws made by *de facto* governments but not abrogated or modified by the Congress are of full force and effect except if they conflict with the Constitution; (c) the point at issue was not the property but the valuation of the property, which should be contested through ordinary channels without interrupting the expropriation through a *habeas corpus* proceeding; and (d) the agrarian reform established by Decree Law 14,444 was not in conflict with the national Constitution.[23]

When Fernando Belaúnde Terry became President in 1963, discussions were initiated for an organic law of agrarian reform. Work was carried out on the basis of various different drafts, the principal debate concerning the question of whether payment in bonds was legal and proper. In 1964 the Constitution was amended to make clear that payment in bonds were authorized (see Section II (4)), and in the same year the new Agrarian Reform Law was enacted.[24] However, that law contained a large number of exceptions, particularly in favor of the great agricultural-industrial land holdings in the coastal areas. Accordingly, the 1964 Agrarian Reform Law had relatively little effect.

The Agrarian Reform Law of 1969. The Revolutionary Governmental Junta that took office as a result of the *coup d'état* of October 3, 1968, decided early in its administration to consider a much more radical agrarian reform law. The result was Law 17,716, promulgated on June 24, 1969. Without discussing the agrarian reform law in detail, a brief description of those portions of the law related to transfer of property to the State and in turn from the State to the new holders is interesting in showing the current attitude toward the issues raised earlier in this paper concerning the relation between state and private property.

The Agrarian Reform Law declares (in Article 7):

The lands hereafter listed shall be utilized for the purposes of agrarian reform: (a) abandoned lands as well as lands reverting to the public domain and lands that are not being cultivated; (b) rural land belonging to the state or to state entities; (c) lands that may be expropriated in conformity with this law; (d) duly qualified land included in private partitions; (e) land made suitable for agricultural purposes either by direct action of the state or through projects financed from public funds; (f) lands resulting from donations, legacies or similar acts in favor of the Agrarian Reform.

There are a number of exemptions from expropriation for agrarian reform purposes: (a) agricultural properties along the coast operated by their owners are subject to agrarian reform only to the extent they exceed 150 irrigable hectares. This limit may be increased to 200 hectares if the proprietor fulfills certain requirements concerning management, labor relations, and taxes; (b) cattle operations located along the coast operated by the owner are only subject to agrarian reform on properties in excess of 1,500 hectares covered with natural grasses, and this limit may be tripled if the proprietor fulfills certain additional requirements similar to those indicated under (a) above; (c) for other regions of the country the size of holdings exempt from agrarian reform varies between 15 and 50 hectares.

Establishment of these categories does not mean that all properties in excess of the limits are immediately taken over. It does mean, however, that the owners know that at any time the Agrarian Reform Institute may undertake procedures, as described below, to deprive them of their holdings in favor of the agrarian reform.

Procedure under the Agrarian Reform Law. In order for a piece of property to be taken over, the area must be declared included within the agrarian reform by a Supreme Decree based on prior

181

studies and reports by the Ministry of Agriculture and Fishery. Once a particular region of the country has been declared to be included in the agrarian reform, the transfers of ownership of particular properties are to follow the following procedures:

(i) the Regional Bureau of Agrarian Reform and Agricultural Settlement notifies the public and the property owners of the initiation of the procedure. Within a period of sixty days the property owners must submit a written declaration stating the rural properties which they own in the territory in question and supplying relevant particulars. (ii) Upon expiration of the sixty-day period the documents presented will be studied, along with appropriate technical reports. (iii) A plan is then prepared indicating which properties will be taken over under the agrarian reform program and whether in whole or in part. The owners have the right to make any observations they may consider necessary through a summary procedure before the General Bureau of Agrarian Reform and Agricultural Settlement. When this stage is passed, the Ministry of Agriculture and Fishery, by means of a Supreme Decree, shall approve the final plan concerning the property or properties affected.

Once these procedures have been completed through publication of the Supreme Decree, the owner is notified and given fifteen days to comply with the decree, under penalty of summons.

Thereafter the law makes three provisions concerning remedies of the owner: no judicial action may obstruct, detain, or stop the expropriation procedure; the decree which completes the expropriation procedure can only be challenged with respect to the amount of compensation awarded, but not with respect to the procedure followed or with respect to a claim for return of the land in question: and in matters not foreseen in the present law, the provisions of Law 9125 and amendments thereto shall be applicable.

Redistribution of the Land Taken. The assignment of land obtained through expropriation as described above is to be made by the General Bureau of Agrarian Reform and Agricultural Settlement in favor of landless peasants or those who have inadequate land. The priorities are to be established in the following order: 1) peasant communities; 2) cooperatives; 3) agricultural companies of social interest. The first measures taken in application of the Agrarian Reform Law have been expropriation of the great agricultural-industrial land holdings on the coast and subsequent distribution of the expropriated land to cooperative organizations established by the workers themselves with technical and financial assistance granted by the Agrarian Reform agencies. Later expropriations have followed similar guidelines, usually with special government committees acting in an advisory capacity in connection with the operation of these cooperatives. On June 24, 1970, the first anniversary of the publication of the Agrarian Reform Law, the cooperative associations were scheduled to be turned over to the new owners for their direct operation.

Valuation and Compensation. Under the Agrarian Reform Law of 1969 the value of lands, buildings, installations, and other property expropriated is to be determined according to the official assessment carried out by the General Revenue Service in preparing the rural tax rolls. Pending completion of the rural tax roll, compensation is to be based on the self-assessment made by the property owner at the time of payment of property taxes for 1968. In cases where this method is inappropriate, additional guidelines may be resorted to, such as the value stated at the last transfer of ownership. The value of cattle, crops, and plantings is to be set on the basis of average market prices, expected yield and data appearing in account books.

Payment for expropriated lands and other property will be made partly in cash and mostly in bonds. The bonds, backed by the Executive Branch and denominated "Bonds of the Agrarian Debt," will be issued in seven denominations from 1,000 to 1,000,000 soles.*The bonds are of three classes:

Class A Bonds	6%	20 years
Class B Bonds	5%	25 years
Class C Bonds	4%	30 years

All agrarian debt bonds and interest thereon are exempt from payment of any taxes. They are nominative and are nontransferable.

As in the Chilean Agrarian Reform Law enacted two years earlier, both the class of bonds received by the former owner and the proportion of compensation payable in cash depend on observance of legal requirements prior to the reform. Thus, lands worked directly by their owners and in accordance with legal

---

*As of the summer of 1970, 1 Sol ⁼ U.S. $0.0235; 1 U.S. dollar ⁼ S / 43.38.

requirements regarding wages, cultivation, housing, public health, etc. are entitled to full cash payment up to 100,000 soles and Class A bonds for any amounts in excess of that sum. Owners of leased lands or of lands operated not in conformity with all the provisions of the law are entitled to a cash payment up to 50,000 soles, with the balance in Class B bonds. Owners of lands deemed feudal or lands that are not currently cultivated are entitled to cash payment up to 25,000 soles, with the balance payable in Class C bonds. When cattle, installations, or agricultural and industrial equipment are expropriated, payment shall be in cash up to 1,000,000 soles, with the balance in Class A bonds if the lands are being worked by the owner and Class B bonds if they are leased.

Provisional Comment. On the very day that the Agrarian Reform Law was promulgated, the President, General Juan Velasco Alvarado, announced that army troops were taking over the seven largest agricultural-industrial complexes located along the Peruvian coast. This measure had considerable impact, since on the one hand it was evident that public opinion supported a sound agrarian reform, but on the other hand no one had thought that its implementation would be so rapid. The problem for the government and the new owners of the agrarian lands has been to maintain the productivity of the agrarian lands and also to maintain the revenues received by the government from tax payments on such lands. After one year's experience only, it is impossible to give an assessment of the success or failure of the Agrarian Reform Program. But whatever the results, there is no doubt that this time Peru has started on the road to a serious and profound change in the system of ownership and cultivation of rural land.

2. Urban Housing

The National Housing Corporation. Law 13,517 of February 14, 1961 declared remodeling, provision of sanitary facilities, and legalization of the marginal districts or shanty towns (*barriadas*) to be of public necessity and utility. The law created the National Housing Corporation, charged with the responsibility for transforming the marginal shanty towns into urban projects of social utility.

To achieve this objective, the law authorized the Housing

Corporation to expropriate, pursuant to Law 9125, the land on which marginal districts had grown up, whether owned by communities, municipalities, or private persons. Once expropriated, this land becomes government property and the Housing Corporation proceeds to have it remodeled and subsequently to sell it to the occupants at appropriate prices. The law provided that valuation for purposes of compensation of lands on which marginal towns had grown up was to be made on the basis of the price of the land at the time that the marginal town was built. Thus, though the basic standards of Law 9125 were to govern, the price paid for expropriation of the properties was in effect frozen through circumstances beyond the control of the owners. In a number of cases, for example, in the case of expropriation of the property "El Agustino" near Lima, it happened that the date on which a marginal district had grown up was not apparent. The Housing Corporation took the view that it had the responsibility for determining this date although Law 13,517 had not said this. When the procedure for expropriation of the El Agustino property was already under way, a decree was issued, providing that the dates of formation of marginal districts would be determined exclusively by the Housing Corporation. [25] The owner of the El Agustino property argued that the application of this decree to an expropriation commenced before the decree had been issued was unconstitutional. The owner prevailed on this issue before the Superior Court of Lima, on the basis of Article 25 of the Constitution, which states that no law has retroactive effect. Accordingly, the date on which the marginal town had been formed for purposes of valuation was not determined by the Housing Corporation but rather by expert assessors. As to expropriations begun subsequent to Decree 35-F, however, presumably the determination by the Housing Corporation will be upheld.

Expropriation in Connection with Urban Planning. Decree Law 17,803 of 1969 authorized expropriation of rural lands for purposes of "urban development and promotion of economic housing." Article 1 of the Decree Law provides that expropriation may be resorted to when considered necessary for the expansion or improvement of towns. The application of this authority is not limited to urban properties, but may extend also to properties nearby which could facilitate urban growth.

It is interesting to see how this Decree Law builds on, but in several significant respects departs from, the basic pattern of expropriation law in Peru as established by Law 9125. Article 4 of the Decree Law provides that expropriation shall be declared by a Supreme Decree countersigned by the Minister of the Treasury, who will (1) outline all the reasons justifying the public necessity and utility of the project in question; (2) designate the agency responsible for the procedure; and (3) stipulate a period within which the project must be completed, counting from the date of termination of the expropriation procedure. Thus under this Decree Law the role of the Congress is eliminated.

Under Article 7, the properties expropriated are to be assessed for purposes of compensation on the basis of a schedule to be prepared in connection with the general regulation of assessments. Thus, the role of expert appraisers appears to be downgraded if not eliminated.

The expropriating agency—generally the Ministry of Housing which succeeded to the rights and duties of the Housing Corporation—is to make its presentation before the court of first instance of the province in which the property is located, enclosing a copy of the Supreme Decree authorizing the expropriation, and enclosing also the relevant assessment. If it considers immediate possession necessary, the expropriating agency may so request. The remainder of the proceeding is substantially similar to the procedure under Law 9125 (see Section III (2)), with notification in person or through publication, with an opportunity for the property owner to contest the government's assessment, and with a precise schedule of steps to prevent a chance of delay at the behest of the private party. Only the appraisal of the expert appointed by the court in case of dispute is subject to appeal to the Superior Court, and the decision of that court is final, without possibility of recourse to the Supreme Court or to any extraordinary remedies. The expropriating agency must deposit in the Banco de la Nacion (see Section II (3)) the amount of compensation awarded, in cash or bonds, as the case may be.

Compensation in Urbanization Cases. Perhaps the most important difference between expropriation for purposes of urban improvement and ordinary expropriation is the manner of compensation. As in the case of agrarian reform, expropriation for urban improvement is to be compensated through a mixture of cash and bonds, depending on the type of property taken. The bonds, however, are all of one class, bearing six per cent interest on declining balance, and amortizable over a ten-year period. Article 22 of Decree Law 17,803 provides a schedule for cash and bond payments. With respect to rural properties, worked lands are to be compensated in cash up to 100,000 soles and the balance in bonds; idle lands are to be compensated up to 25,000 soles in cash and the balance in bonds; and any plantations, installations, or buildings, as well as costs of licenses and the like, are to be compensated entirely in cash. With respect to properties already in towns or cities, the value of land and buildings up to 200,000 soles is to be compensated in cash and the balance in bonds, unless the property in question is the only housing owned by the expropriated party, in which case the entire amount is payable in cash. The urban development law also contains a series of provisions for special cases. For example, if one owner holds several properties, their total value shall be aggregated, with only one cash payment; improvements paid for by the owner are to be compensated in cash; and property taxes paid on assessments in excess of the schedule of assessments on which the compensation under the urban development law is based, are to be refunded. Like the agrarian reform bonds, urban bonds are nominative, backed by the credit of the State, and tax-exempt as to both interest and principal. Unlike the agrarian reform bonds, however, urban bonds may be freely transferred.

Special Legislation. In addition to the general authorizations described above, special legislation has been adopted in a number of particular cases ordering expropriation of real property for purposes of urban housing, and making special provision for compensation. For example, Law 15,959 of December 29, 1965 declared of public necessity and utility the expropriation of urban real estate located on an important Lima thoroughfare which had intense industrial concentration. The National Housing Board was authorized to initiate the procedure for expropriation in accordance not with one of the recent laws, but with the basic expropriation law, Law 9125. Much comment was provoked in the press because the Law 15,959 provided that the national budget for the year 1966 include an amount required for payment of compensation, all of it in cash. While no one could object specifically to resort to the standard procedure for expropriation and compensation, in the context of the amendment of the Constitution and the development of agrarian reform and urban improvement programs, there was considerable sentiment that this particular expropriation constituted a preference.

"**Territorial Conditioning.**" Though not directly pertinent to the subject of expropriation, it is interesting to note that at present the Office of Urban Planning and Development is working on the formulation of a new law designed to create so-called "territorial conditioning" *(acondicionamiento territorial)*. "Conditioning" is understood to refer to the physical aspects of the country's social and economic planning. For purposes of territorial conditioning, it is necessary to regulate property rights, to regulate ownership, use and occupancy of property; to create new rights and legal institutions such as the "territorial reserve," that is, land set aside for particular purposes; and to develop new standards for a Registry of Property that may be used in city planning, zoning, construction of public facilities, and the like. Again, the scope of the proposed reforms is beyond the coverage of this paper. It is clear, however, that Peru is thinking along the lines of a major restructuring of urban life, and that the law of expropriation has been adapted and can be adapted to suit these ends.

VI. Two Recent Cases

Since October 1968, Peru has been governed by a *de facto* government headed by General Juan Velasco Alvarado, which is in many respects quite different from other juntas that have governed the nation in the past. We have seen some of the regime's inclinations in the preceding pages, particularly in the discussion of agrarian reform. But two of its actions, both at least in form expropriations, deserve special mention here, both because they received worldwide attention, if not understanding, and because they illustrate the relationship of law to politics in expropriation cases.

1. Expropriation of the La Brea y Pariñas Petroleum Complex

The history of the oil properties at La Brea is long and complicated, and any adequate discussion would go far beyond the confines of this paper. [26] Only a very brief summary of the history of the La Brea problem is given here.

La Brea was a center of controversy from the time of the

original grant, even before Peru's independence, and throughout the 19th century as well. There was doubt about whether the original grant had been legal or not, and whether it comprised surface property only or sub-surface rights as well. If only surface rights were granted, then the operator of the oil wells was in default of fees for use of the sub-soil. Moreover, the boundaries of the grant were in almost continuous dispute, and with this, the alleged tax liabilities as well.

In 1890 a British company took a 99-year lease on the property. The extent of the property covered by the lease, as well as the taxes and fees due, became the subject of a prolonged controversy, including a number of investigations and decrees in Peru leading to a substantial claim for back taxes. This claim was protested not only by the company but by the British government. After considerable diplomatic pressure, an arbitration agreement was entered into between Peru and Great Britain in August of 1921.

A number of Constitutional authorities in Peru considered at the time and later that the arbitration agreement, although authorized by the Congress, was unconstitutional, in that it subjected the sovereignty of the nation to external control. The arbitration itself was not actually held, but a settlement was negotiated which was on the whole favorable to the company, and this settlement was incorporated into an arbitral award dated Paris, April 24, 1922. [27] Both the authority of the Peruvian representative to enter into the settlement and the authority of the arbitral tribunal to accept the settlement have been debated in Peru ever since. The award was never formally ratified by the Peruvian Congress, but the substance of the award was carried out. Following the arbitral award, the British company sold all its rights to the International Petroleum Company, a wholly-owned subsidiary (incorporated in Canada) of the Standard Oil Company (New Jersey).

During the 1920's the International Petroleum Company (IPC) operated La Brea y Pariñas without interruption. When the government of the dictator Leguia was overthrown in 1930, an attempt was made by the new Peruvian government to reopen the arbitration, but this proved unsuccessful. During the 1930's and 1940's IPC operated La Brea y Pariñas generally in controversy but without direct interference by the government. There were frequent reports that IPC met the recurring budgetary deficits of the national government.

When the Organic Petroleum Law of 1952 was adopted (see Section IV (2)), IPC was expressly excluded. When IPC requested to be brought under the law, the request was denied as contrary to the public interest. In 1959 a long series of debates about La Brea y Pariñas began which have not ceased to this day, and a political movement was launched dedicated primarily to the recovery for the nation of La Brea y Pariñas. A special commission appointed by the Foreign Ministry at the request of the House of Representatives concluded in 1960 that the 1922 agreement and award were null and void, but that since they had been in force for 38 years, "it would be unwise to have a unilateral decision over a matter which had been the subject of international jurisdiction." [28] The Commission suggested, however, that the problem might be resolved by reference to internal law.

The IPC question continued uncertain throughout the administration of President Prado (1956-1962) and the *de facto* government that took office ten days before Prado's term was to expire in 1962. When President Belaúnde Terry was elected in 1963 he announced that a proposal for a "definite solution" of the La Brea y Pariñas problem would be forthcoming within 90 days. In fact, however, it took nearly six years to produce a solution, including long negotiations with the company and a series of laws and decrees which successively repealed the law that authorized the arbitration, proclaimed the nullity of the 1922 settlement agreement and arbitral award, and authorized the President to resolve pending disputes in the La Brea y Pariñas case subject to ratification by the Congress. [29] Finally, in 1967, a law was passed declaring the La Brea y Pariñas wells to be property of the State, and authorizing the Executive Branch to establish the most appropriate system for exploitation of the wells.[30] On the basis of this law, negotiations with the company were intensified, as were pressures on behalf of the company by the United States Embassy in Lima. [31]

It appeared that a solution had been arrived at when a contract was signed by the government and IPC on August 12, 1968. On August 13, 1968 the President of the Republic celebrated a symbolic takeover of the properties at the site, and signed the so-called "Act of Talara" (named for the city near the oil fields). Some days later, however, doubts arose as to the effectiveness of the settlement, because it seemed that in exchange for takeover of the property the government had made even greater concession to the company. The President of the State Oil Enterprise announced publicly that "page 11" of the original contract, on which he had made some important notations, was missing.[32] The Acción Popular party, which had been founded by President Belaúnde Terry, called the contract a "surrender." The Congress refused to ratify the contract, and the political tide rose so high that on October 3rd, less than two months after the signing of the Act of Talara, a *coup d'état* ousted President Belaúnde and sent him to exile in Buenos Aires. The new military government declared the contract and Act of Talara null and void. Decree Law 17,066 of October 9, 1968 declared the Talara Industrial Complex expropriated, and on the same day the area was occupied by military forces. Article 1 of Decree Law 17,066 stated:

> The expropriation of the so-called Talara Industrial Complex is hereby declared to be of public necessity, utility and security . . .

Once the oil wells of IPC were taken over, the government began the administrative procedure for the purpose of determining the compensation to be paid or the back debts to be collected from the company.

As we have seen previously (see Section III (2) and (3)), in compulsory expropriations the expropriated party may not oppose the taking itself, but merely has the right to object to the assessment made. IPC, however, brought an action for *habeas corpus*, asserting that the Constitutional guarantee of property had been violated, and requesting that the Decree Law ordering the expropriation be declared null and void. The Superior Court declined to grant *habeas corpus*, and IPC appealed to the Supreme Court. The Supreme Court declared that

> Civil legislation establishes that expropriation is subject to special laws, and in the case *sub judice,* the general norm contained in Law 9125 is subordinated to the special laws . . . the holder of a right (in this case the state) does not require that a judicial decision thereon be made previously to its exercise, since the existence of the right based on the law is prior to and higher than any judicial pronouncement.

Accordingly, the Supreme Court affirmed the decision of the lower court, stating that the motion presented by the expropriated company was inadmissible.[33]

Some reflections may be in order on the IPC case. In the first

191

place, IPC and its predecessors created, with the complicity of foreign governments and the submissiveness of Peruvian governments, an irregular status outside the framework of the Constitution and the law. The Peruvian governments tolerated and took advantage of this situation although they knew of its questionable origin. After fifty years a *de facto* government, applying laws enacted by a legally constituted parliament, expropriated the La Brea y Pariñas oil complex, following strictly in all pertinent respects the general norms existing in Peruvian law. This fact cannot be debated, and even the representative sent subsequently by the government of the United States to negotiate with the Peruvian government, John N. Irwin, II, admitted this power which every sovereign state enjoys. In this writer's view, the decision of the government of Peru was the decision of a country acting in defense of its own interests.

2. Expropriation of the Newspapers *Expreso* and *Extra*

Lima has eleven daily newspapers, some going back as far as the time of Bolivar. Two new papers, both owned by the same publisher, Editora Nacional S.A., made their appearance in 1961—the daily morning paper *Expreso* and the evening paper *Extra*. From the beginning, both publications had a first-class staff such as had not been seen in the local press in many years. Since both were launched some months before the electoral campaign of 1962, both adopted the slogan "Before and after the election—with no candidate and with no party." However, both supported the candidate who was to become the next president of Peru, Fernando Belaúnde Terry. From the beginning, *Expreso* enjoyed a very wide circulation.

Editora Nacional was subsequently acquired by a financial syndicate headed by Manuel Ulloa, who was Minister of the Treasury and a key man in the government of President Belaúnde. When President Belaúnde was ousted on October 3, 1968, under circumstances described in the preceding section, both *Expreso* and *Extra* joined the opposition to the new military junta. On October 31, 1968 the new regime closed both newspapers, and justified this subsequently with a decree law. [34] The legal representative of the newspapers presented an appeal of *habeas corpus,* and the newspapers were re-opened 15 days later, as had in fact been contemplated in the decree law that ordered the closing.

Some time later the government denounced before the courts the persons responsible for signing the Act of Talara (see page 189) including Ulloa, and they were subsequently imprisoned. However, the Supreme Court declared that former Ministers of State enjoyed a special immunity, and ordered them released. [35] A few days later Ulloa went to Buenos Aires to attend a meeting of the Inter-American Press Association, and he did not return. Depending on the point of view, Ulloa was considered a political exile or a fugitive from Peruvian justice.

Ulloa continued to conduct his newspapers from Buenos Aires by correspondence and telephone, in strong opposition to the government. On December 31, 1969, a new Statute of Freedom of the Press was promulgated which introduced a series of innovations in journalistic activities, including a requirement that only Peruvian nationals hold shares in Peruvian newspapers, a recommendation that newspapers be operated cooperatively, and a requirement—obviously directed at Ulloa—that every owner or shareholder of a newspaper reside in the nation for a minimum of six months per year. [36] In a daring maneuver Ulloa abandoned the position of Chairman of the Board of Directors and arranged to be replaced by his father D. Alberto Ulloa Sotomayor. Some time later the newspapers became involved in a series of labor conflicts with their workers, leading to the intervention of the Ministry of Labor. Thus, at the beginning of 1970, the newspapers were facing two problems: internally with the workers and externally with the government.

On March 4, 1970, at an early hour when *Expreso* was beginning to be distributed throughout the country, members of the *Guardia Civil* occupied the newspaper premises and took over its workshops and presses. On the same day the front page of the official newspaper *El Peruano* displayed Decree Law 18,169, providing that expropriation of the stock of Editora Nacional S.A. is of social interest; that the Ministry of the Interior is authorized to proceed with expropriation in accordance with Law 9125 as amended; that the employees and workers of the publishing house who desire shall constitute a cooperative which shall continue to publish the two newspapers; and that the nominal value of the stock shall be deposited in the Banco de la Nación until the expropriation procedure is completed. On the following day, the newspaper appeared with the headline: "*Expreso* now belongs to the people." A new name appeared as director, and the paper stated that it was a publication of "Editora Nacional S.A. administered by its union." Some days later the cooperative provided for in the decree law was established under the name *Prensa y Pueblo* (Press and People). [37]

The expropriation of *Expreso* and *Extra* gave rise to strong criticism from the press and to an unfavorable reaction in public opinion, both national and foreign, though the new directors of the newspapers also received much support from various sectors of the country. *Expreso* and *Extra* have continued their normal publication, although as was to be expected, the editorial orientation has changed, going from opposition to support of the government. It is fair to state, however, that the support has not been unconditional and that some governmental actions have been subject to criticism. The staff and contributors of the newspapers include well-known theoreticians and leaders of the Peruvian extreme left.

To comment briefly on this case, while the legal forms were followed, in fact Law 9125 was violated in several respects. The decree law had no basis for the statements that the social interest required the expropriation; compensation was not paid in advance, as required by Article 29 of the Constitution (since none of the exemptions in the new part of Article 29 were relevant); and the law was put into effect by the police even before publication, contrary to express Constitutional command. But the seizure of these papers was clearly a political act in a sense different from the use of that term in connection with agrarian reform or urban renewal. As the Minister of Industry and Commerce stated, the norm which expropriated the newspapers was "a law with a proper name."

Conclusion

The right to property as it has been understood since Roman times is possibly the basic institution of western law. However, it has undergone notable changes in response to the needs of each historical period. In Peru, the first Civil Code of 1852 reflected the influence of the Napoleonic Code of 1804, known as the code of the *petit bourgeois*. Its liberal concept subsisted on the whole until 1920, when what is known as "social constitutionalism" made its appearance. The influence of the post-war period became more

194

marked in the Constitution of 1933, which shows the effect of the Mexican Constitution of 1917, the Weimar German Constitution of 1919, and the Spanish Republican Constitution of 1931. This second phase may be characterized as one of a democratic-liberal ideology.

The third phase, the current period, is frankly oriented to cooperativism, which is believed to be the most satisfactory road to achieve not only political but social and economic democracy. Property has begun to be cooperative, as may be seen from the effects of the recent Agrarian Reform Law.

As a consequence of these changes, the institution of expropriation has had a remarkable increase in scope, and the end is not yet in sight. As far as compensation is concerned, bonds have practically replaced payment in cash. As regards the law itself, it must be observed that as a result of the innumerable special laws, Law 9125 has become largely inoperative in practice.

It may be said without exaggeration that the country is now living through a process of revision of its basic institutions. It is clear that the process of development through which Peru, like so many other countries, is passing will make severe demands on lawyers and legal scholars as well.

Notes

1. We utilize the version made by José Pareja Paz-Sóldon in *Las Constituciones del Peru* (Madrid, 1954).

2. *Código Civil*, Art. 866.

3. Decree Law 17716 of June 24, 1969 (*El Peruano*, June 25, 1969).

4. See Humberto Nuñez Borja, *Lecciones de Ciencia de la Administración y Derecho Administrativo del Peru*, (2d ed. 1959) pp. 289-291; Antonio Valdez Calle, "Comentarios sobre algunos aspectos relacionados con la Expropriación" in 272 *Revista de Jurisprudencia Peruana*, 860 (1966); Rafael Bielsa, *Derecho Administrativo* (5th ed., 1966) Vol. IV, pp. 431, Vol. V, p. 599 et seq. See also Bielsa, "El método jurídico en la expropriación," in 123 *La Ley* 1269 (July-Sept. 1966) and Bielsa, "Régimen Jurídico en la expropriación" in 118 *La Ley* 1035 (April-June 1965).

5. See Giorgio Del Vecchio, *Lo Stato Moderno e i suoi Problemi* (G. Giaparelli ed., 1967), pp. 79-103.

6. For the most important laws on expropriation enacted in the 20th century, see Humberto Nuñez Borja, op. cit., note 5, pp. 297-300, *Informativo Legal Rodrigo* No. 25, p. 256.

7. See reports on this incident in Lima's newspapers, *El Comercio, La Prensa,* and *Expreso,* for the month of February 1964.

8. Supreme Decree No. 47 of August 9, 1963, *Informativo Legal Rodrigo,* No. 31, p. 804.

9. Law 15.242 *(El Peruano,* Nov. 30, 1964).

10. Law 9125, Art. 18. This provision has played the role of prototype of laws and decrees ruling like voice in case of public works not involving expropriation. For instance, Law 9866 concerning the construction of sporting grounds in Barranco, a suburb of Lima, authorized a lien or "improvement duty" to be levied on all owners of land favorably affected by the construction of sporting grounds. The government issued a similar decree when the four-lane highways to Chosica and to Ancon were built.

11. Ramirez de Urbina v. Concejo Provincial de Arequipa, 44 *Anales Judiciales* 235 (1948). Supreme Court, May 5, 1948.

12. See Law 9125, Art. 14 and Law 12063, Art. 9.

13. Law 14605 of July 25, 1963, *Ediciones El Peruano,* 1963.

14. Evans v. International Petroleum Co., Supreme Court, *Revista de Jurisprudencia Peruana,* August 1967, No. 283, pp. 960-962.

15. Lozano, *Habeas Corpus,* in 42 *Anales Judiciales* 292 (1946) Sociedad Agrícola San Agustín, S.A., Supreme Court Jan. 3, 1961 in 55 *Anales Judiciales* 212 (1960) Saldivar v. Instituto de Reforma Agraria, Supreme Court, Jan. 15, 1965, 35 *Revista de Jurisprudencia Peruana* 100 (Jan. 1965).

16. The Minister of Energy and Mines has recently declared that a draft for a new Mining Code is being studied (see *Expreso,* April 4, 1970). Until this organic law is enacted, the government has promulgated a "Law of Bases" Decree Law No. 18225 (see *El Peruano,* April 16, 1970).

17. Mining Code, Arts. 34-39.

18. Law 11780 of March 11, 1952. Official edition of the Ministry of Promotion, Lima, 1952.

19. Law 13270 of Nov. 30, 1959. Official edition of the Ministry of Promotion and Public Works, Lima, 1965.

19a Law 18350 of July 27, 1970.

20. Law 12378 of June 8, 1955. Published in *Informativo Legal Rodrigo,* No. 11, p. 103.

21. Law 14238, published in 37 *Normas Legales,* Trujillo 1962. See V. Villanueva, *Un año bajo el sable* (Lima, 1963) especially p. 135 and following.

22. Villanueva, id., p. 137. Decree law 14444 was published in 38 *Normas Legales,* Trujillo, 1963. This law, which served as a pilot project, stated, in speaking of

expropriations, that Law 9125 would be applicable where no other provision was made.

23. Saldivar v. Instituto de Reforma Agrarian, Supreme Court, January 15, 1965, 5 *Revista de Jurisprudencia Peruana* 100 (Jan. 1965).

24. Law 15037 of May 21, 1964.

25. Supreme Decree 35 F of Sept. 26, 1962.

26. For a good collection of the principal documents of this historical controversy, see 27 *Revista Peruana de Derecho Internacional* No. 68, 1969.

27. Id. at 19-20.

28. Id. at 57 and following.

29. Laws 14695 and 14696, both of November 6, 1963, and Law 14863 of Feb. 12, 1964, all in 27 *Revista Peruana de Derecho Internacional* pp. 85-87.

30. Law 16.674 of July 26, 1967, id. at 88-90 *Revista Peruana de Derecho Internacional,* at 85-87 (1969).

31. See Goodwin, "Letter from Perú" in *The New Yorker,* May 17, 1969, p. 41.

32. The information has been taken from *Expreso, La Prensa, El Comercio,* and *El Peruano* of August 12, 1969 and the following days.

33. *Informativo Legal Rodrigo,* No. 96, Feb. 1969, p. 243.

34. Decree Law 17094, in Julio Espino Perez, *Decretos Leyes modificatorios del Código Penal,* 1969, p. 10.

35. Supremo Gobierno v. Ulloa, Carriquirry y Hoyos, *Revista de Jurisprudencia Peruana,* Oct. 1968, No. 297, pp. 1231 et seq.

36. Decree Law 18.074, published in *El Comercio,* Jan. 1, 1970.

37. See *Expreso,* March 5, 7, and 19, 1970.

Venezuela

Enrique Perez Olivares
with
Allan-Randolph Brewer-Carias,
Hildegarde Rondón de Sansó,
and Tomás Polanco Martinez

Contents

I. Theoretical Foundations in Changing Concepts of Property 203
  1. Historical Foundation of the Right to Own Property   203
  2. Constitutions and Codes   205
  3. Doctrine in the Twentieth Century   206
  4. Twentieth-Century Constitutions   208
  5. The Civil Codes   211
II. Expropriation   211
  1. Historical Development   211
  2. The Theoretical Basis of the Power to Expropriate   213
  3. Legislative Bases for Expropriation   213
  4. Types of Property Subject to Expropriation   214
  5. Mining Property   215
III. Public Utility and Social Interest   216
  1. Significance of the Terms   216
  2. The Declaration of Public Utility   218
IV. Compensation   221
  1. The Duty to Compensate   221
  2. Determination of Just Compensation   221
  3. Forms of Payment   223
V. Expropriation Procedure   224
  1. The Judicial Proceeding   224
  2. The Scope of Judicial Review   225
  3. Rights of Third Parties   226
  4. Out-of-Court Settlements   228
VI. The Special Case of Agrarian Reform   229
  1. Scope of Agrarian Reform   229
  2. Compensation   230
  3. Classification of Land Use and Its Consequences   231
  4. Judicial Procedure   232
Conclusion   235
Notes   236

I. Theoretical Foundations in Changing Concepts of Property

1. Historical Foundation of the Right to Own Property

During the whole of the nineteenth century, independent Venezuela accepted without discussion the liberal views on the right to own property as an individual and absolute right. The Constitution of 1811 stated: "The social contract guarantees to each person the enjoyment and possession of his goods, without damage to the rights others have over theirs" (Article 1 (8)). Further, the Constitution spoke of "the right which each person has to enjoy and dispose of goods he has acquired through his work or industry" (Article 2 (8)).

The first national Constitution after the split-up of Gran Colombia (which had embraced what is now Colombia, Ecuador, and Venezuela) also contained the right to property among its basic guarantees: "Civil liberty, individual security, property, and equality before the law are guaranteed to all Venezuelans" (Article 188).

Throughout the political controversy that took place in Venezuela during the nineteenth century, no dissent seems to have been voiced against the right to own property. The issues that absorbed the attentions and passions of Venezuelan writers concerned questions such as the relations between creditors and debtors. Thus, for example, the *Sociedad Económica de Amigos del País,* established with government support toward the close of the year 1829, presented to the government the surprising request that "citizens shall be granted in respect to property of their debtors the same rights that the government has in respect to individuals." Approval of the law of April 10, 1834 on the freedom of contract turned the controversy into a heated political issue until the law was repealed in 1848 due to a large extent to a critical study by Fermin Toro published in 1845.

In 1825 a pamphlet attributed to Thomas Lander was published in Caracas called "The Colombian's Handbook or Explanation of National Law." In the section covering justice, the pamphlet asked:

Q. How does Natural Law prescribe Justice?
A. Through the three physical attributes inherent in the organization of man.

Q. Which are those attributes?
A. Equality, freedom and property.
Q. Why is it said that property is another physical attribute of man?
A. Because since every man was created equal or similar to every other man, and consequently independent and free, each one is absolute owner and legitimate proprietor of his body and the fruits of his work.

The fundamental problem was how to protect adequately the guarantee consecrated by legal doctrine and Constitutional text, and more specifically, how to achieve that protection within the state of social anarchy pervading the country during most of the century. To this end the armed groups which resisted the Government were fought and embargoes or confiscations of their goods were decreed, although in most cases these measures were not put into effect. In some cases this magnanimity on the Government's part provoked irate protest because it was considered the worst way of obtaining the desired protection:

> If great robberies, disasters and ruin are not compensated for by those who caused them, the Constitution's guarantee of property will be reduced to mere words, producing the inconceivable result that criminals have their property guaranteed by Congress while honest, innocent, pacific, harmless men who work to provide their children's sustenance and contribute to the public treasury—robbed, destroyed, annihilated—lose the properties which the Constitution guarantees them. [1]

It is worth mentioning that one important series of state takings, the taking of property owned by the Church, provoked hardly any controversy, although the decree of September 21, 1872, and the subsequent law of May 5, 1874, were in flagrant violation of positive law and of commonly accepted principles. [2]

We can close this brief review of Venezuelan legal thinking in the nineteenth century with a reference to Luis Sanojo, one of Venezuela's distinguished jurists of the period. Sanojo asserted that society has the obligation of guaranteeing the right of property, but also that

> Whoever expects such protection from the law must submit to its restrictions. However, it must not be believed that the legislature can impose any kind of restriction capriciously; it may only impose such restrictions as are required by respect to the property of others

and by the good order of society. Even assuming that the legislature may abuse its powers, it is always a protection to have as an incontestible principle that only the law can restrict the exercise of the right of property. In this way at least owners are safeguarded against arbitrariness . . .[3]

The nineteenth century closed on a consensus about the legitimacy of the right to own property and the obligation of the state to guarantee it and protect it as "one of the firmest bases of human society in general, and particularly of each nation."[4]

What constitutionalist Ernest Wolf holds when referring to the guarantee of property and to the freedom of industries, is true, however:

> Those freedoms did not come to be in actual practice a guarantee for all, but a guarantee for the few landowners; it consisted less in the State's abstaining from diminishing their property than in the protection it lent to the great landowners for keeping the rebel forces at bay, a guarantee based more in fear than in justice.[5]

2. Constitutions and Codes

Each of the three Constitutions in force in Venezuela between the dissolution of Gran Colombia and the adoption of the federal system in 1864 contained a guarantee of property stating that no one can be deprived of his property without his consent or the consent of the Congress on the basis of a public interest (Constitution of 1830, Articles 188, 208; Constitution of 1857, Articles 97, 108; Constitution of 1858, Article 26). The Constitution of 1857 literally stated that the right of property is inviolate.

The later constitutions of the nineteenth century provided that property is subject to taxes established by legislative authority, and to expropriation.[6] On the subject of taxes and their relation to the right of property, it is worth again quoting Sanojo:

> Another one of the attacks committed by the government against property is the imposition of excessive taxes; the poor distribution of taxes; and the diversion of tax proceeds for uses other than in the public interest. The excess in taxation consists not only in relation to the state's needs, but also in relation to the taxpayers' resources.[7]

Perhaps more important than the Constitutional provisions were the Civil Codes in force in Venezuela in the nineteenth century. The first Civil Code of Venezuela was promulgated in 1862 and shows a noticeable influence of the Chilean Civil Code (drafted, incidentally by a Venezuelan, Andrés Bello). [8] The Venezuelan Code of 1862 states in its sections on property (Second Book, Title II, "Del Dominio," Law I, Article 1) that a property right is a tangible thing that may be enjoyed and disposed of at will, subject only to not being against the law or against the rights of another.

The second Code of 1867 was inspired by the draft Civil Code of Spain of 1851. It contained a peculiar provision stating that property is subject not only to limitations established by laws, but also to limitations established by regulations (Article 351). While some authors criticized this provision as being contrary to the nature of regulations and subjecting property to "the most diverse, contradictory and whimsical of restrictions," [9] it does not seem to have had practical consequences. The third Venezuelan Civil Code in 1873 adopted as its model the Italian Code of 1865, and preserved individual rights and absolute control as the basis of the right of property (Articles 444 and 446).

Article 444 of the 1873 Code, which left its mark on subsequent codes, stated:

> Property is the right to enjoy and dispose of things in the most absolute manner, so long as such use does not include a violation of law. [10]

3. Doctrine in the Twentieth Century

Shortly after the turn of the century the controversy raging in Europe on the right to own property and on the proper attitude of the State toward private property began to be felt in Venezuela. [11] While the first 35 years of the twentieth century were spent under harsh dictatorships, there was some writing and a good deal of talk questioning the fundamental assumptions concerning the right of private property. [12] With the death of Dictator Gómez in 1935 and the advent of political parties representing different political doctrines, the controversy about the nature of property rights became nation-wide. Four works published just after the death of Gómez led the way to questioning the absolute character of property rights and, doubtless, paved the way for a new system of law in which the rights of the individual are balanced against considerations of a social nature. [13] None of these writings, however, resolved the critical question of whether the right to own property is an individual right having a social role or whether, on the contrary, property is itself a social function. If the former view prevailed, then all state taking must be compensated; under the latter view, one could justify the right of the State to take privately owned property without compensation in case of the owner's failure to fulfill that property's social function. Four groups emerged from the student movement, some of whose leaders were in exile during the Gómez regime. Of these, the Venezuelan *Communist Party* repeated the traditional thesis of international Marxism-Leninism on the illegitimacy of private ownership of the means of production. However, except in the heat of Parliamentary debates, the Venezuelan Communist Party placed little stress on this position. For the most part, it limited itself to advocating transfer of property to persons fit to make correct use of the property; for instance, advocating theories of land reform involving correct exploitation of agrarian land. [14]

The *Union Republicana Democrática* did not take a specific position on the concept of private property. In 1960, in discussing the new draft Constitution, it simply stated that it approved the draft since "the ideas of decadent and Manchesterian Liberalism do not predominate." [15]

Acción Democrática affiliated with the national socialisms of Latin America, influenced by the program and goals of the *Alianza Popular Revolucionaria Americana* (Apra), one of whose goals is the progressive nationalization of land and industry. In practice, however, this postulate does not appear in the programs of *Acción Democrática,* which refer to the first stage of revolution as "of a democratic type, nationalist, anti-imperialist, and anti-feudal, before being able to be socialist." [16] In the 1947 Constitutional debates, spokesmen for *Acción Democrática* proposed that the State guarantee property as a social function, preferred the theory of the State's eminent domain in property, and proposed that private ownership of land and forest would cease if not in socially useful production. However, the Assembly did not approve these propositions, in part because *Acción Democrática* itself did not press them to the end. Thereafter, the doctrinal disputes were subordinated to more practical questions of the social function of property and the way in which it might be redistributed.

Finally, the *Partido Social Cristiano* (Copei)) took the position that private property and its social function must be distinguished. Property is not a social function, it merely has a social function. If property is not utilized in the most desirable way, taxes or other measures might be in order. The loss of the right to own land for lack of social production, however, could not be admitted since such a doctrine would amount to confiscation.

In the end, the drafting commissions proposed a text along the lines of the position of the Social Christians, and the representatives of the other three parties that had participated in these debates concurred.[17]

In the most recent works of our legal writers, the social functions of property are emphasized:

> The acknowledgement of purely individual ends which do not redound to the collective benefit must not be a part of our juridical institutions. Even for us, under Venezuelan law, modern private property is conceived of as the protection of the relationship between a person and a thing, in the light of a utility of social character, and may be conditioned on the effective fulfillment of ends of a social character.[18]

Again, either the social function of property is added as a footnote in a characterization of property, or emphasis is placed on the present rules restricting the owner's sphere of action "unlike the case of Roman law, which acknowledged ownership as an unrestricted right of the individual ('the sovereign, autonomous, and unlimited power')."[19]

4. Twentieth-Century Constitutions

The Constitution of 1925 provided that owners were "compelled to observe provisions on public health, forest and water conservation, and similar provisions concerning the community benefit" (Article 32 (2)). Thus, it may be said that by 1925 the idea of social welfare contracts in private property was outlined, though the time had not yet come to speak of the social function of property. The Constitutions of 1928, 1929, and 1931 made no changes in the concept of property. The 1936 Constitution added important provisions: first, it contemplated the possibility that the law could for reasons of national interest establish "special restrictions and prohibitions on the acquisition and transfer of certain kinds of property, whether because of their nature, their condition, or their location;"[20] second, the Constitution declared that the nation favored medium and small rural property, and to that effect it was authorized to expropriate idle lands and to divide them or transfer them under conditions prescribed by law; third, two exceptions to the prohibition against confiscation of property were adopted. One exception, traditional in Venezuelan constitutional law, related to international wars and cases of reprisal or where there had been previous confiscation of property of Venezuelans. The other, which occasioned a great public debate, provided for restoration to the national treasury of sums embezzled by high public officials when, in the judgment of the national Congress, they were guilty of offenses against the public welfare and against property. This provision was the result of a proposal made when Congress began its session relating to recovery of improperly acquired goods in the hands of the family of the late dictator Gomez. Though some objected that the provisions were contrary to the Constitution, the pressure of public opinion, revolting after more than three decades of dictatorship, resulted in the acceptance of this provision by a wide margin. The provision was repealed in 1945, however, after it had given rise to contradictory case law relating to the conditions under which the states within the Federal Union could decree confiscation of property.[21]

Another innovation of the 1936 Constitution was to permit expropriation, not only for reasons of "public utility," but also for reasons of "social utility." The reference to social utility was introduced in the parliamentary period with the following argument: "All that is of public utility is also of social utility, but not vice versa. In the future we may be faced with the problem of *latifundia*, and it may not be possible to solve that without the proposed amendment."[22] Eleven years later Venezuela had still another Constitution; this one written by a Congress dominated by the *Acción Democrática*. Though the draft Constitution, as introduced, did not depart from the prior Constitution with respect to private property and state taking, the final version of the 1947 Constitution introduced for the first time the social function of property into the Organic Law. Also, for the first time, the 1947 Constitution made provisions for deferred compensation to former owners of expropriated property. How both of these concepts work in practice will be discussed below.

Two further points about the Constitution of 1947 should be mentioned in this short summary. First, one concrete manifestation of the social function of property appeared in the Constitution in provisions concerning rural property which laid the foundation of agrarian reform (Article 65), although in fact no agrarian reform was begun until almost fifteen years and two Constitutions later. Second, the 1947 Constitution provided for transfer to the nation, and without compensation, of land acquired for exploitation of mining concessions, once the concession lapsed or terminated for any reason (Article 70).

In 1953, following a military *coup d'etat*, another Constitution was promulgated for Venezuela. While in general the 1953 Constitution was more conservative than its predecessor, it made no basic changes in the innovations introduced previously, except that it eliminated all references to agrarian reform.

The Constitution of 1961, which is in force at present, echoes to a great extent the orientation of the 1947 Constitution, including, however, a series of more modern principles. In brief, the drafters assigned to the State the task of leading the country toward economic development, and of seeing to it that "the economic system of the Republic shall be based on principles of social justice that assure to all a dignified existence, useful to the community" (Articles 95 and 98).

The Constitution also provides that the State may reserve to itself specified industries of public interest; in particular, basic heavy industry (Article 97); that it may make economic plans; and that it may rationalize and develop production and regulate distribution and consumption of the national wealth (Article 98). Further, the State must look after the protection and conservation of natural resources and the channeling of their exploitation, principally to the collective benefit of Venezuela (Article 106); it must establish rules concerning the participation of foreign capital in economic development (Article 107); and it must favor the economic integration of Latin America (Article 108).

The regime of *latifundia* is declared contrary to the social interest, and the bases of agrarian reform are set forth (Article 105). Subject to the above general objectives, the Constitution guarantees private initiative, economic freedom, and the right to own property (Articles 96-102).

These provisions were, as we have seen, the fruit of broad agreement within the drafting committee and the result of a very broad consultation and consensus throughout the country, which manifested itself in an almost unanimous vote obtained both in Congress and in the State Legislative Assemblies. For this reason, the social function of property can now be subject to much more precise regulation, as for example, in the Agrarian Reform Law (see Section VI).

5. The Civil Codes

During the twentieth century four civil codes have been in force in Venezuela—the Codes of 1904, 1916, 1922, and 1942. The first three reflect the clear influence of the individualist tradition. But as early as 1931, the desire to overcome this tradition is noticeable. A draft civil code appeared in that year which would have suppressed the absolute character which the prior codes gave to the right to own property on the theory that the absolute character of property was "very ancient." [23] The draft code which appeared in 1941 and was approved the next year placed emphasis on the character of property no longer as an absolute, but rather as an exclusive right (Articles 541 and 525). As Jorge Chapellin noted,

> This change does not, by itself, embody the idea of the social function of property; yet, it was intended as a step along the way to giving the institution of property a truly just meaning. [24]

It is worth noting that Venezuelan writers kept referring to the right to own property as an absolute one, stressing always, however, that absolute and unrestricted are not synonymous and, therefore, that the right of property may be modified by human restrictions, both as to use and as to its relation to social or public utility. The latter concept, as we have seen, was rounded out by the Constitution of 1947 which definitively introduced the concept of social function of property into positive law.

II. Expropriation

1. Historical Development

From the time of Venezuela's independence, Constitutional texts guaranteed private property and established at the same time the power to expropriate. The very first Constitution (1811) states that

No one shall be deprived in the slightest of his property, nor may such property be put to public use without the owner's consent or that of the legislative bodies representing the people; and when any sort of legally proved public need requires the property of any citizen to be put to public use, he shall receive just compensation therefor (Article 2(8)).

The basis of expropriation underwent various modifications in the many subsequent Constitutions. For example, the Constitution of 1819 added general utility legally proved as a cause for expropriation, a concept that disappeared from the Constitution of 1821 and then reappeared in later Constitutions. A requirement of prior compensation appeared for the first time in 1857, but disappeared again in 1860. The Expropriation Law of 1860, based on the 1858 Constitution, established two grounds for expropriation: need, which applied only in time of war, and public utility, which was to be determined by the national Congress if the owner's consent were not given (Article 1). The 1860 Law required that

if controversy arises between the representative of the State and the owner, either over the public utility or the property or over the compensation to be paid, the State shall appeal to the appropriate provincial judge by formally filing a suit against the owner, seeking an order that he transfer the property to the State (Article 10).

The Law also said

the State always pays for privately owned property it takes for public use for reasons of public utility (Article 9).

The first Federal Constitution (1864) made the guarantee of "property with all its rights" to all Venezuelans subject to taking "for public works, through prior compensation and adversary judicial proceeding" (Article 14 (2)). This definition was incorporated in the Expropriation Law of June 13, 1876. Various revisions of the 1876 Law followed up to the end of the nineteenth century and the beginning of the twentieth century. The most important of these, which forms the basis of expropriation law today, was the Expropriation Law of August 2, 1909. Later laws have refined and improved the regulation of the expropriation, specifically with respect to assessment by experts, temporary occupation, the grounds of objection in the judicial proceedings, amicable settlement, provision for improvements, and deferred compensation. But in essence, the Law of 1909 set the standard for the law of expropriation in Venezuela.

2. The Theoretical Basis of the Power to Expropriate

The theoretical basis for the power to expropriate has not been difficult for Venezuelan writers. Some, like Luis Sanojo, have called it "a sacrifice that the general interest demands from the individual;"[25] others have called expropriation "a typical case of the predominance that always exists for the collective over the private interest."[26] The Venezuelan Supreme Court has recently stated that expropriation is justified because "In the conflict of two interests, logically the private interest must yield to that of the collectivity."[27] Of course, the sacrifice of the private interests is not total, since expropriation always requires just compensation.

Efforts to classify the power to expropriate in terms of private law along such lines as forced sale or quasi-contract are doomed to failure since the power to expropriate is, as we have seen, rooted in Constitutional and public law and not in the institutions of private law.[28] One consequence of this is that the power to expropriate is inalienable. Even in cases in which the law invests the power to expropriate in holders of concessions, the State has not relinquished the power and can, accordingly, intervene as expropriating agency.[29]

3. Legislative Bases for Expropriation

Apart from the general authority in the Constitution and civil code, the power to expropriate derives from the Expropriation Law of November 4, 1947, as amended by Decree 184 of April 25, 1958. The Expropriation Law establishes the following requirements for expropriation of immovables:

1. a formal declaration of public utility;
2. a declaration stating that the project to be carried out requires all or part of the property to be transferred;
3. appraisal of the property to be transferred; and
4. payment of the price representing compensation (Article 3).

In addition to the above principles, certain special legislation, such

213

as the Law on Mines and Hydrocarbons and the Agrarian Reform Law provide particular conditions that must be met in expropriations taken under their authority. [30]

As we have seen, the Venezuelan Constitution of 1961 guarantees the right to own property. Nevertheless, this guarantee is modified by the following:

> by virtue of its social function, property shall be subject to the taxes, restrictions, and obligations imposed by law for purposes of public utility or general interest (Article 99).

Expropriation is considered one of these restrictions, subject, however, under Article 101 of the Constitution, to the proviso that expropriation may take place only on grounds of public benefit or social interest through a final judgment and the payment of just compensation. Note that only expropriation, among the qualifications on the right to own property, entitles the property owner to compensation. Other restrictions on the use of property, whether by way of taxation, licensing, zoning laws, food and drug legislation, or even temporary occupation by the police or military, are not thought of as expropriation and therefore do not entitle the owner to compensation under Articles 99 and 101. Where to draw the line between expropriation and regulation or even administrative seizure of property (for example, seizure of food considered unfit for consumption or seizure of weapons carried by unlicensed persons) has been a difficult problem for Venezuelan law. It is interesting to note that the Venezuelan Expropriation Law provides that "judges or public officials who take property or order the taking of property in the name of the state without observance of the requirements of the law shall be personally liable for the value of the thing taken and for any damages caused thereby" (Article 55). This liability is in addition to liability of the State for a taking contrary to the formalities of the law. [31] Even in cases of emergency, justifying suspension of Constitutional guarantees, including the guarantees of right to property, the Expropriation Law calls for compensation to the property owner (presumably subsequent to the taking) "taking all circumstances into account" (Article 54).

4. Types of Property Subject to Expropriation

Article 101 of the Constitution refers to compensation for "every

214

class of property." In general, however, expropriation is carried out only with respect to immovable property and it is to that kind of property that the Expropriation Law of November 4, 1947, as amended, is addressed. Ordinary movables are not covered by the present expropriation law, apparently on the theory that tangible movables are usually not unique, and there is no reason for the State to acquire tangible property through expropriation. As to intangible personal property, the Law of Industrial Property contains an explicit provision regarding expropriation:

> Whenever an invention or discovery is of interest to the State or may be deemed to be of public interest, the executive may for public or social utility decree the expropriation of the right of the inventor or discoverer, subject to the requirements established by law for the expropriation of goods (Article 16).

While there is some debate about unpublished technical knowledge, it would appear that the power of the State to subject inventions or their designs to expropriation is now clear. [32] Similarly, the Copyright Law of December 1962 contains a provision for expropriation on account of public utility or general interest, provided that the special norms laid down by the copyright law are followed (Article 1). In essence, this would seem to mean that the government might take over the rights to a certain publication, but could not thereby infringe those rights personal to the author, such as the right to be recognized as author, and to prevent modifications of this work that might injure his reputation.

5. Mining Property

Of the three general regimes for mining rights—ownership in the State, ownership in the person owning the surface, and ownership in the person staking a claim to a particular mineral deposit—all have had their place in the history of Venezuela, beginning with the earliest ordinances of royal Spain, extending through the early period of independence, the Constitution of 1864 which established the states and gave them certain rights, and up to the latest Constitution of 1961. The current situation in Venezuela is not clear. The Constitution of 1961 states only that "the operation and administration of mines and hydrocarbons . . . and the conservation, development, and utilization of forests, waters, and other natural resources of the country are within the competence of the national power" (Article 136(10)).

It can be stated that apart from stones used in construction or nonprecious jewelry, mineral property may not belong to private persons. Private persons may, however, have a real right not amounting to ownership pursuant to a concession. But it has not been clearly established whether mining property belongs to the states or to the national government, since the Constitution speaks only of operation and administration.

The Mining Law of December 28, 1944, states (in Article 18) that the holder of a concession, if he is in a dispute with the surface owner, shall have the right to expropriation. The law presumes the necessity of expropriation in the absence of proof to the contrary, if it is essential for the drilling of wells or tunnels, the construction of buildings, storehouses, repair shops, dams, and the like, and for the establishment of living quarters or offices incident to the mining project.

It may be asked whether it is possible to expropriate mines or oil wells granted in a concession. Thus far, none of the special laws regarding mining or petroleum production have treated this subject. Undoubtedly, the right acquired by a concession holder over a mine is a real right in immovable property. [33] Thus, mining property comes clearly within the kind of right subject to the expropriation power. Moreover, the Mining Law states that everything concerning mines, breeding stations, or ore deposits is declared to be of public utility (Article 1). The same thought appears in Article 1 of the Hydrocarbon Law. However, both the Mining Law and the Hydrocarbon Law are "special legislation," and it is believed their provisions are controlling against a more general law such as the Expropriation Law. If this analysis is correct, a concession granted under one of the special laws provides within its own terms and subject to the special law pursuant to which it was granted the exclusive means for depriving the concession holder of the subject of the concession.

III. Public Utility and Social Interest

1. Significance of the Terms

The concept of public utility has not been a fixed one in Venezuela, but rather has been the object of constant revision according to changes in the needs of society. As the concept of private property has moved away from its original rigid definitions, and has gradually become imbued with ideas of social function, the range within which the sacrifice of private property interests is permitted has been correspondingly expanded.

Three stages may be distinguished in the evolution of the principle of the power to expropriate: first, when the principle was exclusively shaped by the concept of public necessity; second, when this idea was expanded by the concept of public utility; and, finally, when the concept of social interest was introduced into the law of expropriation.

In the first period, expropriation was confined to those narrow areas of public activity directed to preservation of the body politic and to protection of private persons whose goods or existence was threatened. The theoretical foundation for the limited use of expropriation was derived from Article 17 of the Declaration of the Rights of Man, in which expropriation was rigorously limited to "duly verified public need." Since the right to own property constituted one of the foundations of the social and political order, any move against this right without an absolute public necessity was inconceivable.[34]

In the course of the nineteenth century, the concept of public need, public interest, national interest, state interest, public utility—all these terms were used without distinction—began to take on broader scope. Expropriation was considered in order not only when the property in question was absolutely necessary for a public purpose, but also when it was useful for that purpose. Moreover, the common understanding of what were public purposes continued to expand. It is interesting that the first expropriation law of Venezuela, the Law of July 13, 1860, distinguishes between cases of necessity, "which take place in time of war and are determined by the natural law and the law of nations" and cases of utility, "which are established by the Congress (Article 1).[35]

Finally, in the third stage, reached by the middle of the twentieth century, property is itself deemed to have a social function. The current Law of Expropriation, enacted in 1947 and amended in 1958, is called "Law of Expropriation for Reasons of Public or Social Utility." Whether this title indicates that public and social interest today have different meanings is not clear. One view holds that the distinction depends on what happens to the property after it has become expropriated. According to this view, in expropriation for public utility the expropriated property must become part of the patrimony of a public entity, [36] whereas in cases of expropriation for social interest the expropriated property does not become part of the patrimony of the State, but instead may be transferred from one private owner to another. [37] However, this view does not seem persuasive. For one thing, public entities are not the only expropriating agencies under Venezuelan law. As we have seen, concession holders and contractors engaged in public works as well as corporations so authorized, may exert the power of expropriation (Expropriation Law, Article 9). For another, the procedure for expropriation makes no distinction of the kind that one would expect if the difference between public and social interests were as suggested above. Indeed, when one looks at particular expropriations, for example those in connection with land reform, one sees that the distinction suggested simply does not fit. Land reform typically is started by a public enterprise such as the National Agrarian Institute, but on the other hand is commonly thought of as the classical case of expropriation in the social interest. [38]

The second point of view seeks to distinguish between whether the community benefits directly from an expropriation, considered to be expropriation for public utility, or only indirectly, considered to be expropriation for the social interest. For example, if land is taken for use as a public highway, it would be thought of as expropriation for reasons of public utility; on the other hand, the taking of a business in order to integrate it into a larger state enterprise might be thought of as expropriation for reasons for social interest. But this distinction, too, seems artificial, as was indeed realized by one of its proponents, Alvarez Gendin, who predicted in 1928 that over time, as the judicial conscience of the nation develops, the concept of public utility might well absorb the concept of social interest. [39]

Still another attempt at explaining the distinction between public utility and social interest in the context of expropriation rests on the difference between expropriation to satisfy the needs of society and expropriation as a form of sanction or punishment against the owner who has failed to live up to the social function that the law demands of property ownership. Under this theory, payment for expropriated property should be computed differently in expropriation for public utility than in expropriation in the social interest. While expropriation for public use would require payment of the full value of the expropriated property, expropriation for default by the property owner in fulfilling his social function would, presumably, call for payment of less than the full value or payment stretched out over time. If this thesis were applicable, there would be substantial differences in, for example, application of the Agrarian Reform Law. Thus, the taking of lands which are not fully exploited would be cases of expropriation as a sanction for causes of social interest, while so-called extraordinary expropriation, when lands do fulfill that function, would be expropriation for public use. However, the Expropriation Law does not establish a system of differences concerning the expropriation system to justify an exposition of this kind.

Variations on the attempt to distinguish between public utility and social interest also focus on the difference between benefit to the whole of the nation and benefit to particular classes such as workers or peasants. In this writer's view, however, all efforts to draw a distinction between public utility and social interest must fail, given today's concepts of what is the proper scope of governmental activity; that is, essentially without limit.

2. The Declaration of Public Utility

An expropriation in Venezuela can proceed only upon a declaration of public or social utility. According to Article 10 of the Expropriation Law, such a declaration may be made by the National Congress; in cases of urgency during recess of the Congress by a standing committee of Congress; by the Legislatures of the States; in urgent cases during recess of the Legislature by the State Executives; and for the cities by the City Council.

Throughout the course of Venezuelan history the tug-of-war between the Legislature and dictatorial Executives has, as might be expected, focused in good measure on the power to take private property in the name of the State, and to determine what constitutes state property and what constitutes private property. (It will be recalled that it was this issue which was used against the most recent dictator, Marcos Perez Jimenez, in the successful attempt to have him extradited from the United States and brought to trial in Venezuela following the overthrow of his regime.) In part, also, this tug-of-war has taken place between the national government and the states.

In brief, the situation is at present as follows: (1) Under ordinary circumstances the power to authorize expropriation is vested in the Congress, the State Legislatures, and the Municipal Councils. (2) In cases of emergency the power to make the declaration of expropriation in matters pertaining to the national power is vested in the National Executive Power, whether or not Congress is in session. At the state level such power is vested in the governors of the respective states, subject to the approval of the National Executive if the State Legislature is in session and (paradoxically) without the approval of the National Executive if the State Legislature is not in session. The decision of what constitutes an urgent matter rests entirely with the Executive. (3) With respect to matters of defense or national security, the power to make the declaration of expropriation rests with the National Executive at all times.

To say that the power to issue the declaration of expropriation lies first in the Legislature in certain cases is not, by any means, to answer the question of who makes the decision. A substantial number of activities are by law declared to be of social interest or public utility, so that any given decision to expropriate is considered a decision to implement, and thus purely executive. For example, Article 11 of the Expropriation Law lists railroad construction, highway construction, school buildings, fortresses, hospitals, cemeteries, stadiums, and airports, among many others, as activities "previously declared to be of public utility, as is evidenced by their character . . ." Similar advance declarations are contained in the Forest Law (Article 2), the Civil Aviation Law (Article 37), the Agrarian Reform Law (Article 1), the Law of Mines (Article 1), the Law of Hydrocarbons (Article 1), and numerous similar pieces of legislation. It is interesting also that the Expropriation Law itself waives the declaration of public utility or social interest for works included in the city plan for the city of Caracas and in comparable plans for other cities or urban groupings (Article 11).

Once a given purpose or type of works has been declared to be a cause authorizing expropriation, the decision as to which particular property will be taken to carry out the public purpose rests exclusively with the authorities who administer the type of project in question. To determine who these authorities are is not always easy, particularly in a federal regime in which the national government, the states, and municipalities all may have jurisdiction over the kind of activity in question—for example, road building or construction of parks. The most commonly used criterion for determining the sphere of competence for purposes of expropriation is based on the governmental authority, at whatever level, to which the funds to be used in the expropriation or the project in question have been appropriated.

We have made reference previously to the fact that expropriation is not limited to governmental entities, but that private contractors, mining companies, and the like may have the advantages of expropriation (see Article 9 of the Expropriation Law). When non-governmental entities seek to proceed by expropriation, they apply to the appropriate governmental unit for the declaration of public utility or social interest.

IV. Compensation

1. The Duty to Compensate

As we have seen, the Constitution requires "payment of just compensation" as a condition of expropriation for every class of property for any cause (Article 101). The same requirement is contained in the Civil Code, which provides in Article 547 that "no one may be forced to yield his property nor to permit others to use it except for reasons of public or social utility established through judicial process and upon prior compensation." Again, the Expropriation Law lists as one of the requirements of expropriation "payment of the price representing compensation"' (Article 3). The object of compensation is to repair damage suffered by the property owner through loss of his property without causing him either loss or gain.

2. Determination of Just Compensation

Ordinarily compensation is determined after the other issues in an expropriation proceeding have been settled and all the other steps have been followed. However, in cases of urgency the court may permit immediate occupation of property, and in such cases a preliminary proposal may be made so that an initial payment is paid to the property owner at the time of transfer. In such cases the appraisal is made by a three-member commission of whom one member is appointed by the expropriating agency, one by the court of first instance, and the third either by the first two or (in the Federal District) by the College of Engineers. The decision of this Commission of Appraisal is not binding on the final determination of the price, in part because the property owner does not have the right to appear before the provisional body.

Final determination of just compensation—whether following a provisional assessment, as described above, or following a final decision that expropriation is in order, as is the more usual procedure, is also made by a commission of experts. Two experts are appointed: one by the property owner and one by the judge of first instance. In this proceeding the property owner has the right to appear and make presentations concerning the value of the property to be taken. In agrarian reform proceedings disagreement by the property owner with the appraisal must be taken directly to the Supreme Court in connection with an appeal of the entire case. In other cases a special procedure is provided to challenge the position of the appraisers. However, the scope of review of an expert appraisal is very narrow. Apart from attack upon the motives of the appraisers, as set forth in the Code of Civil Procedure (Article 480), the appraisal by the experts may be rejected by the court only if it is shown that they proceeded unlawfully in open violation of the principles set forth in the law, on the basis of plainly erroneous data, or on the basis of proved bias.[40]

The range within which the experts may work is very broad. Thus, according to Article 35 of the Expropriation Law, they may take into account in arriving at a just value the type of property, its quality, location, approximate dimensions, its probable production and "all other circumstances which may influence the value of the property, provided these influences are spelled out." Among the elements which must be taken into account by the experts are "declared value," that is, the value which the owner declared or accepted in statements made for purposes of property taxes; "commercial or market value," that is, the value derived from any previous transaction concerning the property at least six months prior to the decree of expropriation; and "average value," that is, a value derived from the average sale price of comparable property within the twelve-month period prior to the expropriation decree. [41] These three components, however are not to be used to the exclusion of other factors. [42] For example, "good will" is to be taken into account by the experts. The compensation article of the Expropriation Law (Article 35) also contains a provision concerning the effect of a partial expropriation on the property remaining in the owner's possession. For example, a railroad station or a road built on a portion of the owner's land may substantially enhance the value of the remainder. In such a case, the benefit to the owner with respect to the property remaining in his hands is credited to the amount due him for the portion expropriated. If, however, such credit exceeds one quarter of the compensation due to the owner, the owner may then opt for the expropriation of the entire property on the basis of the appraisal previously made.

Venezuelan law is concerned that the act of expropriation itself not affect the value for which compensation is to be given. Neither increase nor decrease in value resulting from announcement of the projected work may be taken into account, and, as we have seen, commercial value and average value are determined on the basis of events at least six months or within twelve months prior to the decree of expropriation. [43]

3. Forms of Payment

Payment of compensation for expropriation must be made entirely in cash, in legal tender. However, under Article 101 of the Constitution, expropriation under the Agrarian Reform Law (see Section VI(2)) requires payment to be made partly in cash and partly in bonds. These bonds constitute the so-called Agrarian Debt guaranteed by the Nation (Article 172). In addition, in cases of expropriation of immovable property aimed at enlargement and improvement of towns, payments are to be made in installments over a period of up to ten years, with interest and other terms determined in each case by the Executive Branch (Expropriation Law, Article 40). Also, the Forestry Law authorizes payment over periods of up to 15 years in case of expropriation within zones declared national parks (Article 15).

These exceptions comprehend a very substantial portion of the expropriation carried on in Venezuela at the present time. Arguably, they undermine the principle of prior compensation. It might be said on the other side that these kinds of Venezuelan solutions preserve the principle in cases where the state is able to effect payment—typically expropriation of individual pieces of property, and abandon the principle only where the obligation to make payments in very large amounts would hamper the social policy designed to be implemented.

V. Expropriation Procedure

1. The Judicial Proceeding

An expropriation proceeding begins with a petition by the expropriating authority to the court, describing the property to be taken, the name of the owner, and, if appropriate, the names of other interested parties such as tenants or mortgagees (Article 20). The court is the civil tribunal of first instance, except if the Nation itself is the expropriating agency, in which case the proceeding is brought directly before the Supreme Court (Article 19). Within three days of the petition, the court must request all relevant information covering the property to be taken, to the extent this has not been supplied with the petition. As soon as the information is received, the court issues summonses to all persons shown to have any right or interest in the property, and also publishes a notice every ten days for a month in a major Caracas newspaper and in a local newspaper (Article 22). Ten days after the last date of publication the interested parties must appear before the court, in person or by attorney. If they do not appear, a defense counsel is appointed by the court (Article 23).

The respondents then must answer the petition for expropriation. However, the only basis for opposition is violation of law by the expropriating agency, and this has been interpreted narrowly to mean deviation from specific procedures related to the expropriation. [44] In addition, the property owner may ask the court to decree expropriation of an entire piece of property though the government sought only a portion, if he can establish that the remaining portion would be valueless or inadequate for the purpose for which it had been used (Article 26). Though a successful challenge on this ground is rare, an example may be seen in the decision of the Supreme Court of December 12, 1962, ordering total expropriation for a property owner who showed that the partial expropriation requested by the State would have deprived him of water resources and, therefore, would have made his property unusable for residential purposes. [45]

The court first proceeds to determine the legal issues, if any, raised by the opposition to the expropriation. If there has been no opposition or if the determination is in favor of the expropriating agency, the judge next proceeds to a determination of the value of the property—not by himself but either through amicable settlement by the parties within a time period set by the court or, if that fails, through expert appraisal. The experts—one or three— are appointed by agreement of the parties or, if they cannot agree, one by each side and the third by the judge (Article 33 and 34). When the price to be paid has been determined by either of these methods, the expropriating agency deposits the compensation (or, where appropriate, the initial installment) with the court, unless the owner acknowledges receipt of the sum. The court in turn issues an order entitling the expropriating agency to occupy the property and to register its title. Thereafter the court orders that the compensation deposited be paid to the expropriated party (see Title V of the Expropriation Law).

2. The Scope of Judicial Review

The decision of the court concerning the legality of the procedure is appealable (Article 30). But neither the court of first instance, nor any appellate court, has the power to review the Declaration of Public Utility or Social Interest, whether made by the Legislature or the Executive Branch. This has now been firmly established by the Federal and Cassation Court in its decision of May 18, 1945. [46] The immunity from judicial review covers not only the issue of whether a stated purpose is indeed an object of public utility or of social interest, but also the issue of whether a particular piece of property is the one best suited for the public purpose. Interestingly enough, these two issues have not always been treated alike in Venezuelan law. Prior to the Law of June 13, 1876, it was possible for the private party to contest the issue of public utility; thereafter this possibility was eliminated, but the interested party was permitted to argue whether his piece of property was or was not required to carry out the approved work. This division was maintained under the Expropriation Laws of 1891, 1909, 1912, 1918, and 1923. Under the Laws of 1926 and 1936 judicial review of the issue of public utility was again permitted, along with the issue of whether a particular piece of property was required. Under the 1942 Law the issue of public utility was reviewable, but the issue of whether a particular piece of property was required was no longer reviewable. Finally, under the 1946 reform still in effect, both issues were removed from review by the courts, thus confirming the 1945 decision of the Federal and Cassation Court. What is left for the courts, then, is a general supervisory power over the procedure, the limited issue of partial versus total expropriation, and, as discussed below, some determinations concerning the rights of third parties.

3. Rights of Third Parties

It has already been indicated that the entire procedure of expropriation is directed not at particular parties, but at a piece of property. Thus, although at the opening of the proceeding notice must be given to all owners, tenants, creditors, and all others who may have any right in the property (Article 22), only those having a "real right in the estate" have standing to contest the petition for expropriation (Article 27). The other persons, though entitled to notice, can do no more than follow the course of events at the trial with a view to defending their rights when the time comes for allocating the amount of compensation. [47] The definition in Article 27 may involve more than one "party"—for example the legal owner and others having a secured interest such as a mortgage. Both parties may intervene in the proceedings with regard to agreement on the price to be paid, deciding to appeal or to drop appeals, agreeing on the appointment of experts, submission of information to the commission of experts, or attacking the decision of the experts. Persons enjoying only possession, or owning only improvements on plantations, are in a special situation. The law provides that persons in possession of a plantation have the right to be parties in the expropriation proceedings in order to secure a reduction of the price paid to the owner of the portion corresponding to the value of improvements made by them and damages caused to them (Article 28). However, this seems to be the total scope of their right to intervene, and they do not become true "parties." If expropriation affects improvements owned by someone other than the owner of the land, the latter may receive payment directly if there is no opposition from "third parties" (Article 43), [48] i.e., all those not included in the above who may have some right or interest in the property other than a "real right." At the appropriate moment, a third party must present to the judge "convincing proof of his claim" (Article 45) and request that the price assigned to the expropriated party as compensation be deposited with the court pending the determination of the third party's claim rather than be paid out directly. The point is that the law does not seek by transferring property to the State for its social needs to deprive creditors of the security for their debts.

The law does not specify the residual rights of third parties and, in particular, what happens if a judge does not find the proof convincing or for some reason does not order the money deposited in the court. Moreover, except in certain cases of agrarian reform involving mortgaged farms that have fulfilled their social function (Article 33), the law is not clear on what happens to the obligation secured by mortgage. The law states simply that the rights of mortgagees are "transferred to the price." Whether that means that the mortgage expires upon transfer of the property to the State, with the result that full payment comes due immediately, or whether, on the contrary, it means that the loan remains in effect with the security simply being the money paid by the State, has not been established in Venezuelan law. Whichever logical inference one may draw has its difficulties. In one solution, the debtor, no longer in possession of the property, is exempt from further interest payments so that, in effect, he has an interest-free loan. [49] On the other hand, if the debtor is required to pay the full amount at once, he is deprived of the opportunity that he originally bargained for to stretch out his payments over a long time. One point has, however, been established by a recent decision of the Supreme Court. Where under the Agrarian Reform Law the property owner is paid in agrarian reform bonds, his debt to the mortgagee may also be paid in such bonds. [50]

4. Out-of-Court Settlements

In the majority of cases, at least at the national level, once expropriation has been decreed the matter proceeds by amicable settlement without resort to judicial procedures. The reason for this is that since the price is not at issue in the trial before the court, which generally is limited to aspects of the legality of the proceedings, the great majority of property owners have little to gain from going to court. Consequently, the majority of owners prefer to discuss the price and come to terms with the expropriating authority in an informal manner.

It is worth saying that this situation is different in cases of agrarian reform, where appraisal is part of the judicial proceedings and where the form of payment depends on the proof submitted concerning the social function of the property. For these two reasons, owners affected by agrarian reform are interested in taking their cases to court in order to obtain greater compensation and to obtain a greater proportion in cash rather than bonds. This explains why in one hundred years of expropriation the number of cases is quite limited, in contrast to the numerous court decisions handed down under the Agrarian Reform Law, less than a decade old.

It is fair to say that there is a consensus that the rights of property owners are duly safeguarded in the present law. This is true even when in practice property owners often do not utilize all of the means provided for defense of their rights, whether because of ignorance, bad advice, or abuse on the part of government officials. In other instances, the defense of such rights and interests is costly, so that the property owners prefer to arrive at out-of-court settlements even if these may not be entirely satisfactory, and even at some sacrifice of their rights. Despite the above, experience has shown that in the area of urban renewal expropriation can be carried out peacefully and that means not specifically provided for in the law can facilitate the procedure. For example, a common exchange agreed to by both parties is one in which the expropriating agency receives a portion of the property needed for its projects while the condemnee is exempted from payment of the tax on improvements which would be levied on his remaining property (Article 15 and 16 of the Expropriation Law). Again, it often happens that the property owner agrees to give up a certain piece of property without compensation in return for a permit to make improvements on or new uses of the remainder of his property. Sometimes, in fact, owners prefer to give up portions of their property without any return, expecting simply to profit from the improvements brought about by the public works.

VI. The Special Case of Agrarian Reform

1. Scope of Agrarian Reform

In many ways agrarian reform is like other takings of private property for state use. However, the scale is much greater, and consequently it was felt in Venezuela that both the procedure and the means of making payment had to be modified in order not to frustrate the program at the outset. The expropriation provisions of the Agrarian Reform Law of March 5, 1960 (Articles 28-40) accordingly contain a series of variations from the norm prevailing in other types of expropriation.

Under the Agrarian Reform Law the taking agency is the National Agrarian Institute, created by Decree 173 on June 28, 1949, and stated in the 1960 Law to be the primary agency to carry out the agrarian reform. The National Agrarian Institute (IAN) is an autonomous institution annexed to the Ministry of Agriculture and Breeding, but with its own juridical status, right to own property, and prerogatives and privileges. It is independent from the National Treasury.

Property subject to expropriation under the Agrarian Reform Law includes agricultural land and estates, whether privately or publicly owned, improvements on such land, and in certain cases, equipment, livestock, and farm produce on the site of expropriated land. All farms are subject to expropriation under the Agrarian Reform Law except those which come under exemptions; in particular, those that do fulfill their social function as defined.

Under Article 19 of the Agrarian Reform Law, a farm fulfills its social function when all of the following are true:

a. The soil is exploited efficiently and in such a way as to make the best use of the factors of production existing in the zone where it is located and according to its particular characteristics.

b. The farm is worked personally by the owner of the land, who is also financially responsible for the farm, except in those cases where work and ownership are separated for good cause shown.

c. All provisions on conservation of natural resources are observed.

d. Legal norms regulating salaried work and other aspects of labor relations of farm workers are respected.

e. The farm is included in the National Registry of Lands and Waters as prescribed by law.

In addition to expropriation of agricultural properties which do not fulfill one or more of the above requirements, the law provides for expropriation, by way of exception, of farms which do fulfill their social functions, but which nevertheless must be expropriated in order to "resolve an agrarian problem of obvious seriousness" (Article 33). [51]

2. Compensation

Under the Agrarian Reform Law, immediate payment in cash must be made for the value of existing equipment, livestock on the farm, pledges, and secured debts owed mortgagees, and for the land itself when its total value does not exceed 100,000 Bolivares (about $22,500 in U.S. currency). For other property, that is to say, for the immovable property of farms worth more than 100,000 Bolivares, compensation shall be paid partly in cash and partly in bonds (Article 178). These bonds are of three kinds: Class A Bonds have a twenty-year period of amortization, earn 3 per cent, and are not transferable; Class B Bonds have a fifteen-year term, earn 4 per cent, and are transferable; Class C Bonds have a ten-year term, are transferable, and earn interest in accordance with the interest prevailing generally in the financial market (Article 174). Where agricultural property is expropriated although it fulfills its social function as described above, compensation (to the extent it is not in cash) must be paid in Class C Bonds. [52] Class A Bonds are to be used in payment of compensation for agricultural property either not cultivated at all or cultivated indirectly; that is to say, by absentee landlords. [53] If the owner himself exploits his agricultural property, but does not comply with one of the other provisions defining social function, the compensation shall be in the form of B Bonds. [54]

3. Classification of Land Use and Its Consequences

The difference between expropriation of property which does and which does not fulfill its social function is important not only with respect to the means of compensation, but also with respect to the judicial proceeding required. In effect, Article 33 of the Agrarian Reform Law requires that in cases of farms that do fulfill their social functions, the National Agrarian Institute must prove in an appropriate judicial proceeding that the expropriation is necessary to establish an agrarian organization in the particular place, and why the existence of one or more private estates in the area would constitute an obstacle of a technical or economic kind for the successful accomplishment of the Institute's plan.

Moreover, in expropriation of property which is fulfilling its social function as defined, certain grounds of modifying the request by the expropriating agency are available. For example, an owner of agrarian property that is fulfilling its social function may object to the court that the property should not be expropriated partially, because the remaining property cannot be economically utilized. It is possible to have partial expropriation under the Agrarian Reform Law, but the decision on whether to approve partial expropriation or require total expropriation is up to the court. Again, if the expropriation agency seeks to take land, including the 150 hectares of first class land which, under Article 29 of the Agrarian Reform Law are exempt from expropriation, it must follow the procedures for ordinary expropriations and not the procedures under the Agrarian Reform Law.

The lands to be expropriated under the Agrarian Reform Law are classified in an order of preference, starting with lands and rural properties mentioned in Title I, Chapter 1 of the Law— 1) uncultivated land and property in the private domain of the Nation; 2) property belonging to one of the independent national institutes; 3) real property that has become part of the National Wealth by reason or in consequence of illicit enrichment against public policy.[55] If this category of properties is insufficient and the Agrarian Institute has not been able to acquire lands equally exploitable by other means, then expropriation of lands not fulfilling their social function may take place in the following order: First, uncultivated lands, and among these the largest first; those indirectly exploited through tenants, middlemen or squatters; and those lands not exploited during the last five years prior to initiation of the expropriation proceeding. Second, those lands designated to be parceled out into private rural lots when the parceling out has not taken place; subject, however, to preservation by the Agrarian Institute of the rights of those private owners who have benefited from the subdivision. Third, agricultural lands devoted to cattle pasture on a large scale. Finally, expropriation may also take place on other lands when lands falling in the above categories have been exhausted, or in cases where there is no other possibility of solving an agrarian problem of obvious seriousness (Article 27).

In all cases of expropriation of agrarian land the property owner has a so-called right of reserve, defined by Article 30 of the Agrarian Reform Law as "a right to reserve to his own ownership property in an amount equal to estates deemed not subject to expropriation under Article 29," that is, estates up to 150 hectares of first-class land or the equivalent. This right of reserve may be exercised up to the date fixed for the assessment of the compensation due. In cases where the property owner has not himself exercised this right, the judge may determine the location of the reserve property prior to the final assessment.

4. Judicial Procedure

Article 36 states that except as otherwise provided, the procedure of the Expropriation Law shall be followed. In general, the variations are designed to expedite the procedure.

Before the formal expropriation of agricultural property may take place, the expropriating agency must take steps looking to an amicable settlement with the property owner. These steps may not take more than ninety days, after which formal expropriation shall be initiated. What happens if the steps looking to amicable settlement are not taken does not appear from the text of the Agrarian Reform Law. Insofar as judicial decisions have touched upon the point, it appears that the attempt at amicable settlement is not a requirement "of public order" *(de orden publico),* since the law has not provided any sanction in the event it is omitted, and since, for example if the property owner is unknown or absent the expropriation proceeds without attempt at amicable settlement.

It is not necessary in agrarian reform takings to make a prior declaration of public utility as is normally required for urban expropriation. The reason is that the law itself has determined that expropriation of land in connection with agrarian reform is considered to be of public utility. The petition for expropriation is to be directed to the "judge competent in the territory where the immovable is situated" (Article 36 (1)). Note that this is different from the general provision in the Expropriation Law (Article 19), which states that in cases where the nation itself is the expropriating agency the appropriate court is the political-administrative chamber of the Supreme Court of Justice. Upon receiving the petition for expropriation, the judge must accept the petition and set a time limit for interested parties to raise objections. The petition and the setting of time limits must be published twice and notice must also be given by posters in public places and in one newspaper in the Capital of the Republic. Within five court days following the date of final publication the parties summoned must appear before the tribunal in person or by attorney to raise their objections to the petition. The law provides that if by the appointed date no defendant has appeared, the court will name the party defendant.

Assuming that persons have appeared to contest the petition of expropriation, the issues raised may be procedural or go to the question of whether the property is or is not subject to expropriation. Among the procedural issues may be the failure to go through efforts to reach an amicable settlement; the description of the property in question; or inclusion of portions within the prescribed reserve. Fundamental objections relating to the expropriability of the property may be that the property is fulfilling its social function; that in the area there are properties having priority under the Expropriation Law, such as uncultivated farms; that the expropriating agency could acquire equally suitable lands by other means; and that the land subject to the expropriation is less than 150 hectares of first-class property or its equivalent. If the ground of objection is procedural it will be decided on the fifth court day following the raising of the objection, on the basis of all the statements made by the parties. In other cases, if there is a substantive objection, fifteen working days shall elapse for the gathering of proofs and evidence. The next hearing thereafter shall be set by the judge with a view to arriving at an agreement on the amount of compensation. If agreement is not possible the judge shall appoint a future date for designation of expert appraisers, whose work shall proceed independently of the proceedings concerning the substantive objections to expropriation.

Means of proof in contests concerning expropriation include expert appraisals, personal inspection to determine the prior occupancy and social function, and documentary proof concerning ownership of the property. The Supreme Court of Justice has held that testimony is not sufficient to prove the social function of agrarian property. [56] In order to prove social function, it is necessary to undertake a scientific study of the soil—the percentage of the surface under cultivation, the state of conservation of the soil, as well as the quantity, value, and time of commercial exploitation of the property in comparison with exploitation of other properties in the area.

Once the proceeding has gone before the court, the burden of proof concerning social function is on the person objecting to the expropriation. [57] Other requirements established in the Agrarian Reform Law concerning proof of social function relate to evidence about conservation of natural resources, proof of compliance with the regulations concerning wages, hours, and working conditions, and proof of due inscription of the farm in the Registry of Lands and Waters (Article 19).

One of the questions raised by the Agrarian Reform Law, and particularly on the issue of social function, is the date as of which the compliance by the owner with these standards should be judged. In particular, what happens in the case of a landowner whose properties have been occupied by squatters? On this issue the Supreme Court of Justice held on October 23, 1963 [58] that "in the case of a forcible invasion of an estate by groups of squatters, if the petition of expropriation has been delayed for reasons not attributable to the property owner, and if further the property owner is a) practicing conservation; b) personally directing the operation; c) assuming financial responsibilities; and d) observing labor and other social legislation, he will be deemed to have carried out those functions which he could not carry out because of the occupation by *campesinos*. In such a situation the judicial determination about the fulfillment of the social function of the property will be as of the date that acts of force prevented full compliance, assuming that the owner can prove before the judicial and police authorities that he took all appropriate legal steps to enforce his rights of property. If the latter is not proved, the forcible invasion of his property will be interpreted as tolerated by him and will be considered proof that at the time of expropriation the property was not fulfilling its social function.

Following the period provided for proof, the court holds hearings at which the parties make their written submissions. In addition, the judge may hold oral hearings on matters covered in the written submissions. He may give his decision at such a hearing or issue the decision in writing with his opinion.

Appeal from the decision of the court may be made to the Supreme Court of Justice.

Just as in ordinary expropriation, it is possible under the Agrarian Reform Law to occupy the property prior to the completion of the proceeding upon a showing of urgent necessity (Article 37). In such cases, following the provisions of the Expropriation Law (see Section V(1)), the expropriating agency must deposit with the court a sum equal to the just compensation as determined by the expropriating agency. [59] In these circumstances, the basis for deposit of compensation is the category of property subject to expropriation even though the property is fulfilling its social function (see Article 33).

Conclusion

Venezuela in 1970 seems to stand in the middle in Latin America. It has not passed through a violent revolution and has begun to settle into maturity as Mexico has; it has not for over a decade had a right-wing military government as Brazil and Argentina had at the turn of the decade; and it has instituted experiments in agrarian reform similar to those in Peru and Chile, without, apparently, the accompanying political changes.

Venezuela's Constitution authorizes a substantial range of economic activity by the State but guarantees private economic initiative and the right to own property. Expropriation has not, on the whole, been used as an instrument of social transformation, though the foundations for a large-scale redistribution of rural landholdings have been laid in the Agrarian Reform Law of 1960.

The role of the courts in expropriation cases in Venezuela has been maintained as an overseer of procedural requirements. The courts do not, however, have any say over the reason for any particular expropriation, which is considered a legislative or in some cases an executive matter. As for compensation, Venezuelan law endeavors to equalize the losses suffered by private parties through state takings by awarding them sums equal to the value of the property. Determination of compensation is conceived of as primarily a job for experts rather than for judges, with judicial interference only in cases of improper motives. The result of the process appears to be generally fair, given the difficutly of making just valuations.

Altogether it may be said that expropriation law and practice in Venezuela reflect with a fair degree of accuracy the relation between the state and private property generally: private rights are respected and safeguarded, but the state is steadily expanding its conception of its own responsibilities in all phases of the country's economic activity.

Notes

1. For more information see: Tomás Polanco Martinez, *Esbozo sobre la Historia Economica Venezolana*, p. 141 (1960); Nicomedes Zuloaga, "Datos Históricos sobre la codificacion en Venezuela," VIII *Revista del Ministerio de Justicia*, pp. 46-48 (1959); Tómas Lander, "La Doctrina Liberal" (*El Pensamiento Politíco Venezolano del Siglo XIX*, Vol. IV) pp. 45-55, 80-81 (1961).

2. See Rene Lepervanche Parpacér, *Estudios sobre la Confiscación*, pp. 43-51 (1938).

3. Luis Sanojo, *Instituciones de Derecho Civil Venezolano*, p. 20 (1877).

4. Rafael Fernando Sayas, "El Presidente," Madrid (1891). Reproduced in *El Pensamiento Político Venezolano del Siglo XIX*, Vol. XI, p. 127.

5. Ernesto Wolf, *Tratado de Derecho Constitucional Venezolano*, p. 85 (1945).

6. Art. 14, No. 2 of the Constitutions of 1864, 1874, 1881, 1891 and 1893.

7. Luis Sanojo, op. cit. pp. 83-84 (1877).

8. For more information see: Tito Gutierrez Alfaro, "Historia de la Codificación del Derecho Civil en Venezuela," IV *Revista Jurídica*, p. 231-44 (1933).

9. Luis Bastidas, "Historia del Código Civil Venezolano (1862-96)," *Revista del Colegio de Abogados del Distrito Federal*, Vol. III, No. 14, pp. 34-35.

10. For a more detailed historical account see Jorge Chapellin, *El Derecho de Propiedad a Traves de la Historia*, pp. 119-30 (1947).

11. *El Pensamiento Político Venezolano del Siglo XIX*, Vol. XIII, pp. 61-79, 173-190, 267-286. See also Luis Villalba Villalba, *El Primer Insituto Venezolano de Ciencias Sociales*, pp. 46 et seq. (1961).

12. Pedro Manuel Arcaya, "En Defensa de la Propiedad Territorial," *Estudios Jurídicos* (1904).

236

13. Joaquín Gabaldon Marquez, *Concepto del Derecho de Propiedad* (1936); Amenodoro Rangel Lamus, *Estudios de Derecho Privado,* (1937) (especially pp. 87-103); Efrain Ruiz Alfonso, *Organización y Función Social de la Propiedad,* (1938); Luis Alberto Colmenares, *Derecho de Propiedad* (1938).

14. See *Diario de Debates de la Asamblea Nacional Constituyente De Los Estados Unidos de Venezuela 1947,* Month II, p. 24; Month VI, No. 64, p. 16; Month VI, No. 11, p. 17. See also *La Ley de Reforma Agraria en las Cámaras Legislativas,* Vol. I, pp. 390-430 (1961). *Principios,* Journal of the Central Committee of the Communist Party of Venezuela, Vol. III, No. 11 (Oct. 1961).

15. See the *Diario de Debates de la Camara de Diputados de la República de Venezuela,* Oct. 24, 1960, p. 460.

16. Demetrio Boesner, *Socialismo y Nacionalismo,* p. 214 (1965).

17. See *Diario de Debates de la Asambléa Nacional Constituyente,* Cit. No. 42, pp. 11-16, 18-20; Cit No. 70, p. 22; Cit. No. 71, p. 17.

18. Simón Egana, *Manual, Bienes y Derechos Reales,* p. 201 (1964).

19. Gert. Kummerow, *Bienes y Derechos Reales* (Derecho Civil II), p. 211 (Cursos de Derecho, Facultad de Derecho, Universidad Central de Venezuela.) 1965.

20. For a detailed summary, see Ulises Picón Rives, *Indice Constitucional de Venezuela,* pp. 808-809 (1944).

21. See Pablo Ruggeri Parca, *La Supremacía de la Constitución y Su Defensa,* pp. 111-113 (1941).

22. See *Diario de Debates de la Cámara, de Diputados de Los Estados Unidos de Venezuela,* No. 31, p. 3, No. 37, p. 7, Feb.1936.

23. *Exposición de Motivos del Proyecto de Código Civil,* p. 30 (1931).

24. Jorge Chapellin, *El Derecho de Propiedad a Traves de la Historia,* p. 129 (1947).

25. Luis Sanojo, *Instituciones de Derecho Civil Venezolano,* p. 21 (1877).

26. Zoila Graterol, "Nuestra Ley Nacional de Expropiación y su aplicación actual a la propiedad territorial comunera," 85 and 86 *El Profesional Revista Mensual de Derecho. Legislación y Jurisprudencia,* p. 8 (June-July, 1923).

27. Banco Obrero v. Hacienda "La Urbana," Corte Sup. de Justicia en Sala Politico-administrativa, 47 Gaceta Forense 2d 160 (Feb. 24, 1965).

28. See Sucesión Levy Urbano v. Procurador General de la Nación, Corte Federal y de Casación, en Sala Fed., March 14, 1952, 10 Gaceta Forense 2d 133-34 (1952); Efigenia de la Mercedes Herrera de Cunningham v. Carmen Luisa Martínez de Hernandez, Corte Federal y de Casación, en Sala de Casación, May 22, 1951, 8 Gaceta Forense 2d 280-281 (1952).

29. See Judgment of Dec. 16, 1943, Corte Fed. y de Casación, en Sala Fed., (1944)

Memoria de la Corte Fed. y de Casación, V. 1, p. 326 (dealing with the Law of Hydrocarbons).

30. See Instituto Agrario Nacional (hereafter referred to as I.A.N.) v. Federico de la Madriz y Pastor, Corte Federal, Jan. 12, 1961, 31 Gaceta Forense (2d) 11-15 (1961).

31. Nestor Moreno v. Municipalidad Distrito Federal, Corte Sup. de Justicia, Sala de Casación, 10 *Jurisprudencia Venezolana* 386 (July 22, 1964).

32. See Art. 4 of The Law of Industrial Property.

33. See Art. 3 of the Hydrocarbons Law.

34. See Article 2, Ch. 1 of the First National Constitution of 1811: " . . . no one may be deprived of the smallest portion of his property, nor shall it be put to public use, without his consent or that of the legislative bodies representing the people; and when some public need requires that the property of the citizen be applied to such use, he shall receive just compensation therefor."

35. See Enrique Perez Olivares in his foreword to the work of Allen-Randolph Brewer-Carías (1966).

36. See Jesús González Perez, "La Utilidad Pública y el Interés Social en la Nueva Ley de Expropriación Forzosa," *Revista Crítica de Derecho Inmobiliario,* pp. 258-288 (May-June, 1955).

37. See page 221.

38. See Brewer-Carías, *La Expropriación por Causa de Utilidad Pública o Interés Social,* pp. 54-59.

39. See Sabino Alvarez Gendin, Expropriación Forzosa, Su Concepto Jurídico, p. 39.

40. Procuraduría Gen'l. de la Nación v. Guayana Mines Ltd., Corte Fed. y de Casación, Feb. 21, 1950, 10 Gaceta Forense, 2d 101 (1952) and Procuraduría Gen'l. de la Nación v. Fundo "Los Robles," Corte Fed. y de Casación, June 20, 1950, 5 Gaceta Forense 64 (1950).

41. See Compañia anónima "La Unión" v. Sindíco Procurador Municipal del Distrito Federal Corte Fed., April 28, 1960, 28 Gaceta Forense 2d 32 (1961).

42. Banco Obrero v. Urbanización "Las Vegas S.A.," Corte Sup. de Justicia, April 7, 1965, 48 Gaceta Forense 2d 20 (1965).

43. See Florencio Contreras Q., "Algunas consideraciones sobre el justiprecio de los bienes en los juicios de expropriación," *Revista de la Facultad de Derecho,* No. 8, p. 179 (1956).

44. See Urbanización Las Vegas v. Banco Obrero, Corte Federal, March 30, 1960, 27 Gaceta Forense 2d 157 (1960), where the Court ruled that arguments concerning the appraisers' expertise and methods (hidden inspections) were inappropriate for consideration.

45. See Fiscal General de la Republica v. Falco, Nardi, Sindicato Taguaza et al., Corte Sup. de Justicia, Dec. 12, 1963, 42 Gaceta Forense 2d 365 (1963).

46. Procurador General del Estado Carabobo v. Policarpo Clavo Coderido, Sala Fed. Accidental, Corte Fed. y de Casación, May 18, 1945, 1946 1 Memoria de la Corte Fed. y de Casación 224.

47. See Procurador Gen'l. de la Republica v. Benjamin Moore, Decision of Inez de Sustanciación de la Sala Fed. Accidental of the Corte Fed. y de Casación of Nov. 23, 1951, 11 Gaceta Forense 2d 252 (1953) where the Court ruled that lessees of a marble and sand excavation project on a piece of property to be expropriated had no "real right in the estate" and thus did not have standing to contest the petition for expropriation and receive part of the compensation for an unexpired contract.

48. Procurador Gen'l. de la Republica v. Pedro Vallejo Gonzales, Corte Sup. de Justicia, Sala Politico-administrativa, 46 Gaceta Forense 2d 298 (11 / 18 / 64).

49. Compare Art. 40 of the Expropriation Law, requiring the payment of interest so long as the debtor is in possession.

50. I.A.N. v. Compañia Agropecuaria Tacarigia C.A., Corte Sup. de Justicia Sala Politico-administrativa, Oct. 16, 1963, 42 Gaceta Forense 2d 159 (1963).

51. For a detailed description of each of these requisites see I.A.N. v. Dr. Rafael Zomora Pérez, Corte Sup. de Justicia, June 10, 1963, 39 Gaceta Forense 2d 295 (1963).

52. See I.A.N. v. Fundos "Santa Rosa" and "Paraparal," Corte Sup. de Justicia, Aug. 12, 1964, 45 Gaceta Forense 2d 188 (1964).

53. See I.A.N. v. Compañia Agropecuaria Tacarigia C.A., Corte Sup. de Justicia, Oct. 16, 1963, 42 Gaceta Forense 2d 159 (1963).

54. See I.A.N. v. Rafael Lucena y otros, Corte Sup. de Justicia, Feb. 20, 1964, 43 Gaceta Forense 2d 37 (1964).

55. See Arts. 10-18 of the Agrarian Reform Law.

56. See I.A.N. v. Jose Antonio Tamayo Perez, Corte Sup. de Justicia, Oct. 23, 1963, 42 Gaceta Forense 2d 179 (1963).

57. I.A.N. v. Humberto Barrios, B.A.P. et al. Juzgado Primero de Primera Instancia en lo Civil de la Circumscripción Judicial del D.F. y Est. Miranda, Jan. 24, 1967.

58. See I.A.N. v. Jose Antonio Tamayo Perez, Corte Sup. de Justicia, Oct. 23, 1963, 42 Gaceta Forense 2d 179 (1963).

59. See Fundo "Palmera" v. I.A.N., Corte Sup. de Justicia, Feb. 5, 1962, 35 Gaceta Forense 2d 70 (1962) and I.A.N. v. Federico de la Maduz y Pastor, Corte Federal, Jan. 12, 1961, 31 Gaceta Forense 2d 17 (1961).

239

United States
of America

Robert K. Greenawalt

Contents

I. A Brief Introduction to Federalism and the Constitution	245
II. Private Property and Public Welfare	247
1. Changing Concepts of Property	247
2. Modern Restrictions on the Use of Property	249
III. The Power of Eminent Domain	253
1. The Nature of the Government's Right	253
2. "Taking of Property" As Understood	
by the Supreme Court	254
3. Generalizing Theories Suggested by Scholars	263
4. The Meaning of "Public Use"	265
IV. Compensation	268
1. The Right to Just Compensation	268
2. The Problem of Valuation	269
3. The Rights of Third Parties	275
V. Expropriation Procedure	276
1. The Decision to Expropriate	277
2. The Scope of Judicial Review	277
3. The Judicial Method	278
4. The Administrative Method	282
5. "Inverse" Condemnation	282
6. The Law in Practice	283
VI. Rights of Aliens	284
Conclusion: A Summary Evaluation	286
Notes	287

I. A Brief Introduction to Federalism and the Constitution

A lawyer in the United States would be surprised by the title of this paper. "Expropriation," he would think, is something foreigners do —particularly in Latin America, and as likely as not, to property owned by an alien. The subject dealt with, of governmental taking, is known in the United States as "eminent domain." In fact, however, the issues are largely the same as those discussed in the preceding papers—with the exception of certain problems, such as very rapid inflation, that have not yet been seen in the United States. Even the conceptual framework is not as different as one might have supposed, deriving from the term "public use" in the Fifth Amendment of the United States Constitution. The habits of thought engendered by the common law system and the "case method" of legal education tend to direct the United States lawyer more to judicial decisions, and more to challenging governmental acts as in conflict with the Constitution, and rather less to statutes as authoritatives guides. But the conflicts between the common good and individual rights do not depend in any significant way on the difference between the common law and the civil law.

Perhaps the greater difference between a study of this kind devoted to the United States and one devoted to a Latin American country is the consequence of the federal system of the United States. While Brazil, Argentina, Mexico, and Venezuela are all in form federal unions, none has the diversity of legal systems—50 states plus a parallel federal judiciary and more and more overlapping legislative functions—that are characteristic of the United States.

The federal government is, of course, directly bound by the United States Constitution and in particular by the restrictions on governmental power contained in the first ten amendments, the Bill of Rights. The fifth amendment provides that, "No person shall be . . . deprived of life, liberty, or property without due process of law; nor shall private property be taken for public use, without just compensation." Thus, whatever the power under which it acts, the federal government may not take private property without paying just compensation.

When the federal government acts within its granted powers and consistent with the restrictions imposed on it, it can override state assertions of power.[1] It is a corollary of this general principle that the federal government can expropriate property owned by a state,[2] though a state cannot take federal property.[3]

Though not explicit in the Constitution, it was established early in United States history that the Supreme Court could invalidate executive or legislative acts.[4] The federal courts have no power to give advisory opinions, but if in the course of a concrete legal dispute[5] the constitutionality of a Congressional act is challenged, the courts may declare it invalid. The circumstances under which the federal government must compensate for losses to property that it inflicts and the basic principles of fairness in procedures for condemnation are, as a consequence, matters of Constitutional law as developed by Supreme Court decision.

Though the original Constitution contained a number of limitations on state power, some explicit and others implied from grants to the Congress, the fifth amendment and other parts of the Bill of Rights were directed only at the federal government.[6] State exercises of the power of eminent domain were not restricted by any federal requirement of just compensation or due process. Most states had their own constitutions with similar language, however, and under the same scheme of separation of powers that existed at the national level, these restrictions were enforceable by the state courts. In the period after the Civil War the Constitution was amended to give national protection to certain basic rights, particularly those that had been denied to Negroes. The fourteenth amendment, ratified in 1868, provides

> No state shall make or enforce any law which shall abridge the privileges or immunities of citizens of the United States; nor shall any State deprive any person of life, liberty, or property, without due process of law, nor deny to any person within its jurisdiction the equal protection of the laws.

How far this amendment was intended to "incorporate" the Bill of Rights, that is, make its protections applicable against the states, has been, and continues to be, a subject of sharp debate.[7] But it was obvious that the requirements of "due process," whatever they might be, were imposed on the states. In 1897 the Supreme Court held that the due process clause of the fourteenth amendment prohibits states from taking property unless they comply with the just compensation standard of the fifth amendment.[8] Thus for the last seventy years, it has been clear that a state may condemn

246

property only if it conforms with fifth amendement restrictions. A state constitution as written or interpreted may, of course, impose even stricter limits on the power of eminent domain.

Since the principles of federal Constitutional law are applicable to every jurisdiction, and the decisions of the Supreme Court on federal law influence state court determinations of state Constitutional law, the consideration of Constitutional principles will concentrate on Supreme Court cases. Because the ordinary exercise of the eminent domain power is by the state or one of its branches, more attention will be paid to state practices in the discussion of procedures for condemnation and the assessment of compensation within constitutional limits.

II. Private Property and Public Welfare

1. Changing Concepts of Property

Concepts of what may constitute "property" are very flexible in United States law. One reason for this is that legal theorists now generally accept the notion that the "property" protected by law is itself the creature of law. As Jeremy Bentham, the English utilitarian and analytical positivist, wrote:

> Property is nothing but a basis of expectation; the expectation of deriving certain advantages from a thing which we are said to possess, in consequence of the relation in which we stand towards it ... Now this expectation, this persuasion can only be the work of law.[9]

Such "bases of expectation" need not be limited to material objects, and property in the United States can exist in intangibles, such as patents or shares, as well as movables and immovables.[10] The suggestion has been made in recent years that a "new property" should be created for those whose income depends on government largess, in the form of government employment, welfare payments, or licenses, franchises, or contracts.[11] Whatever the merits of this proposal from the perspective of social policy, no theoretical problem would be raised by creating "property" rights to this largess.[12]

Since "property" refers to legal relations between persons, in Anglo-American law different persons can have property rights in the same "thing." Historically, the origin of the law of real property in feudal estates of land, with the ultimate right of property vested in the Crown, and the evolution of the "trust" concept have both contributed to the notion of the divisibility of property among various parties. [13] In the United States, one person may hold a life estate and another a remainder interest with regard to the same land; both would be considered to have "property."

Whether a fee simple is considered full ownership or some ultimate right of ownership is thought to rest in the state [14] is much less important than the extent to which the law allows the holder of property dominion over what he owns. With regard to this question, both theory and actual law have evolved considerably during this century. Holders of property under the feudal system of land tenure had been subject to considerable limitations, particularly in regard to dispositions, but during the eighteenth and nineteenth centuries the idea that property was a natural right conferring upon owners absolute dominion characterized legal thinking in this country. [15] Both Locke and Blackstone were influential. For Locke, writing in 1690, a man's right to property in the state of nature derives from the mixing of his labor with the fruits of the earth. He says:

> Though the earth and all inferior creatures be common to all man, yet every man has "property" in his own "person." This nobody has any right to but himself. The "labour" of his body and the "work" of his hands, we may say, are properly his. Whatsoever, then, he removes out the state that Nature hath provided and left it in, he hath mixed his labour with it, and joined to it something that is his own, and thereby makes it his property. It being by him removed from the common state Nature placed it in, it hath by this labour something annexed to it that excludes the common right of other men. [16]

In Locke's view one of the central purposes in the formation of political society is the protection of property. Though he would allow limited regulation of property, he believed that a government violates the social compact if it significantly impairs property rights. [17] Blackstone, in his famous commentaries published in second half of the eighteenth century and widely used in the colonies as an authoritative exposition of the common law, writes:

> So great moreover is the regard of the law for private property, that it will not authorize the least violation of it; no, not even the

general good of the whole community; . . . The public good is in nothing more essentially interested than in the protection of every individual's private rights, as modelled by the municipal law.[18]

In 1856 this passage was cited approvingly by the highest court in New York, which held that a defendant had a Constitutional right to sell liquor already in the state despite a state statute outlawing such sales. To forbid him to do so would be a destruction of property lawfully acquired.[19]

Whatever the philosophical weaknesses of Locke's and Blackstone's theories, they were relatively well suited to the opening up of a new continent and the early stages of capitalist development. Land was plentiful and the use and disposition of commercial property could be left to be governed, for the most part, by the play of the market. Locke's analysis is less relevant, however, for a complex, urban, and highly inter-dependent society. The value of each person's labor depends very largely on what others do and there are few specific objects that persons can point to and say, "That is mine; I made it." When people live in close proximity and have to rely heavily on each other, the use of property to the social detriment is a serious danger. The need to control private property in the public interest is particularly acute when great concentrations of property, an important form of social power, are owned or controlled by relatively few individuals, as is the case with major companies in United States economy.[20]

Since the late nineteenth century, legislatures have increasingly imposed limitations on property rights thought to be for the general good. After a period of considerable reluctance the courts have left the political branches wide flexibility.[21] Though notions of absolute or near-absolute rights of property are perhaps still a part of popular ideology for much of the population of the United States, few, if any, thoughtful commentators accept that view. The reporter of the American Law Institute's *Restatement on Property* has said that "'Property rights' at any moment of time represent the current wisdom as to how the balance between restrictions and freedom is best served."[22]

2. Modern Restrictions on the Use of Property

At the present time restrictions on property are rather extensive and one would certainly guess that the long-term trend is toward even greater limitation. Some of these restrictions have been developed primarily by judicial decision, though they are now embodied in the statutory law of many states. The power to dispose of owned assests is restrained by: the Rule Against Perpetutities,[23] which limits the amount of time the dead hand of past wishes can control the present; the bar on unlawful restraints on alienation;[24] and the prohibition of illegal or anti-social dispositions.[25] Traditional restrictions on the owner's use of land imposed for the benefit of the other members of society include: easements of necessity, which assure A's access to his own land across the land of B if there is no other way A can reach his land; rules requiring reasonable use of scarce water resources; and the law of nuisance. The last forbids an owner from using his land, for example by creating loud noises or offensive odors, in a way that unreasonably interferes with his neighbors' enjoyment of their land.[26]

What distinguishes the modern era from those preceding is the extent to which statutory and administrative rules limit the use of property. Property rights are subject to the "police power," a short-hand term for the government's power to promote health, safety, morals, and the general welfare. This power is exercised in a variety of ways. Every major city has a detailed code to assure that safe buildings are constructed. Sanitation and sewage are carefully regulated. A landlord's obligations to his tenants are in large part defined by government, and, in New York City, rent control imposed during the housing shortage created by World War II remains in effect, so that for a large number of apartments the amount of rent that can be charged is determined by law. Water is only one of the scarce resources whose use is controlled; states and their subdivisions also protect soil, timber, and grazing land by regulating land usage.

In the last half-century land planning has moved far beyond the protection of natural resources. Most communities with any density of population have zoning laws which restrict the use to which land may be put in any given district. In 1926 the Supreme Court sustained a zoning ordinance against the claim that it deprived a landowner of his liberty and property without due process of law and denied him equal protection of the laws.[27] The area of the village was divided into six classes of use districts. In

U-1, land could be used only for single-family dwellings, parks, reservoirs, and farming; in U-2, two-family dwellings were permitted; in U-3, apartment houses; in U-4, restaurants and theaters; in U-5, warehouses and wholesale markets; in U-6, plants for sewage disposal. Uses were cumulative; that is, in U-6 all uses permitted in the other districts were allowed; in U-2, U-1 as well as U-2 uses were allowed. In the Court's view these limitations on use resembled those imposed by the law of nuisance:

> The question whether the power exists to forbid the erection of a building of a particular kind or for a particular use, like the question whether a particular thing is a nuisance, is to be determined, not by an abstract consideration of the building or the thing considered apart, but by considering it in connection with the circumstances and the locality.... A nuisance may be merely a right thing in a wrong place—like a pig in the parlor instead of the barnyard. If the validity of the legislative classification for zoning purposes be fairly debatable, the legislative judgment must be allowed to control.[28]

In more recent cases some courts have placed greater emphasis on the general welfare aims of zoning than on a theory of quasi-nuisance and have sustained industrial-only zoning, designed to attract industry, and large minimum acreage zoning, intended to protect a community's character.[29] Recognition that aesthetic judgment can justify zoning rules has become increasingly explicit. There are limits to the power to set zoning regulations. They must be reasonable, not discriminatory, and part of a comprehensive plan. They must not, at least in most instances, render the regulated land nearby valueless.[30] When a zoning regulation conflicts with the use of land at the time of passage of the regulation, the prior non-conforming use must be allowed to continue, or the owner at least given a reasonable time to amortize his investment.[31] When a particular attempt to zone is beyond the state's power, it will often be the case that the same objective could be accomplished by expropriation of the protected property rights. The difficult line between regulation of property and taking is discussed below.

A number of states and major northern cities prohibit racial or religious discrimination in the sale and rental of housing, further limiting property rights. Similar legislation was passed by Congress in 1968,[32] and in the same year the Supreme Court interpreted an 1866 Civil Rights act as forbidding such discrimination.[33]

Restrictions imposed on the operation of business enterprises are another sort of limit on property. Business of all kinds must meet state and federal standards for health and safety. Laws in many states and a recent federal act prohibit racial discrimination in choosing customers by hotels and restaurants. Similarly, discrimination in employment is forbidden. Bargaining between employers and unions in businesses affecting interstate commerce is carefully controlled by the National Labor Relations Act. There are federal and state minimum wage laws limiting the hours of employment. Federal antitrust laws are designed to prevent monopolies and other unfair trade practices. At a national or local level the prices and profits of monopolistic public service industries, such as railroad, gas, and telephone companies, are controlled by government. National agencies like the federal Communications Commission, the Interstate Commerce Commission, and the Federal Trade Commission regulate other key industries of the economy.

Taxation is another limit on absolute dominion over property. If one is taxed a large proportion of the value of his property a rather obvious restriction is set on what he can do with the property. In 1964 federal and state revenues were over one-fourth of the gross national product.

The magnitude of tax revenue is in the United States relevant to the power of eminent domain. Since the primary tax burden is borne by the more affluent and the poor benefit from many government programs, some redistribution of social goods is now accomplished through taxation and government expenditures. Even those who believe that this redistribution is much too slight do not propose expropriation of property without compensation, for there are in this society simply much easier methods to achieve the result of economic help for the poor. The strength of the tax base in the United States also puts payment for property taken within the government's means. No pressing need to expropriate must be foregone because it cannot be afforded.

Thus, despite some popular ideology to the contrary, property rights in the United States are far from absolute. In a multitude of ways they yield to what are deemed pressing social interests. Often the government can accomplish its aims with regard to property by regulation or taxation rather than by an exercise of the power of eminent domain. When the government does exercise that power it has the means to pay compensation.

III. The Power of Eminent Domain

1. The Nature of the Government's Right

The power of the sovereign to take property for public use without the owner's consent has been considered in the United States to be an attribute of sovereignty of every independent government, essential to the independent existence and perpetuity of the state. [34] Though not explicitly granted in the federal and state constitutions, the power of the state to take private property "by eminent domain" is implied both by the nature of government [35] and by the Fifth Amendment and similar state constitutional provisions restricting its exercise. While some courts have accepted the theory of Grotius and Pufendorf that the state's power to take private property derives from its ultimate ownership of that property, the predominant view in the United States is that the right to expropriate is the "offspring of political necessity" and distinct from any residual property right. [36] In terms of the practical rights of holders of private property, it apparently makes no difference which of the two theories is used to explain the state's power to condemn.

Courts have held that the power of eminent domain is inalienable, so that one legislature cannot bargain away the power of a subsequent legislature to condemn property for public use. [37] In *Pennsylvania Hospital v. Philadelphia*, [38] the Supreme Court permitted the City of Philadelphia to expropriate part of the hospital's land to construct a street, although sixty years earlier the state legislature has passed an act banning such construction, in return for the hospital's promise to make certain payments and provide grounds for surrounding public streets. The Court declared inapplicable the Contract Clause of the Constitution (Article I, Section 10), which forbids states from passing laws "impairing the Obligation of Contracts," stating:

> The States cannot by virtue of the contract clause be held to have divested themselves by contract of the right to exert their governmental authority in matters which from their very nature so concern that authority that to restrain its exercise by contract would be a renunciation of power to legislate for the preservation of society or to secure the performance of essential governmental duties.

Private contractual agreements are as ineffective as governmental undertakings to limit the power of eminent domain. [39]

Although the power to expropriate resides in the federal and state legislatures, it may be delegated to the executive branch, [40] to governments of local political subdivisions, [41] such as counties and municipalities, to quasi-governmental bodies [42] such as the Port of New York Authority, and to private corporations, such as railroad and telegraph companies. [43] Those delegations, most frequently made to government agencies with specified responsibilities, often limit the exercise of the power to 1) condemnation for a specific purpose, 2) condemnation only of property necessary to effectuate that purpose, and 3) condemnation according to a prescribed procedure.

The power of eminent domain extends to every kind of property right. The state may condemn all, or any part of, the rights to a piece of land, or to movables or intangibles. It may carve out a right, for example an easement, that does not previously exist, and condemn it.

As suggested above, the substantive law of eminent domain is, in the United States, primarily a branch of constitutional law. Apart from issues of procedural fairness, which are important aspects of constitutional interpretation, the major questions covering eminent domain in the United States—both at the state and at federal level—have been presented as problems in interpreting the Constitutional requirement that "private property [shall not] be taken for public use, without just compensation."

2. "Taking of Property" As Understood by the Supreme Court

The first question, framed in Constitutional language, is "when is property taken?" If the government occupies private land for the building of a public road, it is plain that a taking of property has occurred. But suppose it destroys a house to prevent the spread of fire? Or prohibits the only valuable use of a parcel of land? Or requires the owner of land to build structures for public purposes? Or renders land valueless by its use of adjoining land or airspace? Are these "takings of property?" [44] The application of this Constitutional language to specific situations has not been governed by any precise logical rules or definitions. The lines drawn between "taking" and circumstances in which compensation is not required have, rather, reflected social judgments about the proper range

254

of government activity and the place of private property. To the extent these judgments have been rendered by courts, the shifting distinctions also reflect at least an implicit determination of how far such social judgments should be made by judges at all, and of what kinds of rules of decision are appropriate of judicial officers. The Supreme Court has not followed any one coherent and consistent theory in drawing these lines, nor have state courts.

Discussion of what is a "taking" can be approached from a number of perspectives.[45] One can look at historical development, different kinds of cases, different theories advanced by courts for their results, or generalizing principles advanced by commentators to explain what has been, or should be, the course of the law in this area. In this paper, the cases are broken down into broad categories, and historical development and judicial approach are considered in that context. A brief discussion of some general theories advanced by scholars follows.

The cases can be roughly divided into three kinds: 1) When the government appropriates property for its own use or for the use of a third party, such as a railroad, for public purposes; 2) When the government regulates use of property in some way but without appropriation, or imposes a special tax on particular property; 3) When the government neither appropriates nor regulates the use of the property concerned but engages in activity that incidentally diminishes its value.[46]

Appropriation for Use. The first category is the simplest and fits most plainly the language "taking of property." It describes the classic situation in which the government, assuming a consensual transfer cannot be arranged, must act by condemnation and appropriates for public use one's rights with regard to a thing. As long as the government's appropriation of use is complete, it does not matter whether what is appropriated is only a small part of a larger subject matter or is taken for a limited period of time. If the state, for example, in order to widen a road, takes only a small strip of a large tract of land it must compensate the owner even if the reduction of the land's total value is minimal.[47] Similarly, it must pay if it takes only a relatively short leasehold interest.[48] So long as property is appropriated for use, it makes no difference to the duty to compensate how pressing is the public need. In time of war the owner of a steel mill whose property is taken for the construction of war materials must be reimbursed,[49] as must the person whose property is requisitioned in the war theater for use by military forces.[50]

Regulation, Destruction, and Taxation. The second category, when the government regulates the use of property but does not appropriate it, raises much more difficult problems. Plainly not every exercise of the police power limiting the use of property can give rise to a duty to compensate. But the courts have been unwilling to hold that the state is free, even when acting consistently with the public interest, to impose any limitation it chooses on the use of property. If a court holds an attempted regulation to be a deprivation of property without due process of law because it imposes an undue burden on the owner, it is usually saying, in effect, that the state cannot do what it has tried to do without compensating the owner.[51]

In *Mugler v. Kansas,*[52] one of the early cases in which the United States Supreme Court passed on the constitutionality of police power regulations, it upheld a Kansas law prohibiting the manufacture and sale of intoxicating liquor as a beverage, even as the law applied to existing breweries and stocks of liquor. These had been built and produced in accord with the law by persons who had every reason to suppose liquor could be legally sold. The prohibition written into the state constitution deprived them of virtually all value. The Court declared that the state rule was an appropriate way to protect the health, safety, and morals of its citizens and that the diminution of value did not deprive plaintiff of property without due process. The power of eminent domain was not involved, in the court's view, because no one was required to devote his property to the public use,[53] and the state therefore had no need to compensate owners for the reduced value of their liquor. The Court distinguished an earlier case which had allowed recovery by a person whose land had been flooded as a consequence of a state-authorized dam,[54] on the ground that the physical invasion and practical ouster of possession in that case did in effect require devotion to public use. The Kansas legislation, however, "does not disturb the owner in the control or use of his property for lawful purposes, nor restrict his right to dispose of it, but is only a declaration by the State that its use by any one, for certain forbidden purposes, is prejudicial to the public interests." Since the state has power to abate nuisances, and the legislature has wide discretion to determine what are noxious uses that inflict injury on the community, the pecuniary loss sustained did not invalidate the legislation or require compensation.[55]

Mugler v. Kansas suggests two standards for determining whether the value of property can be diminished by the state without compensation. Has a physical invasion occurred? Does the regulation prohibit noxious use? Although courts have since *Mugler* invalidated some state acts diminishing property values that did not involve physical invasion,[56] at least in the ordinary sense,[57] the presence of a continuing invasion almost always requires compensation. Some of the difficulties in determining whether an invasion has occured, and its relevance, are discussed below.

In upholding regulations that diminish property value without compensation, the Court has subsequently relied on the argument that a noxious use has been prohibited. The *Mugler* principle is relatively simple to apply when a particular kind of enterprise, such as the sale of liquor or prostitution, has been altogether prohibited as inconsistent with the public welfare; it becomes more complicated when the objection is simply that an enterprise not considered inherently bad is being carried on in an inconvenient location. In 1915, in *Hadachek v. Sebastian,*[58] the Supreme Court sustained a Los Angeles ordinance forbidding the operation of brick yards or brick kilns in certain parts of the city against someone who had started using his land for brickmaking when the land was outside the city limits and the surrounding area was sparsely settled. What had been an inoffensive use became offensive because of a change in the character of the neighborhood.[59] The ordinance diminished the land's value from $800,000 to $60,000. Nevertheless, the prohibition on brick manufacture was held to be a legitimate exercise of the police power, not entitling the owner to compensation. In *Village of Euclid v. Ambler Realty Co.,*[60] the Court, in upholding a general zoning ordinance explicitly recognized that things perfectly acceptable in some circumstances might be socially harmful in others.

"Nuisance" as a concept may seem to connote some failure by the offender to take into consideration the feelings of others, but if nuisance can be merely the right thing in the wrong place and if it makes no difference whether it was the right thing in the right place when the commitment of resources was made, then any reasonable determination that a particular use is inconsistent with the public interest might be thought to support an uncompensated prohibition on that use.

The courts have not gone this far, however. In the 1922 landmark case of *Pennsylvania Coal Co. v. Mahon* [61] the Supreme Court held invalid a state law that forbade any mining of coal in a manner causing the subsidence of dwelling homes. The mining company had, before passage of the statute, sold property rights to the surface of land it owned while expressly reserving the right to mine the coal under the surface. The purchasers had knowingly agreed to take any risk that might arise from the mining of coal. Justice Holmes, writing for the Supreme Court, noted that the statute attempted to abolish an interest in land recognized by these contracts and would, if sustained, render valueless the property interests of the coal company. The safety of the dwellers could be assured, he asserted, by the simple expedient of adequate notice. If the state chose to protect the home owners who had bought surface rights against the mining of the coal under their homes, it could do so only by condemning the interest of the mining company and paying compensation therefor:

> Government hardly could go on if to some extent values incident to property could not be diminished without paying for every such change in the general law. As long recognized, some values are enjoyed under an implied limitation and must yield to the police power. But obviously the implied limitation must have its limits, or the contract and due process clauses are gone. One fact for consideration in determining such limits is the extent of the diminution. When it reaches a certain magnitude, in most if not in all cases there must be an exercise of eminent domain and compensation to sustain the act . . .
> . . . The general rule at least is, that while property may be regulated to a certain extent, if regulation goes too far it will be recognized as a taking. [62]

Limits on the power to zone in most states reflect an approach similar to *Pennsylvania Coal Co.* Zoning restrictions must, usually, not destroy the value of the land; [63] existing nonconforming uses must be allowed to continue or at least phase out over a reasonable period of time. [64]

In a relatively recent case, *Goldblatt v. Hempstead*, [65] The Supreme Court had before it a town ordinance that in effect prohibited continuance of a prior nonconforming use, the mining of sand and gravel in a residential area. Citing *Mugler* and *Hadachek*, the Court refused to find a taking simply in the fact that the land's most beneficial use, to which it had previously been devoted, was prohibited. But it continued:

> This is not to say, however, that governmental action in the form of regulation cannot be so onerous as to constitute a taking which constitutionally requires compensation . . . There is no set formula to determine where regulation ends and taking begins. Although a comparison of values before and after is relevant, . . . it is by no means conclusive . . .

Finding a "dearth" of evidence on the nature and menace against which the ordinance was meant to protect, the availability of less drastic steps, and the loss in value to the owner's land, the Court decided that he had not met his burden of showing that the ordinance was a taking of his property without compensation. Five months later the Court dismissed an appeal in a similar case in which the trial court had determined that the ordinance in question had destroyed the value of appellant's property. [66]

The Court has upheld state measures that went beyond serious diminution of the value of property and involved its outright destruction. At the common law, a building might be destroyed to prevent the spread of fire; the owner received no compensation. [67] In *Pennsylvania Coal Co. v. Mahon*, Justice Holmes wrote, after stating that regulation that goes too far will be recognized as a taking,

> It may be doubted how far exceptional cases like the blowing up of a house to stop a conflagration, go—and if they go beyond the general rule, whether they do not stand as much upon tradition as upon principle. [68]

Nonetheless, six years later, in *Miller v. Schoene*, [69] the Court rejected a challenge to a Virginia statute that required destruction of all cedar trees infected by cedar rust and located within two miles of apple orchards. Since cedar rust destroys the fruit and foliage of apple trees, but does not harm the cedar trees themselves or any other property, the legislation was a plain choice of the welfare of apple growers over the welfare of cedar tree growers. According to a unanimous Court, which avoided mentioning *Pennsylvania Coal Co.*:

> . . . the state does not exceed its constitutional powers by deciding upon the destruction of one class of property in order to save another which, in the judgment of the legislature, is of greater value to the public . . .
>
> We need not weigh with nicety the question whether the infected cedars constitute a nuisance according to the common law; or whether they may be so declared by statute.

Although the total loss to the cedar tree owners was smaller absolutely and as a percentage of the value of their land than that of the Pennsylvania Coal Co., the loss in terms of the value of the trees infected with rust was complete. [70]

In a more recent case, the Supreme Court had to consider the intentional destruction by the retreating United States army of oil facilities in the Philippines in 1941 to prevent their falling into the hands of the Japanese. The Court compared this action to the destruction of buildings in the path of a fire and denied that it constituted a taking. The owner of property destroyed to promote the war effort has, therefore, no right to compensation, though the owner of property taken for use in the same war effort must be reimbursed in full. [71]

One cannot confidently draw a clear line between regulation and taking on the basis of the Supreme Court's decisions, because they are far from models of clarity. Some threads, however, do stand out. The Court has moved from the basically conceptual approach reflected in *Mugler* and emphasizing appropriation of proprietary interest, physical invasion, and noxious use, to some more flexible standard, as found in *Pennsylvania Coal Co.* and *Goldblatt*. [72] In the absence of physical invasion a number of factors seem to be relevant to the decision whether use can be prohibited without compensation. Is the use one which is considered immoral or whose legal prohibition might reasonably have been expected? The person who runs a house of prostitution or a brewery is not likely to challenge a prohibition successfully even if economic loss is virtually total. How great a threat does the use pose to the community? Apparently the greater the danger, the more likely the prohibition will be upheld even if its effect is severe. [73] How great is the economic deprivation suffered by the property owner? If the use is not immoral, if resources were committed to that use by a person who had no reason to suppose it was inconsistent with the public interest, if the public interest in prohibiting the use is not exceptional, then the owner may be entitled to continue to engage in the use or be compensated if the magnitude of his loss from prohibition would be very great. The destruction cases suggest that a great danger will justify total loss to the property owner. It is not clear why the strength of society's interest in diminishing the value of private property should determine whether the individual or society should bear the loss. The questions whether society should destroy something and whether the loss should be borne by the individual may obviously yield different answers, particularly if the individual is guilty neither of immorality nor lack of reasonable foresight, as in *Miller v. Schoene* and *United States v. Caltex, Inc.*

If the purpose of a regulation is simply to make the exercise of the eminent domain power at some later date less expensive to the state, then anything more than a slight diminution in value would be compensable. Land cannot be zoned for a public park, markedly reduced in value, and then condemned for the lowered value.[74] The rule is different in most states, however, if a municipality plats routes for future roads, and either forbids the subsequent erection of buildings on that particular land or refuses to compensate for buildings that are erected after the date of platting.[75] In these cases, the ordinance does not undermine one's use of a whole tract of land, and the owner may be indirectly compensated by easy access to the street when, and if, it is built.

The application of these principles and some of the problems raised can be illustrated by two classes of cases. Many states have imposed an affirmative duty on railroads to construct bridges or underpasses where tracks cross public roads, and to bear all or part of the cost. This imposition has generally been considered a regulation of the use of property, on the theory that the railroad has introduced the danger and cannot complain about being required to eliminate it.[76] It is true that the danger would not exist absent the railroad but it is equally true that it would not exist absent increased motor traffic. Unless the shift in circumstances was predictable at the time of the railroad's construction, it would seem more accurate to say that the danger is created by changing social conditions rather than by the railroad. As in the cases of the brickmaker and cedar tree owners, however, the Supreme Court has not inquired into reasonable expectations at the time of construction.[77]

Another kind of special duty is often placed on land developers. They are required to set aside land for streets, to build the streets, and, sometimes, to dedicate them to the public. [78] Those impositions have been uniformly upheld, as have exactions for sewers, water mains, and sidewalks, on the theory that the need for the streets is generated by the owner's use of his land. [79] In addition, those to whom the owner sells are the persons who benefit in a direct way from the streets. [80] Some courts have been more hesitant to apply these theories to land exactions for schools or playgrounds. [81] In one leading case the Court reasoned that the needs for recreational and education facilities were not "specifically and uniquely attributable to the intended subdivision;"[82] but a more recent decision, by New York's highest court, found exactions appropriate for park purposes even if it could not be established that the need for facilities was solely attributable to the developer's activities. [83] Two commentators have argued convincingly that careful cost accounting allows a relatively accurate assessment of the added burden placed on the whole community by specific subdivision development and that formulas for fair exactions can be worked out. [84] It seems relatively safe to predict a long-term trend toward imposition upon the developers of large tracts of private property of a duty to satisfy public needs.

Very closely related to such duties are special tax assessments. Indeed one theory for sustaining these exactions is as a legitimate exercise of the taxing power. [85] General taxes are permissible exercises of government power and not "takings of property" within the meaning of the fifth amendment, but were there no limit on special assessments, the just compensation restriction on the government's power of eminent domain could be evaded. Assessments against particular property for public projects will be sustained only if the property stands to benefit in some special way, [86] and the benefit is in proportion to the assessment, [87] though wide discretion is left to the legislature in making these determinations. [88]

The central point to be gathered from the courts' treatment of the police power and the taxing power [89] is that the government has powerful tools to assure use of private property that is consonant with the public interest short of exercising the power of eminent domain.

Activity Affecting the Value of Property. In many circumstances the value of property is diminished by government action that is neither simple appropriation nor regulation. Often the injury is too incidental to give rise to any sort of legal claim. Sometimes the injury creates liability in tort, occasionally it constitutes a taking. [90]

In 1872 the Supreme Court held that a property owner was entitled to compensation after his land had been flooded by water from a lake whose level had been raised by a state-authorized dam. Subsequently, the Court allowed recovery to a property owner injured by a railroad tunnel exhaust fan blowing directly on his house, although it said persons owning land near railroads cannot recover when the value of their property is diminished by the injuries ordinarily incident to railroad operation. [91] In more recent and more significant cases the Court has decided that a taking occurs when the value of property is seriously diminished by low flying aircraft, landing or taking off in a line of flight over complainant's land. [92] What is "taken" in these cases is an air easement which subtracts from the full enjoyment and use of the land owner. [93] The lower courts have refused to grant the same relief to plaintiffs whose land is not in the path of flight, [94] relying on the rather artificial distinction that no physical invasion has occured.

Approximately half the state constitutions require just compensation when property is taken or damaged for public use. The "or damaged" language was added to allow recovery in cases in which a strict interpretation of the elements of a taking would lead to a denial of compensation. [95] But extension of the meaning of "taking" by judicial decision has in a number of other states led to equally liberal rules for recovery, sometimes in circumstances in which an "invasion" in any ordinary sense is hard to find. Almost invariably the property owner must show not only damage of a relatively permanent nature, but some special damage that distinguishes him from other property holders. [96] If, for example, a road is blocked, one whose access to his land is rendered less convenient has no right to compensation, but one whose access is cut off may recover. [97]

3. Generalizing Theories Suggested by Scholars

As the preceding discussion indicates, the courts have not

developed consistent principles for distinguishing between takings and exercises of government power that do not require compensation for inured parties. Professor Joseph Sax, after exposing the weakness of all the existing approaches as general rules of decision, suggests that the proper policy is to require compensation when the government enhances its resource position in its enterprise capacity, as when it acquires land, but to refuse compensation when the government mediates between private parties, as when it prohibits a use offensive to other property owners. [98] Under this approach the cedar tree owners of *Miller v. Schoene* [99] would not recover because the beneficiaries were private apple growers but the oil company whose facilities were destroyed in wartime [100] would recover because destruction directly helped the government as army. This rule, Sax asserts, would limit the risk of discrimination and the possibility of excessive government zeal, both higher when the government acts to benefit its own position, and would also reduce the scope of risks to which property owners are exposed.

There are some problems with this approach, [101] apart from its failure to explain why a private person rather than society should bear the loss for the destruction of property in the interest of his neighbors. It does not provide a basis for determining how great an injury must be to be compensable when the government as enterprise is doing the harm. More serious, perhaps, it fails to take into account, at least sufficiently, the extent to which "government" may be captured by a part of the community and reflect partisan interest rather than serve as an "objective" adjuster of private interests for the general good. This is a particular danger at the local level where much regulation of property takes place. Insofar as it does occur, the risk of discrimination and excessive zeal may be as serious when the government "mediates" as when it operates as enterprise.

A less simple, but in the author's view, more satisfactory theory is developed by Professor Frank Michelman. [102] He begins with principles of "fairness" and "utility" and tries to assess in what kinds of circumstances compensation should be given. Agreeing with David Hume that insecurity of expectation caused by instability of possession is destructive of economic effort and a stable social order, he says that from a utilitarian point of view compensation should be granted when demoralization costs—the costs of insecurity—exceed settlement costs; that is, the costs to society of providing compensation, including not only the compensation itself but the costs inherent in a system to determine appropriate compensation. Adopting John Rawls' thought that justice is fairness and that fairness requires equal treatment except when the person subjected to inequality should be able to see that the social arrangement, including the inequality, are more conducive to his long-run prospects than would be strict equality, Professor Michelman argues that in terms of fairness "A decision not to compensate is not unfair as long as the disappointed claimant ought to be able to appreciate how such decisions might fit into a consistent practice which holds forth a lesser long-run risk to people like him than would any consistent practice which is naturally suggested by the opposite position."

Under either of these standards all of the central factors relied on in particular decisions have some relevance. Cases of physical invasion, great loss in value, the doubtfulness of public gain, the presence of special damage, the sense that no "evil" has been created by the party harmed, are cases in which the failure to compensate will create a greater sense of insecurity among property owners and make a denial of compensation seem less "fair," under the standard set out above, than when these elements are absent. Not one of these factors, however, Professor Michelman contends convincingly, provides the key tool for analysis of every kind of case. The search for some central judicial principle for "taking" cases is, of necessity, doomed to failure. Given the inherent limitations on judicial decision-making, including restricted power to find facts and the need for "principled" decisions, judges are less able than legislatures to weigh all the factors of relevance in particular kinds of cases. A greater part of the burden for determining when compensation is to be provided should be shifted, Professor Michelman concludes, away from the judiciary to the legislative bodies.

4. The Meaning of "Public Use"

The question of what purposes support the exercise of the power of eminent domain is answered in a general way by the Constitutional phrase concerning taking of property "for public use" (U.S. Constitution, Amendment V). Though the federal Constitution does not directly forbid expropriation for private purposes, such as a house for a friend of the President, the language of the fifth amendment, "nor shall private property be taken for public use, without just compensation," precludes by implication use of the power to condemn property for any but public purposes. This limitation is consistent with the accepted premise, reflected in the writings of Grotius and Blackstone among others, that to be legitimate expropriation must be for the public good. The "public use" requirement of the fifth amendment has been held applicable to the states through the fourteenth amendment. [103] Each of the states has its own constitutional "public use" limitation, explicit or implicit, and some of the state constitutions spell out in considerable detail the sorts of purposes that justify condemnation.

Unlike the questions of whether a specific exercise of the power of eminent domain is wise or necessary, questions largely left to the judgement of the political branches, [104] the issue of whether a use is public or not is a judicial one, and can be raised by an individual challenging the validity of the condemnation of his property. [105] Historical expansion of the meaning of "public use," however, has rendered this apparent protection illusory, at least under federal law.

Some cases in the nineteenth century suggested that "public use" required actual use by the public, [106] and that the constitutional standard was not met simply by a purpose to benefit the public. That this view was more restrictive than historical practice is evidenced by the use of expropriation as far back as the prerevolutionary period to condemn land flooded by the structures of private mill owners. The "Mill Acts" permitting the mill owners to build the structures and providing for condemnation of flooded land promoted the public good but involved no actual use by the public. [107]

The Supreme Court has in this century rejected use by the public as too narrow a criterion. [108] In 1905, when faced with an expropriation in Utah of a right of way across the land of a private person for the purpose of conveying water to the land of a private mine owner, the Court sustained the condemnation, emphasizing the importance of considering the peculiar conditions of each case and deferring to the judgment of the state Supreme Court that there was a strong public interest in the conveyance of scarce water resources to the land of persons without their own supply. [109] In more recent cases, the Supreme Court's approach has

266

been much broader, and indeed a virtual rejection of the idea that public purpose is a judicial question. In *United States ex. rel. T.V.A. v. Welch*,[110] the Tennessee Valley Authority, an authority of the federal government, condemned land cut off from access to highways by a government reservoir. Though the land was not needed for any public purpose, the alternative of building a road to restore access was deemed more expensive than expropriating the land itself. The Court said that when Congress has authorized a condemnation, "its decision is entitled to deference until it is shown to involve an impossibility."[111] In *Berman v. Parker*,[112] complainant's property had been condemned as part of a slum clearance project. It did not itself contain slums,[113] but the District of Columbia had decided that the private developer, who was to develop the area cleared of slums according to an approved plan, could put the entire area to better use if some land in addition to that with slums was condemned. The Court upheld the condemnation because, "Subject to specific constitutional limitations, when the legislature has spoken, the public interest has been declared in terms well-nigh conclusive."

This sort of urban development is not unusual. One of the more striking instances is the condemnation of highly valuable real estate in downtown New York City by the Port of New York Authority, a public (but not municipal) corporation, for the construction of a $350 million World Trade Center, composed of twin 110-story office buildings whose space would be rented for government offices and also by private lessees having some connection with foreign trade. This plan was approved by the highest court in New York and the Supreme Court denied review.[114]

An argument can be made that a restrictive definition of "public use" would serve as some sort of check on abuse of the power of eminent domain. But the argument for considerable flexibility on the part of the government is in this writer's view much stronger. The need for thorough land use planning in urban areas is becoming increasingly plain and population growth will intensify the need that already exists. Government must be able to try a variety of approaches to planning, relying on a mixture of public ownership and private enterprise. So long as a reasonable judgment of public benefit is made, the power of condemnation should be at its disposal in promoting that benefit.

While some states retain stricter definitions of public use than

267

the federal one, there can be little doubt that the trend is toward greater liberality, and that the "public use" restraint as embodied in judicial decision will cease to be a significant limitation on legislative or executive judgment.

IV. Compensation

1. The Right to Just Compensation

The fifth amendment of the Federal Constitution conditions exercise of the power of eminent domain upon the payment of "just compensation." The fourteenth amendment makes this restriction applicable against the states; [115] in addition, each state has its own just compensation requirement, imposed by the state constitution or, in the case of two states, by judicial decision. [116] A state may, and many states do, have a more generous standard of just compensation than the federal one. [117]

The judiciary decides what compensation is required by the Constitution. In 1893, the Supreme Court said:

> The legislature may determine what private property is needed for public purposes . . . but when the taking has been ordered, then the question of compensation is judicial. It does not rest with the public . . . through Congress . . . to say what compensation shall be paid, or even what shall be the rule of compensation. The Constitution has declared that just compensation shall be paid, and the ascertainment of that is a judicial inquiry. [118]

This rule does not preclude Congress from giving more compensation than is constitutionally required. Nor does it foreclose the setting of compensation by agreement between the state and the condemnee. But it does mean that anyone who is being offered less than the Constitution requires and is willing to litigate the matter can obtain judicial redress.

Just compensation has always been held to mean full and effective compensation. [119] It has been held by courts passing on the question to mean prompt payment in cash. In 1795, a United States Circuit Court stated that "No compensation can be made except in money," [120] and in later cases state courts have struck down schemes to compensate in the form of land [121] or stocks and bonds. [122] While a property owner may consent to accept some

268

form of deferred compensation in lieu of cash, he cannot be compelled to do so. [123]

Though just compensation is "full," not every economic loss suffered by a condemnee is indemnified. The question of whether a particular interest is compensable is related to the problem already considered of what constitutes a taking. Both require the drawing of lines between expectations that can be destroyed without compensation and those for which the government must pay, and in some cases the underlying considerations may be the same. One illustration of such a relationship is a comparison of two cases involving the so-called "navigation servitude." [124]

In *United States v. Willow River Power Company,* [125] a government dam raised the level of water of navigable river, reducing the operating head of water for a power company's hydroelectric plant, located upstream from the dam. Although recognizing that the company had an economic interest in keeping the river at the lower level, the Supreme Court held that there is a dominant public interest in navigation and that no one has a legally protectable interest against the government's changing the level of a navigable stream. Since the company had no property right in the level of water, there had been no "taking of property." *United States v. Twin City Power Company* [126] involved the condemnation of land, part of the economic value of which derived from the expectancy that the government would approve a private hydroelectric power project. The Supreme Court rejected the argument that compensation should include the power site value of the land because the government has a dominant servitude in navigable water and "to pay for this water-power value would be to create private claims in the public domain." [127] In both *Willow River* and *Twin City Power,* the decision is that an economic expectation is noncompensable because of an over-riding government interest in navigable waters.

2. The Problem of Valuation

The more general problem in regard to "full" compensation is the question of from what perspective "fullness" is to be judged. There is no necessary identity between value to the condemnor, value to the condemnee, and market value. Although the Supreme Court has said that the owner is "entitled to the full money equivalent of the property taken and thereby to be put in as good a position pecuniarily as it would have occupied if its property had not been taken,"[129] the basic standard for just compensation in the federal courts is "fair market value."

In a relatively early case, the Court held:

> In determining the value of land appropriated for public purposes, the same considerations are to be regarded as in a sale of property between private parties. The inquiry in such cases must be what is the property worth in the market, viewed . . . with reference to the uses to which it is plainly adapted . . .[130]

Market value is the price that would be set between a willing seller and a willing buyer and takes into account neither the special value of particular property for the condemnor nor the condemnee's particular need for or attachment to that property.[131] The owner's loss of "idiosyncratic values" has been called a burden of common citizenship.[132]

Market value is easy to ascertain if the thing condemned is a commodity bought and sold on the open market,[133] but the problem is more difficult when anything unique, and this includes most real estate, is taken. The shape, quality, and location of a particular piece of land may cause it to vary considerably in value from another plot of the same size. In making the individualized inquiry required, a court must look not only at the present use of the land but at other more profitable uses that would effect market value.[134] This includes uses to which the land could be put only in combination with other parcels, but such uses will not be considered unless the owner shows a fair probability that combination would have occurred in the reasonably near future.[135]

The market value standard as applied by the federal courts excludes "incidental" or "consequential" damages. Among these are loss of profits, damage to goodwill, and the expense of relocation.[136] The rule has been justified on the ground that "that which is taken or damaged is the group of rights which the . . . owner exercises in his dominion of the physical thing, and . . . damage to those rights of ownership does not include losses to his business . . ."[137] Sometimes courts have said that incidental damages are too remote and speculative.[138]

Almost by definition the market value standard as interpreted by the federal courts gives to the condemnee less than the property is worth to him, unless he is already seeking to sell it. An owner may always sell his property; his very failure to do so indicates that its worth to him is greater than what he could get for it. The difference between a hypothetical market value and the value of property to the condemnee is likely to be particularly great if incidental damages are a significant proportion of total value.

It is easy to understand why courts do not evaluate an owner's personal "attachment" to his property; objective measurement is simply impossible. It may also be that consequential damages are more difficult to assess or more speculative than "market value" as now interpreted, but items such as removal costs are ordinarily no more difficult to estimate than other valuations made by judicial institutions. If the aim is really to indemnify the owner for his loss, allowance of provable items of consequential damage should not be too great a burden to impose upon courts. That non-compensability works hardship on businessmen, particularly small businessmen, [139] is indicated by a Congressional study of condemnation in Southwest Washington, D.C. [140] Of over two hundred businesses displaced, approximately 40 per cent were discontinued; only 10 per cent of the corporate businesses but over 60 per cent of the proprietorships were discontinued. Many of the others had marked losses of income. [141]

The harshness of the market value standard has been moderated in a number of ways. A number of state decisions, interpreting either state constitutions or statutes, have allowed items of incidental damage. [142] Some state statutes have specifically provided relief for incidental losses. [143] Pennsylvania has enacted a law allowing reimbursement for removal and re-installation of equipment and fixtures, for other moving expenses and certain business losses. [144] The constitution proposed for adoption in New York but rejected by the voters on other grounds contained a guarantee that compensation would include the fair value of good will of businesses, as defined by the legislature. Particular federal legislation now gives limited relief; [145] a more comprehensive federal law was proposed in 1965 but not adopted. [146]

Courts generally applying the strict "fair market value" standard have recognized that in certain kinds of cases it is inappropriate. For instance, the Supreme Court has granted more liberal recovery for takings of short duration. In *United States v. General Motors Corporation,* [147] it reviewed the condemnation of a one-year term from a tenant with a twenty-year lease. Affirming a decision that items of actual loss, including removal costs, should be considered, the Court stated that just compensation in such a case required an estimate of the "market" price that would be agreed upon by a tenant and a sub-lessee in these unusual circumstances. Since the tenant would be highly unlikely to sublease the premises at a rate that did not cover removal and storage costs as well as ordinary rental value, the decision in effect allowed recovery for incidental damages. The Supreme Court reached a similar result in *Kimball Laundry Co. v. United States* in the case of condemnation for temporary use of the laundry. The Court reasoned that going concern value can usually be transferred to another location if the taking is permanent but the investment of an owner of a business temporarily displaced remains bound in the reversion of the property. Thus compensation for going concern value is required in the latter instance. [148] One commentator has approved the exception to the market value standard in temporary taking cases because " . . . market price becomes meaningless when most people will not sell. It is not fair to make one owner sell at a price when it is highly unlikely that any owner would sell at such a price."[149] Others argue that *General Motors* and *Kimball* are not logically distinguishable from, and therefore should be extended to, situations in which a permanent interest is taken. [150] Thus far the Supreme Court has been unwilling to do that.

In some circumstances, the nature of the property taken either precludes assessment of market value or renders it a patently unfair test. Highly specialized structures such as churches may have little "market" value in the ordinary sense. Whether the courts hypothesize a "buyer" who wants the property for the same use as the owner [151] or explicitly discard market value as the criterion, [152] in such cases they in fact attempt to ascertain the value of the property to the owner. Bridges, schools, or other public facilities which are condemned may have no "market" value. [153] Or their value in the market may be insufficient to reimburse the government for replacing them. In these cases, when replacement of existing facilities is "necessary," a substitute facility doctrine is applied, under which what the condemnee receives is determined by the amount required to finance a replacement. [154]

Valuing public utilities that are condemned also involves particular difficulties. [155] When the utility is a monopoly and its market value is unclear, great weight will be given to replacement cost less depreciation. Part of the court's task, if the business itself is appropriated, is to assess the value of the utility's intangible assets, its "going concern value." In a 1966 New York case [156] the state's highest court had to pass on the relevance of government policy as it affected expected income and therefore going concern value. New York City condemned the properties of certain privately-owned bus companies operating under city franchises. In the years prior to expropriation the companies had not flourished because the fare had been held by the city to fifteen cents per ride. The companies had made no legal challenge to this fare, in part because their right to any higher fare was doubtful, and in part because they competed with city-owned lines unlikely to have their fare raised. Quite clearly, the actual value of the bus companies as going concerns was sharply reduced for a potential buyer if the realistic prospect was one of unprofitable operation. A bare majority of the seven-judge court held that going concern value should be calculated on the assumption of a reasonable return, since such a return is an unspoken promise of any franchise agreement. The dissent noted that the fare had been kept low for reasons unrelated to any plan to expropriate. It found the claim of a right to a higher fare groundless and questioned whether an increased fare for the private lines would, in view of the competition of city lines, have enhanced the companies' returns. [157]

In an even more recent case [158] the Court of Appeals had to decide upon the appropriate compensation for a dismally unprofitable private company that ran a railroad under the Hudson River to downtown New York City. The physical assets, primarily the tunnel, and the business itself were of little commercial value, but the railroad did perform an important public service. The Port Authority, a government entity, intended to use the tunnels to run a railroad, and it would have cost it a great deal to build new tunnels. The Court of Appeals determined that this special situation required an approach different from that generally followed, and approved an award greater than the value of the business for the condemnee and less than its value for the government.

Another kind of situation in which the "market value" of what is

273

taken is not the sole standard for compensation occurs when the value of adjoining land owned by the same person is affected by the condemnation. If the parcels have been put to an integrated use and the value of the adjoining tract is reduced, the condemnee receives "severance damages" in addition to the value of the land actually taken. [159] If the value is increased, the award may be diminished by a set-off of benefits. [160] Severance damages and set-off of benefits seem appropriate when the condemnee suffers or gains in a special way—as when his remaining land is so small it can be put to no profitable use, or when he receives a particular benefit not enjoyed by other landowners. There is an apparent inconsistency in providing recovery or set-off only for the person whose property was taken when the result of the state taking has led to changes in value for all the land in the community. Other landowners are not paid for identical consequential damages and are free to enjoy any enhancement in value caused by proximity to the new public project. The resolution of this inconsistency lies, in this writer's view, in the approach suggested by Professor Michelman. Courts cannot attempt to assess every change in value caused by government condemnation. When, however, an actual condemnee with adjoining land is before the court, the added effort in assessing the total impact on him is slight.

The value that concerns courts in condemnation cases is value at the "time of taking." [161] Changes in value before this time caused by the government's decision to condemn property are, however, sometimes disregarded. No rule has been held compelled by the Constitution, so considerable variance exists among the states. Federal law, and that of most states, excludes from calculations of value enhancement or diminution that results from the government's commitment [162] to a project that will probably involve condemnation of complainant's land. [163] If, for example, the government commits itself to building a dam but initially expropriates only part of the necessary land, an owner whose parcel is later condemned cannot recover for an increase in value caused by the expectancy of its being condemned. [164] If, on the other hand, land subsequently condemned but not contemplated in the original commitment has risen in value only because of its expected proximity to a government project, the condemnor must pay for this enhancement. [165]

In the determination of the value of particular property, courts have developed complicated rules of evidence. These are only summarily touched here. The evidence most heavily relied on is the opinion of qualified witnesses. [166] Other rules as to admissibility of offered proof vary. Actual sales of similar property in the neighborhood are usually considered [167] but mere offers to buy even for the property being condemned are generally not.[168] The assessed valuations of tax officials are generally not admissible in evidence, but the owner's statement of value on tax returns are admitted against him. [169] If the property is rented, income from the rent is considered,[170] but business profits are usually not,[171] on the theory that they provide little evidence of the value of the real property involved. When property has been improved by structures, courts will ordinarily receive evidence on the cost of reproduction. [172]

3. Rights of Third Parties

Special problems of valuation arise when what is condemned is divided into interests held by more than one person, for instance if property is leased or mortgaged. If only the leasehold interest is condemned, the solution is relatively simple. The lessee receives the fair market value of his lease if his obligation to continue paying the lessor is not terminated by the condemnation. [173] If that obligation is terminated, then the lessee would receive the difference between the fair market value and the rental he has been paying. [174] Thus, if the market value of the lease he has is greater than the reserved rental, the lessee would not be deprived of the benefit of his advantageous lease. If the market value is the same as or less than the reserved rental, the lessee would get nothing. [175] In the latter instance, he would in effect be relieved of a disadvantageous lease at the expense of the condemnor.

More complex difficulties occur when the condemnor takes a proprietary interest that is subject to a leasehold. The market value of the property as a whole may vary from the value of its component interests. If a lessor has given a long-term lease at twice the rent he could obtain, the value of his interest is much greater than the value of the unencumbered property. [176] The general approach, at least in theory, has been to value property as if it were unencumbered and then apportion the award. [177] Many courts, however, have avoided the difficulty this procedure poses for the lessor with a highly advantageous lease, either by explicitly considering continuance of the favorable lease as a "possible use" of the property, or by in fact valuing the property with an eye toward the terms of the lease.[178]

When an unencumbered property with a long-term lease has been valued, courts first value the lessor's interest, normally by treating it as a secured right to a perpetual annuity equal to the yearly reserved rental. This approach is used, rather than a capitalization of the expected income from the lease and the expected value of the reversionary interest at the end of the lease, because valuation of the reversionary interest is considered too speculative. If market value of the lessee's interest is in excess of the reserved rental, the award to the lessor will not exhaust the compensation, and the lessee receives what remains.[179] In the case of a short-term lease, the lessee's interest is first valued and the remainder awarded to the lessor.[180]

Like a lease, a mortgage does not directly affect the valuation of property to be condemned, although as a relevant financial transaction it may be evidence of the property's worth.[181] If there is a complete taking of mortgaged property apportionment of an award between the mortgagor and mortgagee is simple. If the award is less than the amount due on the mortgage, the mortgagee receives it all. If the award is more than the amount due the mortgagee is entitled to that amount and the mortgagor receives what is left. Courts in various jurisdictions differ on the appropriate apportionment if only a part of mortgaged property is taken. Some hold that the mortgagee has a claim on the award up to the entire amount due; others say that he must first exhaust all possibilities of receiving the amount from the remainder area; still others assert that he is entitled to only as much of the award as is required to compensate him for his interest in the part taken.

V. Expropriation Procedure

To some extent the Constitutional guarantees already discussed prescribe minimum checks against arbitrary action throughout the nation. Within these broad guarantees of due process of law, public purpose, and just compensation, however, there is a surprising amount of variety in the procedure for governmental takings—between federal and state action, among the different

276

states, and even within one state among various public or semipublic agencies. This section accordingly concentrates on the procedures followed in one state—New York—with some observations on the variations in other jurisdictions.

1. The Decision to Expropriate

The process of condemnation of a particular piece of land commences with a decision that the land is needed for public use. This decision can be made by the federal or state legislature, but usually it will be made by a public agency, an organ of municipal government, or a corporation to which the authority to expropriate has been delegated. The delegation may be either for a specific project [182] or to enable a public or quasi-public agency to carry out its general functions over a continuing period of time. [183]

The federal Constitution requires no hearing for affected property owners over this initial decision to condemn, since this decision is considered essentially legislative or administrative. [184] However, public hearings commonly precede acts of state legislatures, and municipalities and other bodies with the power to expropriate are often compelled to provide public hearings before specific projects are approved. [185] Some states even require that owners of property to be affected be given personal notice and an opportunity to be heard before the decision-making body. [186]

2. The Scope of Judicial Review

Once the decision to expropriate particular property is made, the owner has as a matter of federal Constitutional law the right to a judicial hearing on whether the purpose for which the property is taken is a public use [187] and on whether he is being afforded just compensation. [188] Many states, by constitution, statute, or judicial decision, allow property owners to litigate other issues as well, such as whether the agency was within its authority to expropriate. If, for instance, a highway commission with authority only to take "underdeveloped land" for "highway purposes" decided to take land for a parking lot, an owner might claim that his land was "developed" or that a parking lot is not a "highway purpose." [189] Similarly, in most states, the property owner can ask the court to determine whether the expropriating authority followed specified procedures in making its decision, or whether the condemnation of the particular property was necessary to accomplish the purpose.[190]

The stage of the condemnation proceeding at which owners are given the opportunity for a judicial hearing varies. The two basic types of procedure are the so-called "judicial method" and the so-called "administrative method."[191] In the former, a taking can be effectuated only upon court order, issued after the condemnor has instituted a court proceeding and the owner has had a chance to appear. In the latter, title may rest in the condemnor after a nonjudicial proceeding at which the owner may or may not have had an opportunity to appear. If the owner wishes to challenge the legality of the taking or have compensation determined by a court, he must initiate judicial proceedings.

3. The Judicial Method

New York's general condemnation law [192] is an example of the judicial method.[193] Most of the state's public agencies, as well as public utilities and other corporations granted the power of eminent domain, follow the procedure outlined there.

The Petition. The expropriating agency must file a petition in the county court or supreme court [194] of the county in which the property is located. The petition, like the Declaration of Public Utility in the Latin American countries, contains a description of the property, the proposed use, the necessity for condemning the particular property, the condemnor's authority and its adherence to proper procedures, the name and addresses of known owners, a statement that the condemnor has been unable to agree with the owner on purchase of the property, [195] and a request that the court adjudge the property required for public use and that a tribunal be set up to ascertain appropriate compensation. [196]

When the petition is filed the expropriating agency must give adequate notice of the proceedings. As a matter of Constitutional interpretation this notice must extend to all parties known to have an interest in the property, giving them an opportunity to be present and submit evidence at the judicial proceeding. [197]

Under the New York law interested parties must be served with a copy of the petition at least eight days before judicial proceedings;[198] ordinarily service is by personal delivery but if that is unsuccessful or impossible, service by mail or even publication may be used.[199] Once notified, the owner may file an answer to the petition challenging any of its allegations. After the answer, the court, or a referee appointed by it,[200] will try the disputed issues other than the question of compensation, thus avoiding that difficult determination until it is clear that the condemnation is permissible.[201] There is no right to trial by jury of these issues. The burden of persuasion is on the expropriating agency to establish the truth of the matter alleged in the petition.[202] If the expropriating agency fails to establish the validity of the condemnation, the court will dismiss the petition;[203] this dismissal is a final judgment and appealable.[204] If the expropriating agency prevails, the court enters an order that the property is necessary for a public use and may be taken upon determination and payment of just compensation.[205] Unlike the dismissal, this order is not considered "final" and the property owner cannot appeal on the issues decided until after the determination of compensation.[206]

Appraisal. The federal Constitution requires that proceedings to determine compensation be fair and that owners be given an opportunity to present evidence and be heard on the question of value.[207] New York's general condemnation law, like that of most states, provides for a court-appointed panel of commissioners or appraisers to determine compensation.[208] When the requested expropriation has been found to be proper, the court appoints three "disinterested freeholders" to ascertain the compensable value of the property.[209] The commissioners, like a court, have the power to subpoena witnesses and compel testimony. Interested parties appear before the commissioners and present evidence on the property's value.[210] But commissioners are not restricted to the written record; they also view the property and rely on their first-hand observations.[211] In reaching a decision, the commissioners must make judgments of both law and fact, measuring the owner's losses against applicable legal principles. Their decision is incorporated in a report which, with the record of testimony, is submitted to the court.[212] Before the report is confirmed, parties have an opportunity to appear in court and offer objections to it. The court may set aside a report "for irregularity, or for error of law in the proceedings, or upon the ground that the award is excessive or insufficient." [213] As in all states, a clear error concerning the law of just compensation will lead to a refusal to confirm, [214] but review of the report's conformity with the evidence presented is relatively narrow. [215] Though assessments of compensation have occasionally been set aside as unsupported by the evidence, [216] this will be done only when the error is obvious and shocks the sense of justice. [217] If a report is set aside the court orders a new hearing by the same or a different group of commissioners. [218] It has been held in New York that the court lacks the power to modify a report, but can only confirm or dismiss it. [219] The practice in other states varies on this point. [220]

Appeal. When a report is confirmed, the court issues a final order directing payment of the determined amount of compensation and providing that upon such payment, the condemnor shall be entitled to possession of the condemned property for the stipulated public use. [221]

Upon issuance of an order confirming the report of the commissioners, the condemnor has three alternatives. It may pay the assessed compensation to the owner, in which case it becomes entitled to possession. [222] If the condemnor thinks the award of compensation is excessive, it may appeal to a higher court, in the first instance the Appellate Division of the Supreme Court. [223] The scope of that court's review of the order of confirmation resembles that of the trial court reviewing the commissioners' report. [224] If it holds the judgment below to be in error, the court can direct a new appraisal by the same or new commissioners. [225] Appeal from the Appellate Division to the Court of Appeals is possible, but that court will reverse the decision below only if it is based on an erroneous theory of law. [226] If the condemnor is dissatisfied with the trial court's award or has, in the period since initiating the condemnation process, decided not to take particular property, it may seek to discontinue the proceedings. [227] New York, like a number of other states, gives the courts discretion whether or not to grant a discontinuance. [228] Discontinuance will not be granted where it is believed that the condemnor's abandonment is not being made in good faith but is instead being made with the intention of re-instituting a condemnation proceeding in the future when the price may be more favorable. If the motion is granted, the condemnor must pay the owner's cost and expenses; other conditions, such as a bar on subsequent condemnation of the property, may be imposed to protect the owner's interests. [229]

A property owner may also appeal from confirmation of the commissioners' report, raising any issues regarding the validity of the condemnation as well as the adequacy of compensation. He cannot, however, postpone the taking of his property by filing an appeal. The court will not halt transfer of possession, though it may stay the condemnor from proceeding with the intended use until a decision is rendered. If an appeal by the owner is pending, he gets no compensation, even though he has had to surrender possession. Thus the owner who considers that he has been unfairly treated is faced with the dilemma common in litigation. He can accept the award and get paid immediately, or forego payment until the appeal is decided—which may well be years later.

If the owner is satisfied with the award and is not promptly compensated, he may sue on the judgment to compel payment. The compensation award in such case is treated like a money judgment in an ordinary civil suit. [230]

In summary, the "judicial method" of condemnation, as formulated, gives an owner an adequate opportunity to contest the validity of a condemnation and to be assured of fair compensation before his property is taken. If disappointed, he may seek vindication of his rights before appellate courts, though he cannot, at that point, delay the transfer of possession.

"Quick-Take" Statutes. New York, like many other states, has a special procedure that displays somewhat less solicitude for the rights of property owners but retains the requirement of a court order. This provides for so-called "quick taking." Upon a showing that the public interest will be prejudiced by delay, the court, at any time during expropriation proceedings, may allow the condemnor temporarily to enter the property and put it to the desired public use. [231] Under this procedure the owner loses possession of the property before a full hearing on the issues or receipt of compensation. [232] This procedure contains important safeguards against abuse. Entry prior to an award will be allowed only if the court is convinced that the use is "public" and that the need for immediate action is clear; [233] and the condemnor must post a bond in an amount stipulated by the court to satisfy the amount of compensation finally awarded. [234] Should the condemnor subsequently abandon his suit, the owner will be paid from the bond for the temporary use of his property for any damage he has suffered and for his costs and expenses in the proceeding.

4. The Administrative Method

In New York, the administrative method for condemnation is used in numerous special statutes that carve out exceptions to the general condemnation law. One of the most significant of these is the Highway Law, which governs condemnations by the state for highway purposes. [235] Under it, "appropriations" may be effected summarily, with notice to the property owner only after title has been vested in the state.

The State Superintendent of Public Works, who decides on the sites for new roads, makes the initial decision to condemn. He may not proceed, however, until he receives the approval of the Boards of Supervisors, the governing legislative bodies of the counties through which the road is to pass. [236] The Boards may, but need not, conduct public hearings on the proposed condemnation, for which notice is required for "persons deemed interested in the project." Once approval is obtained, the Superintendent may have title vested in the state simply by filing a detailed map and description of the desired properties with appropriate public officers. [237] Only at this point must a "notice of appropriation" be given to persons with an interest in the property. [238] Having fulfilled these administrative steps the state may take possession of the property. [239] If the owner resists, the Superintendent may proceed in the same way as a landlord against a tenant holding over illegally. [240] In these proceedings, the owner may challenge the legality of the taking, [241] but not the amount of compensation. Only after appropriation of his property may the owner obtain judicial determination of compensation. If agreement on an amount is not reached between the state and the owner, he may sue for compensation in the Court of Claims. [242] That court's judgment may be appealed to higher courts in the same manner as an ordinary legal action. [243]

5. "Inverse" Condemnation

There are generally no special procedural remedies for the person who claims that his property has been "taken" by a government act other than through formal condemnation, though it is clear that he is entitled to a judicial hearing on that Constitutional claim. If the government act is framed as a regulation, such as a zoning law, or a legitimate tax, the offended person may get into court by refusing to obey the government's command—in which case the government will seek enforcement by the application of ordinary civil or criminal sanctions. Or he may apply for affirmative relief, most commonly an injunction or declaratory judgment against enforcement. When the government does not try to compel the property owner to do anything but engages in activity that reduces the value of his property, for example, as in cases growing out of complaints by property owners that low-flying planes have reduced the value of their land and thus resulted in a taking, [244] or as in flooding cases, the owner may sue under provisions of federal or state law allowing suits against the government.

6. The Law in Practice

Analysis of the substantive and procedural rules governing eminent domain suggests some harshness in the standards for compensation, but nevertheless reveals a system that gives adequate assurance that the condemnee will obtain what is due him. Though empirical evidence is limited, it indicates that only with important modifications does this theoretical model accurately describe what ordinarily happens. Lewis Orgel, [245] probably the outstanding authority on valuation, asserts that judges frequently take into account the hardships faced by condemnees and the substantial resources of the government and in practice inflate "market value" so that the actual award is more than a strict application of the relevant rules would yield. Often expert witnesses make implausible claims on behalf of the owners, or of the condemnor, and a decision is reached on the basis of some arbitrary compromise between conflicting estimates of value rather than on a reasoned calculation of actual worth. Occasionally more serious abuses, such as fraudulent evidence or corruption of government officials, affect what is paid to condemnees.

If actual awards often diverge from what the rules seem to require (and usually do so in favor of condemnees), a recent study by Curtis Berger and Patrick Rohan of condemnation in a heavily populated area in suburban New York City concludes that those who settle out of court fare much less well. [246] The procedure used by Nassau County, N.Y., provides for vesting of title in the condemnor before compensation is determined; [247] that is, ownership and the risks of gain or loss of value are passed, although the previous owner is permitted to remain temporarily in possession. After the county has title, it directs an appraiser to value the property. Once this is done, a county negotiator tries to arrive at a settlement price with the condemnee. The appraiser's figure is not made known to the condemnee, nor is the fact that the negotiator starts at a considerably lower figure than that of the appraiser. For those who hold out for a judicial hearing, the prospect is an award at or above the county's appraisal value, but for a variety of reasons most owners do not hold out. The value of land in Nassau County has risen rapidly, and many owners do not have clear idea of the worth of their property. It costs money to hire one's own appraiser and many landowners may trust the fairness of the county negotiator. Lawyers and legal proceedings are expensive, particularly in comparison with the value of an award for the holder of a small plot. A court hearing is likely to be delayed for a year or more, and many condemnees may need ready cash to restart a business or purchase new land. As a consequence of all these factors, the vast majority of land owners settle [248] with the county, and most of these settle for well below the value set by the county's appraiser. In Nassau County, at least, most property owners, and especially those with small holdings, settle for compensation that is significantly less than that to which they are entitled as a matter of constitutional right. Insofar as generalization is warranted, it appears that with regard to condemnation as well as many other legal problems, the person with the incentive and resources to litigate is much more likely to have his theoretical rights vindicated than one who does not go to court.

VI. Rights of Aliens

A question of general concern in regard to a country's treatment of property is whether aliens and nationals are treated equally. In the United States the fifth and fourteenth amendments apply to all "persons," aliens as well as citizens, and give aliens the same protection against unjustified or uncompensated takings of property as are enjoyed by nationals. State and federal statutes on condemnation draw no distinction between aliens and nationals.

An exception to the normal rules for taking property is the disposition of property owned by enemy aliens in wartime. [249] The Supreme Court has said, "Unquestionably to wage war successfully, the United States may confiscate enemy property." [250] In fact, in both world wars such property was put in the custody of the federal government and eventually part of it was used to satisfy U.S. claims against the enemy. No one questions the power of the government to take custody of the property, but some commentators argue that confiscation violates the fifth amendment and international law. [251] Judicial ears, thus far, have not been receptive to these arguments. In a recent case, a federal court of appeals sustained the freezing of assets of a national of Cuba, a country with which the United States is technically at peace. [252] Although stating that the fifth amendment protects nonresident aliens, the court indicated that in order to protect United States nationals whose property had been expropriated, the United States could seize and eventually confiscate property owned by nationals of the expropriating country. The language of the opinion leaves the Executive Branch wide discretion to interfere with the property of aliens of countries with which the United States is involved in some international dispute.

The Constitution has been interpreted to permit limited restrictions on alien ownership of property and means of livelihood. In a 1923 decision, *Terrace v. Thompson*, [253] the Supreme Court sustained a Washington statute that forbade aliens who were ineligible for citizenship or who did not intend to become citizens from owning or leasing agricultural land. It reasoned that "the quality and allegiance of those who own, occupy, and use the farm lands within its borders are matters of highest importance and affect the safety and power of the state itself." Other Supreme Court decisions have been less permissive, however, and the vitality of *Terrace* has probably been sapped by later cases. As early as 1915, the Court, invalidating a law setting a limit of 20 per cent on the percentage of aliens an employer could hire, had said that an alien's right to equal protection of the laws included the "right to work for a living in the common occupations of the community." [254] After World War II, the Court, in *Takahashi v. Fish and Game Comm'n.*, [255] invalidated a California statute barring aliens ineligible for citizenship from earning a living as commerical fishermen in the ocean waters off the state coast. Finding no "special public interest" in this discrimination and holding that *Terrace v. Thompson*, "assuming" its "continued validity," was not controlling, the Court commented:

> The Fourteenth Amendment and the laws adopted under its authority thus embody a general policy that all persons lawfully in this country shall abide 'in any state' on an equality of legal privileges with all citizens under non-discriminatory laws . . . the power of a state to apply its laws exclusively to its alien inhabitants as a class is confined within narrow limits. [256]

In its only post World War II case concerning limits on the ownership of property by aliens, the Supreme Court in *Oyama v. California* decided in favor of the alien on relatively narrow grounds. [257] A few years later the California Supreme Court decided that *Oyama* and *Takahashi* undermined the authority of *Terrace* and declared California's Alien Land Law invalid under the fourteenth amendment. [258]

While it is hazardous to generalize confidently on the basis of scattered decisions, it seems clear that aliens can be barred from vocations that peculiarly involve public responsibility, such as government employment at the higher levels or the practice of law. They might also be forbidden from owning property of vital concern to the national interest, such as a defense plant. Probably other restrictions would now be held inconsistent with the Constitution. [259] At any rate, few if any states still retain laws that discriminate against aliens in regard to common kinds of property ownership and employment.

Conclusion: A Summary Evaluation

The body of law concerning expropriation in the United States can be criticized on a number of specific grounds. Some of the procedures by which condemnation is accomplished do not permit a full hearing on all relevant issues before a taking of property occurs. The length of even totally fair procedures may lead property owners, either out of ignorance or a need to reach a speedy settlement, to accept less compensation than that to which they are entitled. The lines that distinguish taking from regulation and permissible interference are not always clear, and it can be argued that too great a reduction of property value is permitted in some circumstances without compensation. It may also be that some property holders, especially owners of small business, are insufficiently compensated for their losses.

Although such specific criticisms are frequently made, the broad outlines of the law of eminent domain—including an expansive definition of public use, the requirement of full compensation, and the principle of judicial determination of full compensation—are generally accepted. At first blush, it may seem surprising that a system which operates to maintain the economic resources of property owners should not be attacked by those who urge a redistribution of wealth. But there are other ways to accomplish this purpose, such as heavier taxation of the income and estates of the wealthy and greater spending for the poor, that are far more widely supported than is expropriation with no compensation or partial compensation. The reason, perhaps, is that these measures operate more evenly among those with wealth than limited expropriation, whose incidence on one property owner rather than another may be fortuitous. Wholesale expropriation of classes of property would, of course, apply more evenly, but a very small percentage of United States citizens favor the kind of extreme alteration of the society that such expropriation would imply. It is, of course, true that the need for full compensation may deter government officials from undertaking socially worthwhile endeavors, such as public housing, that might seem more feasible if no or lesser reimbursement were required; and to this degree the present law may be a restraining influence on social reform. Nevertheless, even those who do favor more vigorous reform would prefer to have it financed in a more rational way than as a selective tax on those who have the bad fortune to own the particular property to be used. And most of those who approve expropriation without full compensation in countries with more limited resources would not propose it here.

In short, there is a remarkable degree of consensus about the basic principles underlying the law of expropriation as it applies inside the United States, and most criticisms relate to narrower aspects of it.

Notes

1. U.S. Constitution, Art. VI, cl. 2: "This Constitution, and the Laws of the United States which shall be made in Pursuance thereof . . . shall be the supreme law of the Land."

2. Oklahoma ex. rel. Phillips v. Guy F. Athinson Co., 313 U.S. 508, 534 (1941).

3. United States v. City of Chicago, 48 U.S. (7 How) 185 (1849).

4. Marbury v. Madison, 1 U.S. (Cranch) 137 (1803).

5. The judicial power of the United States extends only to cases and controversies, U.S. Constitution, Art. III, Sec. 2. The line between a "case" and an "advisory opinion" is by no means simple. See, e.g., Aetna Life Ins. Co. v. Haworth, 300 U.S. 227 (1937); Nashville, Chattanooga and St. L. Ry. v. Wallace, 288 U.S. 249 (1933).

6. See Barron v. The Mayor and City Council of Baltimore, 32 U.S. (7 Peters) 243 (1833).

7. See, e.g., Palko v. Connecticut, 302 U.S. 319 (1937); Adamson v. California, 332 U.S. 46 (1947); Pointer v. Texas, 380 U.S. 400 (1965). As these cases indicate, the trend is toward incorporation of at least all the fundamental protections.

8. Chicago, B.&O. R.R. v. Chicago, 166 U.S. 226 (1897).

9. J. Bentham, *The Theory of Legislation,* 111-113 (London ed. 1931). Bentham apparently excludes the possibility that the term "property" can have meaning within a system of nonlegal moral obligations or within a system of ideal legal obligations, i.e., natural law. He says, "property and law are born together, and die together. Before laws were made there was no property; take away laws and property ceases." One can reject this aspect of Bentham's analysis and still accept the central thesis that the "property" protected by a system of positive laws is the "property" defined by that system.

10. See W. Friedmann, *Law in a Changing Society,* 67-71, (ed. 1959), for a comparison of civil law concepts with those of Anglo-American jurisprudence.

11. Reich, "The New Property," 73 *Yale L. J.* 733 (1964).

12. In practical terms such a characterization would compel the government to follow more exacting procedures than it now does before depriving someone of a job or franchise and, in certain circumstances, to compensate the person deprived of benefits he has been receiving.

13. See W. Friedmann, op. cit., note 10, at 67; Hecht, "From Seisin to Sit-In: Evolving Property Concepts," 44 *Bost. U.L. Rev.* 435 (1964).

14. See Hecht, op. cit., note 13, at 448-452.

15. Absolute dominion has never, in fact, existed. Some limitations on the use and disposition of property have always been present. See Hecht, op. cit., note 13.

16. J. Locke, *Two Treatises of Civil Government,* Book II, Chapter 5, Sec. 27 (p. 130, Everyman ed., 1924).

17. Id., chapter 11, Secs. 138-40 (pp. 187-189).

18. I. W. Blackstone, *Commentaries* 139.

19. Wynehamer v. People, 13 N.Y. 378, 385-386.

20. Cohen, "Property and Sovereignty, 13 *Cornell L.Q.* 8, at 11-14 (1927). See A. Berle and G. Means, *The Modern Corporation and Private Property* (1932); Berle, "Property, Production and Revolution," 65 *Colum. L. Rev.* 1 (1965). Berle suggests that companies whose shares are widely distributed are controlled by the managers.

21. Compare Allgeyer v. Louisiana, 165 U.S. 578 (1897), Lochner v. New York, 198 U.S. 45 (1905), and Coppage v. Kansas 236 U.S. 1 (1915), with West Coast Hotel Co. v. Parrish, 300 U.S. 379 (1937), and Day-Brite Lighting, Inc. v. Missouri, 342, U.S. 421 (1952). Some state courts, however, have not emulated the degree of permissiveness reflected in Supreme Court opinions. See Hetherington, "State Economic Regulation and Substantive Due Process of Law," (pts 1-2), 53 *NW. U.L. Rev.* 13,226 (1958); Paulsen, "The Persistence of Substantive Due Process in the States," 34 *Minn L. Rev.* 91 (1950).

22. Powell, "Property Rights and Civil Rights," 15 *Hast. L.J.* 135, 140 (1963).

23. 4 Restatement of Property, Secs. 370, 401 (1944); 5 R. Powell, Real Property, Secs. 759-90 (1962).

24. 4 Restatement of Property, Secs. 404-23 (1944); 6 R. Powell, Real Property, Secs. 839-48 (1958).

25. 4 Restatement of Property, Secs. 424-38 (1944), 6 R. Powell, Real Property, Secs. 849-58 (1958).

26. See R. Powell, "Property Rights and Civil Rights," 15 *Hast. L.J.* 135, 142-143 (1963). Sometimes the state's attempt to prohibit a "nuisance" may give rise to a claim that property has been taken without just compensation. This problem is considered below.

27. Village of Euclid v. Ambler Realty Co., 272 U.S. 365 (1926).

28. Id., at 388.

29. See Heyman and Gilhool, "The Constitutionality of Imposing Increased Community costs in New Suburban Residents Through Subdivision Exactions," 73 *Yale L.J.* 1119 1123 (1964), and cases cited therein. Large minimum acreage zoning has recently been attacked as effectively barring the poor, and indirectly most members of minority racial groups (who tend to be less affluent), from desirable communities. See People v. Stover, 12 N.Y. 2d 462, 240 N.Y.S. 2d 734, 191 N.E. 2d 272, app. dism., 375 U.S. 42 (1963); Reid v. Architectural Bd. of Review, 119 Ohio App. 67, 192 N.E. 2d 74 (1963); Agnor, "Beauty Begins a Comeback: Aesthetic Considerations in Zoning," 11 *J. Pub. L.* 260 (1962); "Comment, 'Zoning Aesthetics, and the First Amendment,'" 64 *Colum. L. Rev.* 81 (1964).

30. See Heyman and Gilhool, op. cit., note 29, at 1124-25, and cases cited therein.

31. Matter of Harbison v. City of Buffalo, 4 N.Y. 2d 553, 176 N.Y.S. 2d 596, 152 N.E. 2d 42 (1958).

32. 42 U.S.C. Sec. 3601 et seq. (Supp IV 1968).

33. Jones v. Alfred Mayer Co., 392 U.S. 409 (1968), interpreting 42 U.S.C. Sec. 1982.

34. 1 P. Nichols, Eminent Domain, Sec. 1.11 (rev. 3rd ed., J. Sackman, 1962); see, e.g., Marin County Water Co. v. Marin County, 145 Cal. 586, 79 Pac. 282 (1904). Boom Co. v. Patterson, 98 U.S. 403, 406 (1879); United States v. Jones, 109 U.S. 513, 518-19 (1883). Kohl v. United States, 91 U.S. 367, 371-374 (1876).

35. Congress in performance of its granted powers may "make all Laws which shall be necessary and proper for carrying into execution the foregoing Powers." U.S. Constitution, Art. I, Sec. 8, cl. 18, Laws authorizing condemnation of land are obviously appropriate means of exercising the powers spelled out in the Constitution. See Kohl v. United States, 91 U.S. 367 (1876). The states, which have all governmental responsibilities not granted to the federal government, have an even clearer need to condemn property.

36. See, e.g., Todd v. Austin, 34 Conn 78 (1867); Beekman v. Saratoga and Schenectady R.R. 3 Paige Ch. 45, 22 Am. Dec. 679 (N.Y. 1831). Kohl v. United States, 91 U.S. 367, 371 (1876). See, e.g., Shoemaker v. United States, 147 U.S. 282 (1893); Sholl v. German Coal Co., 118 Ill. 427, 10 N.E. 199 (1887).

37. See, e.g., West River Bridge Co. v. Dix, 47 U.S. (6 How) 507 (1849); Sholl v. German Coal Co., 118 Ill. 427, 10 N.E. 199 (1887); People v. Adirondack R.R., 160 N.Y. 225, 54 N.E. 689 (1899), aff'd. 176 U.S. 335 (1900).

38. 245 U.S. 20, 23 (1917).

39. Cincinnati v. Louisville and Nashville R.R., 223 U.S. 390 (1912).

40. See Kohl v. United States, 91 U.S. 367 (1866).

41. See, e.g., N.Y. Gen. Mun. Law Secs. 74, 126, 161 (McKinney 1965).

42. See, e.g., N.Y. Unconsol. Laws Sec. 6558, (McKinney 1961).

43. See, e.g., N.Y. Trans. Corp. Law, Art. 2, Sec. 11 (McKinney Supp. 1967); Boom Co. v. Patterson, 98 U.S. 403 (1879); Cincinnati v. Louisville and Nashville R.R., 223 U.S. 390 (1912).

44. A determination that no "taking of property" has occurred may be phrased as a conclusion that whatever has been "taken" is not a *property* right or that whatever property rights exist have not been *taken*. Since this distinction is almost entirely semantic, no attempt will be made to separate cases along this line.

45. Among the better treatments of this subject are Dunham, "Griggs v. Allegheny County in Perspective: Thirty Years of Supreme Court Expropriation Law," 1962 *Sup. Ct. Rev.* 63 (1962); Kratovil and Harrison, "Eminent Domain—Policy and Concept," 42 *Cal. L. Rev.* 596 (1954); Michelman, "Property, Utility, and Fairness: Comments on the Ethical Foundations of Just Compensation Law," 80 *Harv. L. Rev.* 1165 (1967); Sax, "Takings and the Police Power," 74 *Yale L.J.* 36 (1964).

46. The notion that "property" is really a cluster of rights undermines the apparent cleanness of these conceptual divisions. A prohibition of any building over 100 feet might be characterized as an appropriation for the public of a free view through

290

that space. Nonetheless, because one intuitively thinks of "property" as the subject matter with regard to which rights are held and because that is at least the primary meaning of the term in the fifth amendment, United States v. General Motors Corp., 232 U.S. 373, 378 (1945), these distinctions provide a good starting point for analysis.

47. See Calor Oil & Gas Co. v. Withers' Admir., 141 Ky. 489, 133 S.W. 210 (1911); 3 P. Nichols, Eminent Domain, Sec. 10.7[1] (rev. 3rd ed., J. Sackman, 1965).

48. See United States v. General Motors Corp., 323 U.S. 373 (1945), (point not actually at issue since the government instituted proceedings to condemn).

49. See United States v. Peewee Coal Co., 341 U.S. 114 (1951).

50. See Mitchell v. Harmony, 54 U.S. (13 How.) 115 (1852); United States v. Russell, 80 U.S. (13 Wall) 623 (1871); United States v. Caltex, Inc., 344 U.S. 149 (1952).

51. This is not true, of course, for cases in which the state act would be unreasonable even if accompanied by compensation. See discussion of the "public use" requirement below.

52. 123 U.S. 623, 668-69 (1887).

53. For a contrary result on similar facts, see Wynehamer v. People, 13 N.Y. 378 (1856).

54. Pumpelly v. Green Bay Co., 80 U.S. (13 Wall) 166 (1872). See below for further discussion of that case.

55. For a similar conclusion in an earlier case, see Fertilizing Co. v. Hyde Park, 97 U.S. 659 (1879), sustaining an ordinance prohibiting the manufacture of fertilizer and the transportation of offal within city limits. The ordinance severely diminished the value of the property of the complaining fertilizer company.

56. See, e.g., Pennsylvania Coal Co. v. Mahon, 260 U.S. 393 (1922); Miller v. City of Beaver Falls, 368 Pa. 189, 82 A. 2d 34 (1951).

57. Conceptually a limitation on use such as a prohibition of construction within a certain distance of the street might be considered a physical appropriation of a "scenic easement" for public use. See Michelman, op. cit., note 45, at 1185-1188.

58. 239 U.S. 394 (1915).

59. In Fertilizing Co. v. Hyde Park, 97 U.S. 659 (1879), see note 55, the operation of the "offensive" fertilizer plant had also preceded the movement of residents into the area.

60. 272 U.S. 365 (1926), see notes 27 and 28 and accompanying test.

61. 260 U.S. 393 (1922).

62. Id., at 413, 415.

63. See, e.g., Arverne Bay Const. Co. v. Tatcher, 278 N.Y. 222, 15 N.E. 2d 587 (1938).

64. Matter of Arbison v. City of Buffalo, 4 N.Y. 2d 553, 176 N.Y.S. 2d 598, 152 N.E. 2d 42 (1958).

65. 369 U.S. 590, 594, 595, (1962).

66. Consolidated Rock Products v. City of Los Angeles, 371 U.S. 36 (1962). Though dismissal of an appeal is technically administered on the merits, it has not always been viewed this way: thus the significance of the Consolidated Rock Products was not clear. In an earlier case, United States v. Central Eureka Mining Co., 357 U.S. 155 (1958), the Court allowed the government to forbid the mining of nonessential gold in wartime in order to reallocate scarce labor. This exercise of the war power rendered the owners' gold mines completely unproductive for the duration, though because of its temporary nature, the regulation did not destroy the underlying value of the land.

67. See Bowditch v. Boston, 101 U.S. 16 (1879).

68. 260 U.S. 393, 415-416 (1922).

69. 276 U.S. 272, 279-80 (1928).

70. This suggests a more general problem with any test that turns on the magnitude of the injury. The court must first decide what is the standard of value against which one assesses the magnitude, the value of all property owned by the complainant, the value of the particular piece of land affected, the value of a particular thing on a particular piece of land. One might, of course, even argue that the appropriate standard should be the value of a particular right in a particular thing, but this leads to the absurd conclusion that so long as the right is narrowly enough defined, the magnitude will always be 100 per cent. See Michelman, op. cit., note 45, at 1191-1193.

71. United States v. Caltex, Inc., 344 U.S. 149 (1952).

72. See Sax, op. cit., note 45, at 37.

73. See Michelman, op. cit., note 45, at 1193-1196. Professor Michelman, id., at 1234-35, suggests that when net social improvement is obvious, the pain for the person bearing the loss is reduced and that requiring compensation in cases where social improvement is more doubtful may protect against society's causing loss unwisely or unfairly.

74. See Miller v. City of Beaver Falls, 368 Pa. 189, 82 A. 2d. 34 (1951); Morris County Land Improvement Co. v. Township of Parsippany-Troy Hills, 40 N.J. 539, 193 A. 2d 232 (1963); Sax, op. cit., note 45, at 72-73.

75. See, e.g., Harrison's Estate, 250 Pa. 129, 95 AT1. 406 (1915); Town of Windsor v. Whitney, 95 Conn. 357, 111 AT1. 354 (1920); S.S. Kresge Co. v. City of New York, 194 Misc. 645, 87 N.Y.S. 2d. 313 (Sup. Ct. 1949); Kratovil and Harrison, op. cit., note 45, at 638-641. For some older cases voiding this kind of ordinance, see Moale v. Mayor and City Council of Baltimore, 5 Md, 314 (1854); Edwards v. Bruorton, 184 Mass. 529, 69 N.E. 328 (1904); Forster v. Scott, 136 N.Y. 577, 32 N.E. 976 (1893).

76. See Atchison, T. & S. F. Ry. v. Public Utilities Comm'rs 346 U.S. 346 (1953). Erie R.R. v. Public Utilities Comm'rs. 254 U.S. 394 (1921). In Nashville Central & St. L. R.R. v. Walters, 294 U.S. 405 (1935), the Supreme Court overturned a Tennessee decision that foreclosed the railroad from introducing evidence that the grade crossing would not contribute to the safety of local traffic but merely to the efficiency of national highway traffic. The Court stated, " . . . W hen particular individuals are singled out to bear the cost of advancing the public convenience, that imposition must bear some reasonable relation to the evils to be eradicated or the advantages to be secured . . . " 294 U.S. at 429. It is doubtful whether this decision imposes any significant limit on the state's power to put the burden on the railroad, so long as it is careful to present the acceptable reasons for its decision. Compare Georgia Ry. & Elec. Co. v. Decatur, 295 U.S. 165 (1935), with Georgia Ry. & Elec. Co. v. Decatur, 297 U.S. 620 (1936). See also Georgia Ry. & Elec. Co. v. Decatur, 297 U.S. 620 (1936) (sustaining a special assessment for street repair on the ground that company tracks contributed to the need for repair).

77. It did in 1935 refuse to extend the railroad cases to a requirement that a gas company modify its underground pipelines, Panhandle Eastern Pipeline Co. v. State Highway Comm's., 294 U.S. 613. The state argued that the modifications were necessary to prevent gas leaks from endangering the safety of a new road crossing the pipeline. The Court responded that the danger was not comparable with that posed by the grade crossing cases. Given the subsequent reaffirmance of the duty placed on railroads and the tenuous distinction drawn by the Court in Panhandle, it is hard to know how much strength it has today.

78. See Heyman & Gilhool, "The Constitutionality of Imposing Increased Community Costs on New Suburban Residents Through Subdivision Exactions," 73 *Yale L.J.* 1119, 1130-33 (1964).

79. Ayres v. City Council of Los Angeles, 34 Cal. 2d 31, 207 P. 2d 1 (1949); Brous v. Smith, 304 N.Y. 164, 106 N.E. 2d 503 (1952).

80. See Heyman & Gilhool, "Constitutionality," note 78, at 1133.

81. See Pioneer Trust & Savings Bank v. Village of Mount Prospect, 22 Ill. 2d. 375, 176 N.E. 2d 799 (1961). But see Billings Properties Inc. v. Yellowstone County, 144 Mt. 25,394 Pac. 182 (1964); Jenad Inc. v. Village of Scarsdale, 18 N.Y. 2d 78, 218 N.E. 2d 673, 271 N.Y.S. 2d 995 (1966); Jordan v. Village of Menomonec, 28 Wisc. 2d 608, 137 N.W. 2d 442 (1966).

82. Pioneer Trust & Savings Bank v. Village of Mount Prospect, 22 Ill. 2d 375, 379, 176 N.E. 2d. 799, 801 (1961).

83. Jenad Inc. v. Village of Scarsdale, 18 N.Y. 2d 78, 218 N.E. 2d 673, 271 N.Y.S. 2d 995 (1966).

84. See Heyman & Gilhool, "Constitutionality," note 78.

85. Id., at 1146-1154.

86. Shoemaker v. United States, 147 U.S. 282, 302 (1893). But cf. Georgia Ry. & Elec. Co. v. Decatur, 297 U.S. 620 (1936).

87. Bauman v. Ross, 167 U.S. 548 (1897).

88. The rule of the Supreme Court and most state courts is to give conclusive effect to the legislative determination of benefit and its amount. See, e.g., French v. Barber Asphalt Paving Co., 181 U.S. 324 (1901); Flynn v. Chiappari, 191 Cal. 139, 215 P. 682 (1923).

89. There are, of course, other government powers which support action in the public interest at the expense of economic expectations of private individuals. Among these for the federal government is the power "To Coin Money [and] regulate the Value thereof," U.S. Constitution, Art. I, Sec. 8, cl. 5. In 1935, after the dollar had been devalued in terms of gold, the Court in Norman v. Baltimore & O.R.R., 294 U.S. 240, upheld statutory provisions voiding contractual terms that required payment equivalent to a certain weight in gold. These contracts had been formed with the express purpose of protecting the obligee from a devaluation of the dollar, and yet the government was permitted to destroy the contractual rights without compensation. In Perry v. United States, 294 U.S. 330, the Court dealt with government debts similarly framed. It held that the government could not vitiate its own obligations, but it characterized the government's failure to pay the amount indicated as a breach of contract and assessed damages on the basis of what a private party could legally do with gold. Since at the time of the repudiation of the contract (which preceded devaluation), holders of gold coin were compelled to turn the gold in to the government and receive dollars at the old rate, the Court held that no financial damage had been suffered. It thus reached exactly the same result as if it had held the government free to breach its obligation. The fifth amendment apparently provides little protection against the power to regulate money.

90. One's property rights may be quite different if damage is done or authorized by the government rather than by purely private action. For example, the legislature may legalize what would otherwise be a public nuisance, Richards v. Washington Terminal Co., 233 U.S. 546, 553 (1914), and incur no liability, either in tort or under the just compensation requirement. The government may also reduce the head of water in a navigable stream, without liability, though the owner of the damaged property would be protected against identical injury by a private party. See United States v. Willow River Power Co., 324 U.S. 499 (1945); compare United States v. Cress, 243 U.S. 316 (1917) (held a taking when government dam left unworkable head in nonnavigable stream). See text accompanying notes 99-103.

91. Richards v. Washington Terminal Co., 233 U.S. 546 (1914).

92. United States v. Causby, 328 U.S. 256 (1946); Griggs v. Allegheny County, 369 U.S. 84 (1962).

93. United States v. Causby, 328 U.S. 256, 264-67 (1946).

94. See Batten v. United States, 306 F. 2d 580 (10 Cir. 1962), cert. denied, 371 U.S. 955 (1963); Avery v. United States, 330 F. 2d 640 (Ct. Cl. 1964).

95. See Kratovil and Harrison, op. cit., note 45, at 611.

96. See Richards v. Washington Terminal Co., 233 U.S. 546 (1914).

97. See Kratovil & Harrison, op. cit., note 45, at 611-612, 648.

98. Sax, op. cit., note 45, at 61-76.

99. 276 U.S. 272 (1928), see text accompanying notes 69-70.

100. United States v. Caltex, Inc., 344 U.S. 149 (1952), see text accompanying note 71.

101. That the approach does not correspond with all of existing case law is something the author recognizes and is not, in itself, a defect in a theory which attempts to explain what should be the ground of decision, not what always has been.

102. Michelman, op. cit., note 45.

103. Missouri Pacific Ry. v. Nebraska, 164 U.S. 403, 417 (1896).

104. See Rindge Co. v. Los Angeles County, 262 U.S. 700, 709 (1923).

105. See Shoemaker v. United States, 147 U.S. 282 (1893).

106. See, e.g., Bloodgood v. Mohawk & H.R.R. 18 Wend. 9, 60-61 (N.Y. Ct. Err. 1837).

107. See Comments, "The Public Use Limitation on Eminent Domain; An Advance Requiem," 58 *Yale L. J.* 599, 604-605 (1949).

108. Clark v. Nash, 198 U.S. 361 (1905); Mt. Vernon Woodbury Cotton Duck Co. v. Alabama Interstate Power Co., 240 U.S. 30 (1915); United States *ex rel.* T.V.A. v. Welch, 327 U.S. 546 (1946); Berman v. Parker, 348 U.S. 26 (1954).

109. Clark v. Nash, 198 U.S. 361 (1905).

110. 327 U.S. 546 (1946).

111. Id., p. 552. See also Old Dominion Co. v. United States, 269 U.S. 55, 66 (1925).

112. 348 U.S. 26, 32 (1954).

113. The absence of slums on his land might have been relevant to complainant's case because courts have frequently held that elimination of harmful uses is an appropriate purpose for exercise of the power of eminent domain. See Dunham, op. cit., note 45, at 67.

114. Courtesy Sandwich Shop v. Port of New York Authority, 12 N.Y. 2d 379, 240 N.Y.S. 2d 1, N.E. 2d 403, app. dism., 375 U.S. 78 (1963). The dismissal is technically a decision on the merits, not a discretionary refusal to review. For a case upholding the Port of Authority's plan for the World Trade Center as a taking for public purpose see In re Real Property in County of New York, 48 Misc. 2d 365, 264 N.Y.S. 2d 802 (Sup. Ct. 1965) Aff'd 25 App. Div. 2d 620, 268 N.Y.S. 2d 957 (1st Dept.) Aff'd 18 N.Y. 2d 250, 273 N.Y.S. 2d 337, 219 H.E. 2d 797 (1966); cert. den. 385 U.S. 1006 (1967). For a case holding that the Congressional compact establishing the Port Authority did not forbid the Authority from building the World Trade Center see Port Authority Bondholder Pro Com v. Port of New York Authority, 387 F. 2d, 259 (20 Cir. 1967).

115. Chicago, Burlington & Quincy R.R. v. Chicago, 166 U.S. 226 (1897).

116. In a period when fewer constitutions had explicit provisions requiring compensation, courts held recompense was due to the private owner of property taken as a matter of "natural law." See, e.g., Bonaparte v. Camden & A.R.R., 3 F. Cas. 821 (No. 1617) (C.C.D.N.J. 1830); Petition of Mt. Washington Road Co., 35 N.H. 134 (1857); Gardner v. Village of Newburgh, 2 Johns, Ch. 162 (N.Y. 1816).

117. 26 Am. Jur. 2d *Eminent Domain* Sec. 151 (1966); see, e.g., Ill. Constitution, Art. II, Sec. 13.

118. Monangahela Nav. Co. v. United States, 148 U.S. 312, 327 (1893). But cf. United States v. Commodities Trading Corp., 339 U.S. 121 (1950). In that case the government condemned black pepper and paid the price set for black pepper as a part of wartime price administration. The Supreme Court said it would accept the ceiling price in the absence of a showing of special circumstances and hardship. See also United States v. Cors, 337 U.S. 327 (1949); United States v. John J. Felin & Co., 334 U.S. 624 (1948); Dunham, op. cit., note 45, at 91-93.

119. See, e.g., United States v. Miller, 317 U.S. 369 (1943).

120. Van Horne v. Dorrance, 2 Dall. 304, 28 F. Cas. No. 16, 857. See also Commonwealth v. Peters, 2 Mass. 125 (1806).

121. Beveridge v. Lewis, 137 Cal. 619, 67 P. 1040 (1902); see Reynolds v. State Board of Public Roads, 194 Atl. 535 (R.I. 1937).

122. Martin v. Tyler, 4 N.D. 278, 60 N.W. 392 (1894).

123. See generally Recent Cases, 51 *Harv. L. Rev.* 742 (1938).

124. See generally Morreale, "Federal Powers in Western Waters: The Navigation Power and the Rule of No Compensation," 3 *Nat. Res. J.* 1 (1963).

125. 324 U.S. 499 (1945).

126. 350 U.S. 222 (1956).

127. Id., at 228.

128. The Twin City Power rule is sharply criticized in Dunham, op. cit., note 45, at 98-105.

129. United States v. New River Collieries Co., 262 U.S. 341 (1923). See also United States v. Reynolds, 90 S. Ct. 803. (1970).

130. Boom Co. v. Patterson, 98 U.S. 403, 407-08 (1879).

131. United States v. Petty Motor Co., 327 U.S. 372, 377 (1946).

132. Kimball Laundry Co. v. United States, 338 U.S. 1, 5 (1949).

133. See United States v. New River Collieries, 262 U.S. 341 (1923); Vogelstein & Co. v. United States, 262 U.S. 337 (1923).

134. See Olson v. United States, 292 U.S. 246 (1934).

135. Id., Act 255; see also United States *ex rel.* T.V.A. v. Powelson, 319 U.S. 266 (1943); McGovern v. New York, 299 U.S. 363 (1913).

136. United States v. Petty Motor Co., 327 U.S. 372, 377-78 (1946); Mitchell v. United States, 267 U.S. 341, 344 (1925); 1 L. Orgel, Valuation Under Eminent Domain Secs. 66-80 (2d ed. 1953).

137. United States v. General Motors Corp., 323 U.S. 373, 380 (1945). If the government actually appropriates a business as a going concern, it has to compensate for at least some of the business losses.

138. See, e.g., St. Louis v. St. Louis etc. Ry. Co., 266 Mo. 694, 182 S.W. 750 (1916).

139. See generally "Just Compensation for the Small Businessman," 2 *Colum. J. of Law and Social Problems* 144 (1966).

140. Staff of House Comm. on Public Works, 88th Cong., 2d Sess., Study of Compensation and Assistance for Persons Affected by Real Property Acquisition in Federal and Federally Assisted Programs 473-485 (Comm. Print 1964).

141. For a discussion on the appropriateness of judicial redress for the factor of human disruption see Klein, "Judicial Response to the Humans' Disruption," 46 *J. Urban L.* (1968).

142. See, e.g., Harvey Textile Co. v. Hill, 135 Conn. 686, 67A. 2d 851 (1944); Blincoe v. C. O.&W. R.R. Co., 16 Okla. 286, 83 P. 903 (1905).

143. See "Just Compensation for the Small Businessman," op. cit., note 139, at 151-162.

144. Pa. Stat. Ann. Tit. 26, Secs. 1-608, 1-609, 1-610 (Supp. 1966). The Draft of the Model Eminent Domain Code Sec. 610, 2 Real Prop. Prob. T.J. 365 (1967), provides compensation for reasonable moving expenses from both a residence and a place of business. For a discussion of the appropriateness for an award for moving expenses see Note "Compensation For Moving Expenses of Personal Property in Eminent Domain Cases," 20 *Hastings L. J.* 749 (1969).

145. See, e.g., 66 Stat. 606, 624 (1952); 78 Stat. 788 (1964), 42 U.S.C. Sec. 1465 (1964); 78 Stat. 305 (1964), 49 U.S.C. Sec. 1606(a) (1964) as amended, 49 U.S.C. 1606 (Supp IV 1968) "Just Compensation for the Small Businessman," op. cit., note 139. at 152.

146. See H.R. 3421, 89th Cong., 1st Sess., Secs. 101-118 (1965). See "Just Compensation for the Small Businessman," op. cit., note 139, at 157.

147. 323 U.S. 373 (1945).

148. 338 U.S. 1 (1944). But cf. United States v. Westinghouse Elec. & Mfg. Co., Inc., 339 U.S. 261 (1950).

149. Dunham, op. cit., note 45, at 98.

150. See Krativil and Harrison, op. cit., note 45, at 615-19; "Just Compensation for the Small Businessman," op. cit., note 139, at 150-151.

151. See, e.g., Producer's Wood Preserving Co. v. Comm'rs. of Seerage, 227 Ky. 159, 12 S.W. (2d) 292 (1928).

152. See, e.g., in re Simmons, 127 N.Y.S. 940 (Special Term, Ulster County 1910).

153. See generally "Just Compensation and the Public Condemnee," 75 *Yale L.J.* 1053 (1966).

154. See, e.g., United States v. Certain Lands, 246 F. 2d 823 (3d cir. 1957); United States v. Arkansas, 164 F. 2d 943 (8th cir. 1947); 27 Am. Jur., 2d, *Eminent Domain* Sec. 329 (1966); "Just Compensation and the Public Condemnee," op. cit., note 153, provides critical analysis of some of the subtleties of the substitute facility coctrine.

155. See generally 2 L. Orgel, Valuation under Eminent Domain, Ch. 16-19 and cases cited therein (2nd ed. 1953).

156. In re Fifth Avenue Coach Lines, Inc., 18 N.Y. 2d 212, 273 N.Y. Supp. 2d 52, 219 N.E. 2d 410 (1966).

157. The minority opinion also contended that even if the companies had a theoretical right to a higher fare, their failure to assert that claim in proceedings prior to condemnation precluded them from doing so after condemnation was accomplished. This point, in my view, is not well taken. Had the value of the property been reduced by a patently illegal act, the condemnor should not have been able to profit from this reduction simply because the illegal act had not earlier been contested in legal proceedings.

158. Application of the Port Authority-Trans Hudson Corp., 20 N.Y. 2d 457, 231 N.E. 2d 734, 285 N.Y.S. 2d 24 (1967) cert. den. 390 U.S. 1002 (1965). For discussion of the case see Comment, 68 *Colum. L. Rev.* 977 (1968).

159. Sharp v. United States, 191 U.S. 340 (1903); United States v. Grizzard, 219 U.S. 180 (1911).

160. Bauman v. Ross, 167 U.S. 548 (1897); McCoy v. Elevated R.R., 247 U.S. 354 (1918). Some state constitutions or statutes forbid set-off of benefits; e.g., N.Y. Condemnation Law, Art. 2, Sec. 14 (McKinney Supp. 1969).

161. "Time of taking" has different meanings in different jurisdictions, some of them are the date of filing the petition, the date of trial, the date of summons, and the date of judgment. See 27 Am. Jur. 2d, *Eminent Domain,* Sec. 252 (1966).

162. "Commitment" apparently contemplates some formal and final decision. See United States v. Virginia Elec. & Power Co., 365 U.S. 624, 636 (1961). Since property values may drop when it is learned that projects are being considered or appear likely, losses may be suffered before the date of commitment that will not be compensable. See House Study, op. cit. note 140, at 64-67, discussing this problem and suggesting a more liberal rule.

163. See United States v. Miller, 317 U.S. 369 (1943). In the federal courts the question of whether land taken was "probably within the scope of the project" is for the judge, not the jury. United States v. Reynolds, 90 S. Ct. 803 (1970).

164. It does not matter whether the increase is caused by a certainty or only a probability of later condemnation. Id., p. 377.

165. Ibid. However, in a case involving the requisition of tugboats in wartime, the Court approved a refusal to include in compensable value the enhancement resulting from the reduction of the number of private tugboats caused by earlier requisitions. Cors. v. United States, 337 U.S. 325 (1949). It is difficult to distinguish in principle this increase in value from other increases, such as proximity to a project, unrelated to the expectancy that the property in question will be condemned. Perhaps the result may be attributed to the special exigencies of wartime conditions and the unusual shortages in supply of kinds of commodities needed by the government.

166. See generally 1 L. Orgel, Valuation Under the Law of Eminent Domain, Ch. XI, (2d ed. 1953); see also Fiorini v. City of Kenosha, 208 Wis. 496, 243 N.W. 761 (1932). But cf. Sands v. City of New York, 104 Misc. 427, 429, 172 N.Y.S. 16, 18 (1918).

167. 1 L. Orgel, Valuation Under the Law of Eminent Domain, Sec. 137 et seq. (2nd ed. 1953); Village of Lawrence v. Greenwood, 300 N.Y. 231, 90 N.E. 2d 53 (1949).

168. 1 L. Orgel, Valuation Under the Law of Eminent Domain, Sec. 198 and cases cited therein (2nd ed. 1953).

169. Id., Secs. 150, 151, see, e.g., Texas & St. Louis R.R. v. Eddy, 42 Ark. 527 (1854); United States v. 711.57 Acres of Land, 51 F. Supp. 30 (N.D. Cal. 1943).

170. 1.L. Orgel, Valuation Under the Law of Eminent Domain, Sec. 151 (2nd ed. 1953); see, e.g., Manning v. Lowell, 173 Mass. 100, 53 N.E. 160 (1899); McCardless v. United States, 74 F. 2d 596 (9th Cir. 1935).

171. 1.L. Orgel, Valuation Under the Law of Eminent Domain, Ch. XV and cases cited therein (2nd ed. 1953). Id., Ch. XIV.

172. 2 L. Orgel, Valuation Under the Law of Eminent Domain, Ch. XVI and cases cited therein.

173. 4 P. Nichols, Eminent Domain Sec. 12.42 [3] (rev. 3rd ed., J. Sackman, 1962); Matter of Delancey Street, 120 App. Div. 700, 105 N.Y.S. 779 (1907).

174. See 4 P. Nichols, Eminent Domain Sec. 12.42 3 (rev. 3rd ed., J. Sackman, 1962); Matter of City of New York, 196 App. Div. 451, 188, N.Y.S. 197 (1921). It should be noted, however, that it is quite common in urban leases to have a clause that provides that the lessee's interest terminates upon a condemnation of either the leased interest or the entire fee. Where such "condemnation clauses" are indluded in a lease, the lessee has no extant interest at time of the condemnation and is entitled to no compensation. See 4 P. Nichols, Eminent Domain Sec. 12.42[1] (rev. 3rd ed., J. Sackman, 1962) and cases cited therein.

175. See, e.g., Application of Bronx River Expressway, 278 App. Div. 813, 104 N.Y.S. 2d 554 (1951).

176. One might, of course, say that the lessee has an interest that is worth less than nothing, but the condemnor cannot capitalize his expected loss and compel him to pay that sum to the lessor to supplement the condemnation award.

177. 4 P. Nichols, Eminent Domain, Sec. 12.36 (rev. 3rd ed., J. Sackman, 1962); see

also 1 L. Orgel, Valuation Under the Law of Eminent Domain Secs. 107, 123 and cases cited therein (2d ed. 1953).

178. 1 L. Orgel, Valuation Under the Law of Eminent Domain, Sec. 123, and Ch. XIV and cases cited therein (2nd ed. 1953). The trend is to look to all factors involved in the case of the fee to indemnify the parties for all their compensable positive interests in the property taken. Condemnation of Leasehold Interest, 3 Real Prop. and T. J. 226 (1968).

179. 1 L. Orgel, Valuation Under the Law of Eminent Domain, Secs. 122, 125 and cases cited therein.

180. Id., Sec. 126 and cases cited therein.

181. See generally 4 P. Nichols, Eminent Domain Sec. 12. 43 (rev. 3rd ed. J. Sackman, 1962).

182. See, e.g., N.Y. Public Authorities Law, Sec. 557A(2), (McKinney 1961).

183. See, e.g., N.Y. Public Authorities Law, Sec. 553(4), (McKinney 1961) which gives the Triborough Bridge and Tunnel Authority a general power of condemnation for carrying out its general purposes.

184. See Georgia v. Chattanooga, 264 U.S. 472, 483 (1924); Bragg v. Weaver, 251 U.S. 57, 58 (1919).

185. See, e.g., Nassau County, N.Y. Administrative Code, Sec. 11.-22.0(b) (1952).

186. See, e.g., Charles Tomas Inc. v. Police Jury, 231 La. 1, 90 So. 2d 65 (1956) construing La. Constitution Art. I, Sec 2.6. See also Nassau Code, Sec. 11-22.0 (b).

187. Shoemaker v. United States, 147 U.S. 182 (1893); see text accompanying notes 134-47. As suggested above, under present doctrine almost any purpose will be sustained as a matter of federal law.

188. Bragg v. Weaver, 251 U.S. 57, 59 (1919); see text accompanying notes 148-205. The Supreme Court will reverse state court decisions on just compensation only if they are founded on an erroneous interpretation of the federal requirement, or on a "gross and obvious" error in computation. See Roberts v. New York City, 295 U.S. 264 (1935); McGovern v. City of New York, 229 U.S. 363, 370-71 (1913).

189. The Supreme Court, in Georgia v. Chattanooga, 264 U.S. 472, 483 (1924), suggests by implication that the right to have a judicial hearing on the authority of the condemnor is guaranteed by the federal Constitution but the determination of the authority is one involving construction of state law.

190. See, e.g., N.Y. Condemnation Law, Art. 2, Secs. 9, 11 (McKinney 1950), Board of Educ. of Central School Dist. No. 3 v. Gorga, 9 Misc. 2d 58, 171 N.Y.S. 2d 162 (Sup. Ct. 1957); Cemetery Co. v. Warren School Township, 236 Ind. 171, 139 N.E. 2d 538 (1957); 27 Am. Jur. 2d, *Eminent Domain,* Sec. 404 (1966). The extent to which a New York property owner may challenge the necessity of an appropriation is not completely clear. Sections 4 (d.3), 9, 11, and 13 of N.Y. Condemnation Law, Art. 2, read together, suggest that whether appropriation is reasonably necessary is a trouble issue. Accord New York Tel. Co. v. Wood, 145 Misc. 481, 259 N.Y.S. 365

(Sup. Ct. 1931). In Cuglar v. Power Auth., 4 Misc. 2d 879, 163 N.Y.S. 2d 902 (Sup. Ct. 1957), the court indicated that determination of necessity is essentially a legislative judgment, but it acknowledged that it would interfere if an appropriation was wholly irrational and in disregard of public necessity.

191. See 6 P. Nichols, Eminent Domain, Sec. 24.11 et seq. (rev. 3rd ed., J. Sackman, 1962).

192. N.Y. Condemnation Law (McKinney 1950 and Supp. 1969).

193. Compare the federal procedure set out in Rule 71A of the Federal Rules of Civil Procedure. The Supreme Court adopted Rule 71A in April 1951. It became effective in August of that year, 90 days after it was reported to Congress in conformity with the requirements of 18 U.S.C. 3771 and 28 U.S.C., Secs. 2072-2073. Prior to enactment of this rule, the federal courts had followed the procedure of the state in which they sat in accordance with 25 Stat. 351. When that statutory provision was repealed it was left to the Court to fashion a rule of procedure under the authority granted it by the Enabling Act 28 U.S.C. 723.

194. New York's courts are confusingly named. The Supreme Court is the state trial court, the Appellate Division of the Supreme Court is an intermediate appellate court, and the Court of Appeals is the highest court in the state.

195. This requirement has been held to impose on the condemnor a duty of good faith negotiations with the owner. See Long Beach v. Long Beach Water Co., 209 App. Div. 902, 205 N.Y.S. 420 (1924); Electric & Gas Corp. v. Morrison, 44 Misc. 2d 145, 252 N.Y.S. 2d 979 (Sup. Ct. 1964). 44 Misc. 2d 145, 252 N.Y.S. 2d 979 (Sup. Ct. 1964). If negotiations are unsuccessful and the condemnor files an official offer of payment, the condemnee will not recover court costs (that would be his in the absence of such an offer) from the condemnor if he refuses the offer and the final award is less than the offer. N.Y. Condemnation Law Art. 2, Sec. 16 (McKinney 1950).

196. N.Y. Condemnation Law, Art. 2, Sec. 4 (McKinney 1950). Most states follow a similar practice; see 27 *Am. Jur.* 2d Eminent Domain, Sec. 379 (1966), as does the federal government; see Fed. Rules of Civ. Pro., Rule 71A(c).

197. Schroeder v. New York City, 371 U.S. 208 (1963).

198. N.Y. Condemnation Law, Art. 2, Sec. 5 (McKinney Supp. 1967).

199. N.Y. Condemnation Law, Art. 2, Sec. 6 (McKinney Supp. 1967); N.Y. C.P.L.R., Secs. 301-318 (McKinney Supp. 1967). In order to protect those who may not actually have received notice, when service is not by personal delivery and the owner fails to appear, the court must appoint a lawyer to represent his interests. N.Y. Condemnation Law, Art. 2, Sec. 7 (McKinney 1950).

200. N.Y. Condemnation Law, Art. 2, Sec. 6 (McKinney 1960). If a referee is used, the court will review his determinations.

201. City of Syracuse v. Benedict, 33 N.Y.S. 944 (Sup. Ct. 1895).

202. The U.S. Supreme Court has held this separation of issues consonant with due

process. Louisville & Nashville R. R. v. Western Union Tel. Co., 250 U.S. 363, 365 (1919).

203. The property owner in this event recovers his court costs. N.Y. Condemnation Law, Art. 2, Sec. 13 (McKinney 1950).

204. Marshall v. Hatfield, 138 N.Y.S. 733 (Sup. Ct. 1912).

205. N.Y. Condemnation Law, Art. 2, Sec. 13 (McKinney 1950).

206. Electric & Gas Corp. v. Smith, 269 App. Div. 725, 54 N.Y.S. 2d 287 (1945); Erie R.R. Co. v. Steward, 59 App. Div. 187, 69 N.Y.S. 57 (1901).

207. Bragg v. Weaver, 251 U.S. 57, 59 (1919); United States v. Jones, 109 U.S. 513, 519 (1883).

208. As in the great majority of states, the property owner has no right to a jury trial. Compare Rule 71A of the Federal Rules of Civil Procedure, which permits either party to request a jury, though the judge may deny the request.

209. N.Y. Condemnation Law, Art. 2 Sec. 13 (McKinney 1950). These might include one lawyer, one person familiar with real estate values, and one expert on buildings.

210. N.Y. Condemnation Law, Art. 2, Sec. 14 (McKinney Supp. 1967). Relevant evidence may include expert testimony on the property's value; see, e.g., Matter of Luzerne Lake George County Highway, 145 Misc. 736, 261 N.Y.S. 894 (Cty. Ct. 1932), offers to buy and sell at a given price, see 27 Am. Jur. 2d, *Eminent Domain,* Sec. 428 (1966). Sparkhill Realty Corp. v. State, 238 App. Div. 656, 266 N.Y.S. 72 (3d Dept., 1933). Records of the property's income yielding capacity, 27 Am. Jur. 2d, *Eminent Domain,* Sec. 431 re State at Niagara Reservation 16 Abb. N.C. 159 (1884), off'd 37 Hun 537 (1885), app. dism. 102 N.Y. 734, 7 N.E. 916 (1886), and the sale price on similar pieces of property, see Village of Lawrence v. Greenwood, 300 N.Y. 231, 90 N.E. 2d 53 (1949). But cf. Manhattan Ry. v. Stuyvesant, 126 App. Div. 848, 111 N.Y.S. 222 (1908), (suggesting restrictions on the use of such evidence).

211. N.Y. Condemnation Law, Art. 2, Sec. 14 (McKinney Supp. 1967). Most states permit or require such observation. See 27 Am. Jur. 2d, *Eminent Domain,* Secs. 413, 418 (1966).

212. N.Y. Condemnation Law, Art. 2, Sec. 14 (McKinney Supp. 1967).

213. N.Y. Condemnation Law, Art. 2, Sec. 15 (McKinney Supp. 1967).

214. See, e.g., Hawley v. Village of Elmira Heights, 163 Misc. 787, 297 N.Y.S. 732 (Sup. Ct. 1937).

215. In many states, though the standards differ, review of factual determinations of the commissioners is limited. See 27 Am. Jur. 2d, *Eminent Domain,* Sec. 447 (1966). However, in others the court has the power to conduct a de novo trial and to substitute a decision of its own for that of the commissioners. 6 P. Nichols, Eminent Domain, Sec. 26.731(1) (rev. 3rd ed., J. Sackman, 1965).

216. See, e.g., Janeski v. State, 22 App. Div. 2d 845, 254 N.Y.S. 2d 73 (1964).

217. Application and Petition of Huie, 2 Misc. 2d 38, 154 N.Y.S. 2d 824 (Sup. Ct. 1954), aff'd., 2 App. Div. 2d 631, 153 N.Y.S. 2d 610 (1955); Tennessee Gas Transmission Co. v. Conti, 100 N.Y.S. 2d 309 (Cty. Ct. 1950).

218. N.Y. Condemnation Law, Art. 2, Sec. 15 (McKinney Supp. 1967).

219. See in re New York Municipal Ry. Corp., 189 App. Div 814, 179 N.Y.S. 238 (1919), aff'd., 228 N.Y. 561, 127 N.E. 917 (1920) (construing Code of Civ. Pro., Sec. 3371, the predecessor stat. to Art. 2, Sec. 15 of the N.Y. Condemnation Law).

220. See note 215. See also Rule 71A of the Federal Rules of Civil Procedure.

221. N.Y. Condemnation Law, Art. 2, Sec. 15 (McKinney Supp. 1967).

222. If, upon receipt of compensation and service of a copy of the court's final order, the owner fails to deliver possession, the condemnor can secure a writ of assistance from the court of force delivery. N.Y. Condemnation Law, Art. 2, Sec. 17 (McKinney 1950).

223. N.Y. Condemnation Law, Art. 2, Sec. 19 (McKinney Supp. 1969). If the condemnor is unsuccessful, it must bear the appeal costs of the condemnee, though the converse is not true. Id., Sec. 20.

224. Compare, e.g., Matter of New York School Site, 222 App. Div. 554, 226 N.Y.S. 536 (1928); in re site for Public School 46, 279 App. Div. 600, 107 N.Y.S. 2d 463 (1951), with cases cited in notes 214, 216, 217.

225. N.Y. Condemnation Law, Art. 2, Sec. 21 (McKinney Supp. 1967). Many other states allow the appellate tribunal to modify the award. See 6 P. Nichols, Eminent Domain, Sec. 26.732 (rev. 3rd ed., J. Sackman, 1965).

226. In re Fourth Avenue in the City of New York, 255 N.Y. 25, 173 N.E. 910 (1930). From the Court of Appeals, review may be sought, but only on federal Constitutional issues, to the U.S. Supreme Court. Generally review in the Supreme Court of judgments in state condemnation cases is by discretion rather than of right.

227. N.Y. Condemnation Law, Art. 2, Sec. 18 (McKinney Supp. 1967). The condemnor must act within thirty days after entry of the order.

228. Id. In some states, confirmation of the commissioner's award gives the owner a vested right in the compensation and discontinuance is possible only upon his consent. See Kelly v. Waterbury, 83 Conn. 270, 76 Atl. 467 (1910); Chicago Western Ry. v. Ashelford, 268 Ill. 87, 108 N.E. 761 (1915); Cunningham v. Memphis R.R. Terminal Co., 126 Tenn. 343, 149 S.W. 103 (1912).

229. N.Y. Condemnation Law, Art. 2, Sec. 18 (McKinney Supp. 1969).

230. N.Y. Condemnation Law, Art. 2, Sec. 17 (McKinney 1950).

231. Id., Sec. 24.

232. The Supreme Court has consistently held that the federal Constitution does not compel the ascertainment or payment of compensation before property is

taken, so long as adequate provision is made for assessment and payment without unreasonable delay: e.g., Sweet v. Rechel 159 U.S. 380, 400 (1895); Bragg v. Weaver, 251 U.S. 57, 62 (1919); Cherokee Nation v. Southern Kansas R. Co., 135 U.S. 641, 659, (1890).

233. Long Island R.C. v. Jones, 151 App. Div. 407, 135 N.Y.S. 954 (1912).

234. If the bond is insufficient, the owner is entitled to a judgment for the outstanding amount. See N.Y. Condemnation Law, Art. 2, Secs. 23, 24 (McKinney 1950).

235. Art. 1, Sec. 30 (McKinney 1961 and Supp. 1967).

236. Id., Sec. 30 (1) (b). Inaction, within a given period, ninety days, is deemed approval.

237. Id., Sec. 30 (4)-(9).

238. Id., Sec. 30 (10-(11).

239. Id., Sec. 30 (5).

240. Id., Sec. 30 (12). An owner who refuses to move after receiving notice of appropriation is liable to the state for use of the property after that date. Id., Sec. 30 (13) (c).

241. In many states, these issues are most commonly raised by certiorari, a mode of challenging administrative acts. 6 P. Nichols, Eminent Domain, Sec. 253, (rev. 3rd ed., J. Sackman, 1965).

242. N.Y. Highway Law, Art. 1, Sec. 30 (14) (McKinney 1961).

243. In contrast to the rule with regard to judicial condemnations, the appellate court may substitute its own award. Godfried v. State, 22 App. Div., 2d 973, 254 N.Y.S. 2d 755 (1964); McHale v. State, 278 App. Div. 886, 104 N.Y.S. 2d 981, aff'd., 304 N.Y.S. 674, 107 N.E. 2d 593 (1951).

244. United States v. Causby, 328 U.S. 256 (1946); Griggs v. County of Allegheny, 369 U.S. 84 (1962).

245. See 2 L. Orgel, Evaluation Under Eminent Domain, Secs. 247, 248 (2d ed. 1953).

246. Berger and Rohan, "The Nassau County Study: An Empirical Look Into the Practices of Comdemnation," 67 *Colum. L. Rev.* (1967). The county has moved to correct some of the practices described which bear unfairly on property owners.

247. Id., 433.

248. This is not true in all jurisdictions. See id., p. 456, note 56.

249. See Bishop, *Cases and Materials on International Law,* 791,98 (1961).

250. Silesian-American Corp. v. Clark, 332 U.S. 469, 475 (1947).

251. See Jessup, "Enemy Property," 49 *Am. J. Int. L.* 57, n. 2, (1955).

252. Sardino v. Federal Reserve Bank, 361 F. 2d 106 (1966), cert. den. 385 U.S. 834 (1967).

253. 263 U.S. 197, 221 (1923).

254. Truax v. Raich, 239 U.S. 33.

255. U.S. 410 (1948).

256. Id., at 420.

257. 332 U.S. 633 (1948). The California Alien Land Law, similar to that sustained in Terrace, created a presumption of intent to evade the law's prohibition when an ineligible alien paid for property transferred to someone eligible to own it. In this case, an ineligible father had paid for land purchased in the name of his minor son, a citizen. The Court held that the son was denied equal protection of the laws because a different presumption attached to his father's act than the normal presumption created when a father pays for a conveyance to his child. Justice Jackson, in dissent, admonished the Court that the special rule made sense as a means of effectuating the underlying alien land law.

258. Fuji v. California, 38 Cal. 2d 718, 242, P. 2d 617 (1952).

259. But cf. Ohio ex rel. Clarke v. Deckenbach, 274 U.S. 392 (1927).

Concluding Remarks

Andreas F. Lowenfeld

1. A study based chiefly on contributions from civil law writers but edited in the United States and published in the first instance in English inevitably provokes some thought about the comparison of the two great systems of law in Western civilization. In the area we have focused on, with elements of civil, administrative, and Constitutional law, and by definition bridging the public and private sectors, it is perhaps not surprising that the common generalizations do not hold. Typically, the civil lawyer prizes the static aspects of law as embodied in codes and classical treatises, whereas the common lawyer emphasizes the dynamic aspects of case law development. In the areas we have touched upon here it is interesting that the pattern is reversed. The development of United States law with regard to state taking of property has been slow and traditional, with some exceptions (notably the cases affecting devaluation of the dollar in the 1930's). Professor Greenawalt's paper would have been substantially the same if it had been written in 1918. While the United States and its law are undergoing profound transformation in many areas—notably in welfare legislation, protection of consumers, and protection and expansion of individual rights—the law and practice of taking of private property by the state seem likely to be quite similar in the year 2000 to what they are today. In contrast, every Latin American country studied here—and most of the others as well— seems to be in the process of change with respect to the legal relation between the government and private property. Each of the papers here published had to be brought up-to-date in some important way since its original submission, and some may be overtaken by events before they appear in print. In part, of course, this is so because of political uncertainty. But even in the nations that have not had political upheavals in the past decade—Mexico and Venezuela, for example—fundamental questions of law, such as the requirement of compensation in cash or the scope of judicial review of public utility, are untested or confused. This does not, or at least not necessarily, reflect a failure of law. Law may be ahead of, with, or behind the temper of the country. But

the civil law system as seen in Latin America turns out to be much more in motion than had generally been supposed.

2. One of the difficulties with papers such as the ones presented here—as indeed with lawyers' approaches to social problems generally—is that certain words come to have accepted meanings, and attempts to subdivide and classify the concepts they embrace do not succeed in changing long-held habits of thought. Each of the papers in this volume, for example, begins with a discussion of the concept of property. All the Latin American papers here begin with the origins of the concept of property in Roman law, proceed to discuss the consistency of the Roman idea of absolute ownership with colonial and nineteenth-century concepts of reversion and eminent domain, and then explore the twentieth-century idea of the social function of property. While the history varies somewhat from country to country and the characterizations of expropriation also differ, the definition of property in each case ends up as a tautology: property is anything that is owned.

It may well be that our vocabulary, Spanish and Portuguese as well as English, is in need of expansion. Agrarian land, mineral deposits, urban housing, commercial enterprise, private automobiles, popular songs, and savings accounts—all are property within the understanding of the papers in this volume, as of lawyers everywhere. It seems not too far-fetched to ask whether the essence of these disparate subject matters is contained in a single word, or whether the differences, particularly in the context of this volume, do not outweigh the common features. If the concept of "property" could be replaced by several concepts, the experience of rural landholding under Chile's Agrarian Reform Law need not, for instance, signify the breakdown of security for all ownership interests, as seems to be implied by the conclusion of Professor Avila Martel's paper. Again, the state could take over coffee estates in Brazil or slum apartments in Caracas without by that very act threatening automobile factories, oil wells, or pharmaceutical production.

To some extent the Latin American countries that have recently amended their constitutions in contemplation of agrarian reform or urban renewal have acted consistently with this thought. The basic property guarantees are maintained—for instance in Chile and Peru—but with provisions for long-deferred compensation

310

and discriminatory treatment for certain classes of property holding. The Mexican solution of removing large portions of rural and village land from the rule of the civil code is another example. Even in the United States the increasing participation by the government at various levels as buyer, builder, lessor, pre-emptor, and financier of urban housing suggests a shift in the traditional property concepts.

3. A common truism about civil law countries—particularly in Latin America—is that governments and constitutions come and go, but the basic foundations of the law remain as set forth in the codes inspired by the French Civil Code. This assumption too is drawn into question by the present study. Whereas it was thought that the civil codes were bodies of neutral and technical rules governing interests in property, succession, family law, business associations (in some cases), and judicial procedures, it turns out in the last third of the twentieth century that the rules are far from neutral. Each of the papers from Latin America in this volume observes that the civil codes represented a nineteenth-century liberal and individualist philosophy which appears equally out of date in the countries moving to the right, like Argentina and Brazil, and the countries moving to the left, like Peru and Chile. And the elaborate judicial machinery that graces most of the countries discussed is seen as a set of devices for obstruction and delay. So far as this writer is aware, there is no present effort in any of the countries studied to develop a new set of codes. Probably the effort to combine professional expertise and scholarship with political skills and reliability would not work. Thus even as the United States moves in the direction of a code system—notably with the Uniform Commercial Code—Latin America seems to be moving toward more and more special laws, more and more special tribunals and agencies, with the codes filling in the interstices of the special laws instead of vice versa.

4. Apart from great questions such as the proper system of landholding, the most effective path to industrialization, or the "social function of property," all the countries studied seem to have a set of common technical problems related to expropriation. For instance, none of the seven countries here represented has come up with a satisfactory system of valuation of property. Some leave the task to courts, some to appraisers; some countries adopt elaborate guidelines which turn out to include so many factors as

to be no guidelines at all, others try to remove the guesswork by focusing on objective criteria developed for unrelated purposes, such as declarations to tax authorities or corporate statements of "book value;" recognizing that such "objective" criteria may be unfair, some countries provide for adding 10 to even 30 per cent to the objective figure, while others consider that "turnabout is fair play."

All countries seem to struggle with the problem of going concern value or future profits—the most interesting solution being the Brazilian one, whereby the owner of commercial property is entitled to lost profits for a period estimated to be equal to the time it would take him to reestablish the business elsewhere. No country studied has really solved the question of what to do about third parties with interests in expropriated properties—typically secured creditors or tenants.

The countries studied handle differently the question of what to do in terms of valuation with change in the value of property caused by the valuation itself. Most provide that an owner left with a parcel of property no longer usable because of the portion expropriated can demand that the entire property be taken by the state. But if the remaining property is increased in value (for example, as the result of a highway coming in), some countries deduct this increase from the compensation due, others disregard it and attempt to spread the gain among all the property owners in the area, not just those whose property was taken for the project in question.

One point, however, seems easily communicable and worthwhile. As quick full cash compensation becomes more and more rare, the problem of loss in value of the currency takes on ever greater importance. Mexico, Venezuela, and the United States have not experienced rapid inflation, but in the other countries studied here, as well as in most of the rest of Latin America, even a year's delay in making a payment—whether while an appeal is pending or pursuant to a deferred compensation plan—can be ruinous to the payee and can undo all the elaborate efforts at valuation and adjudication. Argentina, after long reluctance, adopted by judicial decision a reference to a cost-of-living index; Chile issues its Agrarian Reform Bonds in two series, so that at least a portion of the compensation is protected against devaluation. Whether such a system should be applicable to government bonds generally is a question that requires more economic analysis than we are able to present here. For the problem of balancing the requirements of just compensation with the desires for social change within budgetary constraints in time of inflation, however, the Argentine or Chilean examples could well be followed in other states.

5. The introduction to this volume, written as the project was getting under way, suggested the possibility of a model law of expropriation, and raised the question of whether there was a consensus or "common law" of expropriation, at least in Latin America. The results of our inquiry indicate that while there are a number of common problems, and while for all but the two biggest countries in the Hemisphere the heritage was substantially the same, the solutions have tended to diverge rather than converge. A study such as this one made in 1910 would have had much more uniform answers than the present one. Thus all the Latin countries studied begin expropriations with a declaration of public utility, but in some countries the executive and in others the legislative issues it, and in some countries the criteria are fixed, in others not. Similarly, all countries have some kind of judicial proceeding in the course of expropriation, but in some the court has essentially a registrar's function whereas in others it has a truly judicial role. All countries provide for some kind of compensation to expropriated parties, but the extent to which an effort is made to leave the property owner fully indemnified—i.e., without damage—varies widely. Finally, every country here studied has a written constitution which speaks expressly to the subject of expropriation, but again the thrust and interpretation of these provisions are different in each country and within each country change over time.

Since the details of expropriation procedure often differ as a result of variations in judicial procedure not here discussed, a comprehensive attempt to summarize all the differences among the countries would probably be more misleading than instructive. It is interesting, however, to see on one page (at the risk of over-simplification) the solutions adopted by the countries studied to the principal questions reflecting the relation of the state to the individual and the distribution of functions among the several branches of government. (See table, page 314).

Expropriation Law—Solutions to Common Problems

	Argentina	Brazil	Chile	Mexico	Peru	Venezuela	United States
Constitutional Guaranty of Property	Yes	Yes	Yes	Qualified	Yes	Yes	Yes
Prior Compensation Required	Yes	Yes	Yes, with important exceptions	Not always	Yes, with important exceptions	Yes, with important exceptions	No
Compensation Required in Cash	Yes	Yes, with exceptions	Yes, with important exceptions	Not always	Yes, with important exceptions	Yes, with important exceptions	Yes
General Expropriation Statute	Yes	Yes	No	Yes	Yes	Yes	No
Special Legislative Act Required	No	No	Yes	No	No	Yes, with exceptions	No
Judicial Review of Public Purpose	In doubt	No	No	In doubt	No	No	Yes
Judicial Review of Compensation	Yes	Yes	Limited	No	No, with exceptions	No, with exceptions	Yes
Delayed Compensation Adjusted for Inflation	Yes	Yes	Yes	No	No	No	No
Recent Constitutional Change to Permit Social Reforms	No	No	Yes	No	Yes	Yes	No

314

6. The travel pages of the newspapers are full of announcements of international theater tours, ballet tours, museum tours, restaurant tours, opera tours, ski tours, and the like. In each case the idea is that lovers of a particular type of institution or event shall go together with qualified guides through five or six countries, concentrating on their specialty. Such tours, of course, have a built-in hazard. The intermediate slopes on the Austrian, Bavarian, French, Swiss, and Italian Alps (as well as those in Chile) are not altogether different one from the other; the Marriage of Figaro is still the Marriage of Figaro, whether in New York, Paris, Vienna, Milan, or Buenos Aires. And yet, by focusing on a particular subject in a variety of settings, one may discover features that would escape him with only a single vantage point. But if the tour is well conceived something more should emerge: Not only should the participants' understanding of opera or ballet or skiing deepen; by looking at the same subject in a number of countries, they should also get some insight into the countries themselves.

Our tour here has been only on paper. The subject is not skiing or opera, however, but one of the central problems facing every nation today. While we realize that the legal analysis alone cannot give a complete picture, our hope is that each nation emerges through these pages just a bit clearer, both to its own readers and to its friends abroad.